WALKING THE JUNGLE

John Coningham

BURFORD BOOKS

Printed in Canada.

10   9   8   7   6   5   4   3   2   1

Library of Congress Cataloging-in-Publication Data
Coningham, John.
    Walking the jungle / John Coningham.
        p.   cm.
    Includes index.
    ISBN 1-58080-108-0 (paperback)
    1. Hiking—Amazon River Region—Guidebooks.   2. Jungles—
Amazon River Region—Guidebooks.   3. Jungle survival—Amazon
River Region.   4. Amazon River Region—Description and travel.
I. Title.

GV199.44.A45C66   2003
918.1'1—dc21
2003001036

CONTENTS

INTRODUCTION

*Man shall live in such a manner as not to harm
other living beings*
—FIFTH COMMANDMENT OF BUDDHISM

It is with real pleasure that I write this guidebook, which is to me almost an autobiography.

In today's urban world most of us don't know how to identify a snake, build a fire, survive in the wild—or find our way out of it. Yet we may be faced with these needs, be it as a result of a voluntary penetration of the jungle or an air or boat accident landing us there unexpectedly. The intention of this manual is to help you make do when and where there's little or no other assistance.

There will be a number of anecdotes and personal experiences interspersed, to illustrate the points and give you a realistic idea of the conditions, plants, and animals you may encounter, especially those that can either help or harm you.

WHO STANDS TO GAIN FROM THIS GUIDE
All those who travel, work, live in, or fly over tropical American jungles can benefit from this book—airplane crews in general, bush pilots in particular, air force pilots, biologists, campers, doctors and nurses, ecologists, fishermen, hikers, jungle inn and dude ranch managers, missionaries, naturalists, nature-watchers, policemen, ranchers and farmers, readers interested in the region, reporters and TV crews, researchers

who prod, touch, dig, collect; riverboat captains, sailors, scouts—boy and girl, soldiers training in jungle warfare, students, tourist guides, tourists visiting the Swampland, Amazon, and other wild regions, writers, both visitors and residents, universities and research institutions.

Remember, you may quite suddenly and painfully find yourself out there entirely on your own someday, to do or die with what mental and physical resources you may be able to summon. That's when it ought to feel good to have read this guidebook, and to have it on hand.

I cannot help you up in the high Andean altitudes, or down in sheer-walled, whitewater canyons. Those aren't my areas. My area is the jungle. Here I am at home, and trust I can extend you a helping hand where necessary.

PART ONE

Thinking About the Jungle

1

ADVANCE PLANNING

With due precautions, walking in the jungle promises rich experiences. But tragedy lurks for the unwary, as will be described in a great number of real-life experiences throughout these pages.

A WORD OF WARNING

An early warning on a few matters is in order here, before we go any farther.

First, our larger tropical American carnivores—the jaguar, puma, crocodile, alligator, anaconda, boa constrictor, and harpy eagle—do not normally attack adult humans, except defensively.

But all of them feed on monkeys, whenever they can catch them. If you intend to take small children with you into the jungle, as I have done many times, it will no doubt be a great and unforgettable experience for them—provided they are old enough to absorb it, and as long as you bear in mind that small children look very similar to the monkeys these animals hunt. Redouble all precautions and always keep an eye on them!

Second, snakes: Small children are no match for our venomous serpents, especially the larger and more aggressive urutu, jararacuçu, fer-de-lance, and surucucu—the bushmaster—probably the world's largest poisonous snake. This is true even when they wear boots, because their upper legs, hands, and arms remain within striking reach.

And since the toxicity of snake venom is, like other poisons, inversely proportional to the victim's weight, the risk to a child's life is multiplied.

Third, piranhas: Children are fond of playing in the water with sticks, pebbles, and other toys, kicking and splashing about. To a piranha these sporadic vibrations may suggest there's a wounded, edible animal in the water.

Fourth, dogs: Taking a dog along calls for a few special considerations. In the first place, remember that if your dog has lived all its life in your garden, then that is the size of its world. It knows nothing of the jungle and pertinent dangers, and can easily be attacked or get lost after following the scent of some animal that has crossed the trail. My family and I lost a wonderful little dog in the Swampland many years ago due to my ignorance.

Wild boars and giant otters (see chapter 7) call for special precautions. Where there is any possibility of an encounter with the potentially aggressive white-lipped peccary—queixada (*Tayassu pecari*)—a dog should not be taken along. This hog hates dogs, and in its quest to get at its enemy it may overrun and seriously lacerate anyone in the way. Especially dangerous is a dog so large that you are unable to quickly climb a tree with it upon hearing the telltale rumbling interspersed with sharp clicking of teeth, and perceiving a musky smell in the air.

The giant otter—ariranha (*Pteronura brasiliensis*)—which lives in packs, will fall upon dogs swimming across rivers and simply tear them apart.

LANGUAGE

The tongue spoken in Brazil is Portuguese, whereas in the rest of Latin America (except the Guianas) it's Spanish. These are sister Latin languages, and once you know one it's easy to learn the other. In Paraguay people mostly speak their native Indian tongue, Guarani—Spanish is their second language.

Tupi-Guarani was once the English of eastern South America, spoken from northern Argentina to southern Venezuela. Even tribes of different linguistic groups such as the Arawak used to have someone who spoke Tupi in order to do business, much the way foreign firms do today.

Thus Tupi-Guarani names of fauna and flora are the most prevalent and descriptive—so much so that scientific classifications usually coincide with the natives' observations.

Most of these names remain, though slightly modified due to Iberians' inability to pronounce the *ü* sound, which in Spanish countries is registered with a *y*, and in Brazil with either an *i* or an *u*. Thus the suffix *tüba*—the place of—is spelled *tuba*, *tiba*, or *tyba*.

Since many vernacular names in Spanish and Portuguese change from one region to another in this vast continent, I will mention only those generally accepted, sticking to Tupi-Guarani wherever possible.

Today the most widely spoken language throughout the tropical South American jungles is Portuguese, since Brazil occupies the greater part of our region of interest and has borders with all the other countries except Ecuador.

The two Spanish-speaking countries with the best literature on fauna and flora are Argentina and Venezuela. Since Argentina lies almost entirely south of the tropic of Capricorn, with jungle only in the northern Chaco swamps and Iguazu, where Tupi-Guarani used to be spoken, I will resort to the Venezuelan Spanish vocabulary. This is well established since so many of the world's great naturalists were attracted to the vast region between the Amazon, Negro, and Orinoco Rivers, the two latter interconnected by the Casiquiare channel. Baron Alexander von Humboldt was there at the dawn of the 1800s, followed by Drs. von Martius and von Spix twenty or so years later, then Drs. Alfred Russel Wallace and Henry Bates in the mid-1800s—to mention only a few. Thus today we have excellent reference material available, such as the very complete *Guide to the Birds of Venezuela* by Drs. Rodolphe Meyer de Schauensee and William H. Phelps Jr.

Colombia, a country of dramatic beauty and friendly people, is unfortunately not recommended for jungle excursions due to the narcotics traffic war. In the Quéchua countries—Ecuador, Peru, and Bolivia—the jungle constitutes their backyard along the eastern foothills of the Andes.

Of the names adopted in English, the French *fer-de-lance* is unknown outside the Guianas. *Bothrops* snakes are generally known by their Tupi-Guarani names, with minor variations: *jararaca* in Portuguese and *yarará* in Spanish. *Anaconda*, on the other hand, used in the Spanish countries, is unknown in Brazil, where again the native *sucuri* prevails.

If you are coming to the jungle on a one- or two-week tour that includes an English-speaking guide, you don't have to worry about local language if you don't want to, although being able to communicate with the people makes your trip more interesting and gives you greater autonomy. A Latin language also helps you to understand the meaning of scientific botanical and zoological names.

But do make sure you are given a written itinerary in English, clearly stating in U.S. dollars what is included and what is not when you buy the package. Above all you must be clear on who is going to be responsible, so that you aren't skinned by urban man-eaters on account of some "misunderstanding" attributed to language or currency. Fast-buck operators have a marked presence in jungle tourism, especially when you are in a hurry.

If you plan to go it alone and perhaps for a greater length of time, it's advisable that you either learn the language or hire local interpreters—teachers or students of English—to accompany you where necessary. July (winter and dry season here) and December–January (summer and rainy season) are school-vacation months; it's easy to find interpreters in any city, most of which have English-language schools.

MEASUREMENTS
This guide is intended for English-speaking people of all the world. Measurements are therefore given in both the metric and English systems, as compared below, while money is in the universal U.S. dollar.

METRIC		ENGLISH
1 mm (millimeter)	=	0.039 in. (inch)
1 cm (centimeter)	=	0.39 in.
2.54 cm	=	1 in.
30.48 cm	=	1 ft. (foot)
1 m (meter)	=	3.28 ft. or 1.09 yd. (yard)
1 km (kilometer)	=	0.62 mi. (mile)
1.6 km	=	1 mi.
1 kg (kilogram or kilo)	=	2.2 lb. (pound)
453.59 g (gram)	=	1 lb.
1 l (liter)	=	1.05 qt. (quart)
1 ha (hectare)	=	2.47 a. (acre)
2.590 square km	=	1 square mi.

PRELIMINARY PLANNING
Health hazards in the jungle are numerous, but being armed with knowledge and acknowledging the importance of advance planning can minimize the risks. A hazard is most dangerous when you are not familiar with it and therefore don't expect it. If your defenses are down, it can catch you off guard, like someone suddenly attacking you in a crowded street.

While an apparent danger such as a snake or a large spider may turn out not to constitute a hazard at all, a single *Anopheles* mosquito or a beautiful little *Micrurus* coral may, on the other hand, bring your health and perhaps even your life to an end.

Thus advance knowledge of what to expect and how to prepare for it is *sine qua non*: You cannot do without it. In preparing your trip to the jungle you are the general, planning a campaign: You've got to know the terrain, what potential enemies live there and how they may react to your presence, and what friends you must not upset. That should eliminate anywhere from 75 to nearly 100 percent of the danger, depending on what this might be.

The greatest safety is to be found in the attitude that you and those accompanying you bring to the jungle. Patience and care mean safety; rashness and inattention spell trouble. Every step you take in the jungle is a step onto fresh ground and requires renewed precautions, step by literal step, that you won't slip on that rock, the branch you're climbing won't snap, those thorns won't hook you, that vine won't snare your foot, that machete you're wielding (if you use the stupid tool) won't get hung up in the creepers and swerve in at you or get torn from your hand and hurled at a companion, that gun is securely uncocked or on safety so as not to be discharged by a twig, and so forth. Much of people's suffering in the jungle is the result of their own impatience and unpreparedness.

When coming to the Swampland—the Pantanal or Chaco—you need nothing more in the way of gear than your hammock and mosquito net, about which I'll talk in detail in chapter 11. Still, there are some critical health issues to think about and plan for.

In the Amazon basin there is malaria, against which no vaccine has as yet been approved. So preventive pills must be taken besides standard mosquito protection. These pills—known as Aralém or Plaquinol in Brazil—are generally based on quinine. *Begin taking them a fortnight before entering the danger zone and stop a fortnight after leaving.* Take them for short periods only—say, up to a month or two. You cannot keep on taking preventive medicine indefinitely, for it ends up jeopardizing your liver, eyesight, hearing, and more.

Throughout tropical America in general you also want to keep an eye open for the daytime-biting *Aedes aegypti* mosquito, which transmits dengue fever where there are human concentrations (see page 107) and, most threatening of all, yellow fever. Vaccination against yellow fever is necessary (see page 112).

In the rather populous semi-arid northeast region of Brazil, where there is much reuse and contamination of stagnant water, snail-transmitted schistosomiasis is endemic (see page 110). Another danger is leptospirosis (see page 108), transmitted mainly through the urine of rats, wherever there exists a combination of *Rattus norwegicus* and low hygiene.

My friend Frank Rough was a fine English cattle-ranch manager who spent many years in the wild, open savannas of Mato Grosso, where he used to drink straight out of any creek. Then the company sent him to look at some land in the north, where he apparently quenched his thirst in the same manner. He returned with belatedly diagnosed leptospirosis, and died within three days.

Hantavirus is found in the south (see page 108).

Humidity

If you wear humidity-sensitive gear such as a hearing aid, be sure to bring along a bottle of dehydrating silicone pellets in which to keep it for the night, so that it won't fail you out in the middle of nowhere. In the summer you will at times catch as much as a whole week of continual rain here, especially during the full and new moons.

Physical Fitness

A friend of mine visited the Inca ruins at Machu Picchu in Peru in December, including a three-day hike up the Andes. He spent a good preliminary couple of weeks walking around our district hugging a rucksack containing the equivalent in bricks to the weight he expected to be hauling. It would do the prospective hiker no harm to follow his example—for an even longer period if you're not a habitual walker—plus getting in plenty of swimming practice as well.

Teeth

Have your teeth examined about a month before you travel. A trip into the Serra do Mar cloud forest near Santos, Brazil, with my friend Milton when we were in our late teens was completely spoiled by toothache from an inflamed nerve channel. And we depended, for our return, on a man to pick us up by boat on a given day and time, so there was no way to cut the trip short. Not even Milton's whiskey, held in my mouth, did any good.

JUNGLE PHILOSOPHY

"Green Hell" and other such silly exaggerations were created by sensationalists and lazy outsiders who didn't bother to equip themselves adequately for the Tropics. The unprepared might likewise call the polar regions "White Hell," the deep sea "Black Hell," or the concrete city "Gray Hell."

Here in the Tropics the fittest have not yet wholly prevailed like in temperate forests, where a few select species dominate; in the jungle the quest for space and survival is an intense, ongoing process.

Still, if the jungle were all that hellish, our indigenous peoples wouldn't be living there stark naked and thinking nothing of it! Getting caught on vines, branches, or roots, and having tacky seeds on your clothes is simply one of nature's ways of scattering plants, seeds, saplings, and fungi, just like wind, water, birds, and bats do. It must be seen as normal and purposeful rather than an irritating hindrance.

Bear in mind that the white man—who came up with the "Green Hell" epithet—is adapted to temperate, often cold and snowy climates.

That's why he is of a light color, just like polar bears, Siberian tigers, snow leopards, mountain goats, snowy owls, foxes, and other animals not found in the Tropics.

For thousands of generations his ancestors had to provide for the winter in order not to starve or freeze to death; only the fittest, with a developing capacity of foresight, survived. This is why he is today capable of planning ahead, whereas his equatorial cousins never had much need to worry: Food and warmth are available year-round, thus nature has been complacent in her selection process. This is something we ought to stop and think about before tagging natives of warm climates "indolent" and "backward." For although they are by nature less developed in the fields they never needed, they are on the other hand advanced in patience and gentleness, areas in which the more aggressive northerner lags behind. It is said in Bolivia that anyone who mistreats an animal must have foreign blood.

Why, on the other hand, is the black African such a gifted athlete? Because for thousands of generations his ancestors had to outrun fierce animals too large for the individual to stand and fight: elephants, Cape buffalo, lions, rhinos. Mother Nature felt he needed additional help in the form of an extra-dark color, to help him out at night, when he could not outrun these animals. Curiously, several African mammals are black as well: buffalo, hippopotamus, rhino, gorilla. In tropical America, on the other hand, brown is much more prevalent.

Thus if to the primitive European survival meant hoarding for the winter, to the African it was a swift foot to run for his life, while the tropical American native had little to gain from speed in the dense tangles of equatorial rain forests. His needs to survive consisted of well-developed senses of perception to locate food in the forest penumbra, and the stealth and astuteness to ambush his game and enemies, for which purpose his brown skin—the color of tree bark and dead leaves—is best suited.

The fact is that we develop only the qualities we need. Consequently, there is now an inverse process under way: Pressed by the requirements of new tasks, tropical minds are picking up sprightliness, whereas children brought up in the comfortable organization of rich northern nations are getting out of touch with the basic ability to survive on their own. It functions much like physical fitness: Those areas of the body that you exercise, develop; those you don't, atrophy.

White Man Versus Indian

The following anecdote illustrates the point. A discussion of whether primitive forest peoples should be integrated into modern society leads to a request, by a commission of the most erudite professors of social sciences, for a tribe in the jungle to send them one of their most brilliant young men, to be given an aptitude test.

The chiefs hold a council and choose the boy they most admire for his all-around prowess: a deadly archer, stealthy hunter, patient fisherman, valiant and cunning warrior, able tool- and canoe maker. He is conducted to the white man's metropolis and tested . . .

. . . and the result is an absolute zero. The test scorers make remarks such as: "Subject was found incapable of the most elementary mathematics, crossing a street, operating a vehicle, elevator, or computer, locking a door, lighting a gas stove, understanding money, copying a word (or even holding a pen, for that matter), speaking on a telephone, using a bathroom, and so on, and so forth." The professors look at each other with pained *What did I tell you?* smiles.

The Indian chiefs are amazed and at first think they haven't understood. But once the stark truth dawns on them, they become curious, and respectfully request that the distinguished whites send *their* best man to the tribe, for a similar aptitude test.

This request is received with some derision, but, all right, the man with the highest I.Q. is chosen for the test: a real whiz kid, computer hacker and site designer, car racer, Ph.D. in physics, fast thinker . . .

The result of his test in the jungle? Another absolute zero, of course, with the comments of the chiefs: "Pale face is unable to either make or use hunting and fishing weapons; recognize game by their calls, tracks, dung, smells, diggings, holes, nests, or urine; find fruit, roots, larvae, or honey; walk silently; construct a shelter; and so on, and so forth." So there you are.

A Matter of Opinion

In discovering the Northwest Passage, Sir John Franklin (1786–1847) perished with all his 129 officers and men of the ships *Erebus* and *Terror*. According to author Roland Huntford, in *The Last Place on Earth*, "while Franklin and his men were dying of hunger, Eskimos around them were living off the land in comparative plenty. But Franklin was hampered by grotesquely unsuitable methods, the product of rigid thought and incapacity to adapt to circumstances." He maintained that an intelligent, educated white man should have no cause to bow to illiterate natives.

So the saying holds true: When in Rome, do as the Romans do; for they are adapted to their environment.

2

A TOUR OF THE REGION

Let's take an imaginary trip beginning in Venezuela in northern South America (as noted, beautiful Colombia is not now a country in which to explore jungles due to the drug traffic war). You will find the terrain gradually rising south of the Orinoco River toward the Brazilian border, which follows the watershed along the Gurupira, Parima, and Pacaraima Mountains to the Guianas.

This is the region of the tepuys—mesa mountains and buttes in a jungle setting—where Angel Falls, the world's highest with a drop of 980 meters (3,212 feet), gives a pretty good idea of the kind of terrain. This Angel was an American bush pilot, one of whose planes remains on top of a tepuy where he made an emergency landing.

Here is also the home of the Guianan cock-of-the-rock (*Rupicola rupicola*)—called gallito de las rocas in Venezuela and galo-da-Serra in Brazil—and the giant tarantula (*Theraphosa blondi*).

Open savannas with clear, cascading rivers meet you as you enter Brazil at Roraima and move toward the east. These are the southernmost reaches of the double-striped thick-knee (*Burhinus bistriatus*), a ploverlike ground bird called dara in Venezuela and téu-téu-da-savana in Roraima.

As you move on along the watershed of the Tumuc Humac Mountains you now have the Guianas on your left with much the same tepuys and spectacular falls until you reach the coastal state of Amapá, where the ground gradually drops off toward the Atlantic, with some of the world's largest mangrove and grass swamps dotted with lagoons where the tarpon (*Megalops atlanticus*)—a game fish usually identified with Florida—abounds.

TROPICAL SOUTH AMERICA NATIONAL & STATE PARKS

ARGENTINA (Tropical)
1. Iguazu Falls
2. Baritu

BOLIVIA
1. Amboro
2. Carrasco
3. Noel Kempff
4. Beni Biological Station
5. Madidi

BRAZIL
1. Lagoa do Peixe
2. Aparados da Serra
3. Serra Geral
4. Sao Joaquim
5. Serra do Tabuleiro
6. Iguazu Falls
7. Ilha Grande
8. Superagui
9. Caverna do Diabo
10. Serra da Bocaina
11. Itatiaia
12. Tijuca
13. Serra dos Orgaos
14. Restinga de Jurubatiba
15. Serra do Caparao
16. Serra do Cipo
17. Serra da Canastra
18. Abrolhos
19. Descobrimento, M. Pascoal, P. Brasil
20. Grande Sertao Veredas
21. Emas
22. Pantanal

23. Chapada dos Guimarães
24. Brasilia
25. Chapada dos Veadeiros
26. Canudos
27. Serra da Capivara
28. Serra das Confusoes
29. Araguaia
30. Xingu
31. Gorotire Forest Reserve
32. Guapore Biological Reserve
33. Pacaas Novos
34. Serra do Divisor
35. Abufari Biological Reserve
36. Mundurucania Forest Reserve
37. Amazonia
38. Tapajos National Forest
39. Gurupi Biological Reserve
40. Lencois Maranhenses
41. Sete Cidades
42. Ubajara
43. Jau
44. Serra da Mocidade
45. Virua
46. Tumucumaque Indian Res.
47. Piratuba Biological Res.
48. Cabo Orange
49. Pico da Neblina
50. Roraima National Forest
51. Monte Roraima
52. Chapada Diamantina

ECUADOR
1. Rodocarpus
2. El Cajas

3. Yasuni
4. Machalilla
5. Cuyabeno Wildlife Reserve
6. Sangay

PARAGUAY
1. Defensores del Chaco

PERU
1. Manu
2. Pacaya Samiria Reserve
3. Amotape

COLOMBIA
1. La Paya
2. Sanquianga
3. Picachos
4. La Macarena
5. Sumapaz
6. El Tuparro
7. Darien
8. Paramilo
9. Sierra Nevada

VENEZUELA
1. Serrania de la Neblina
2. Parima-Tapirapeco
3. Cerro Guaiquinima
4. Canaima
5. Cinaruco-Capanaparo
6. Sierra Nevada
7. Aguaro-Guariquito
8. Duida-Marahuaca
9. Jaua Sarisarinama

These swamps stretch south across Marajó Island at the mouth of the Amazon, where Indian water buffalo are the main product and transport. Children ride them to school and policemen on their rounds.

There follows a broken coastline of inlets until you reach the vast 100-by-40-kilometer (62-by-25-mile) dunefield Parque Nacional dos Lençóis Maranhenses east of São Luis, after which come endless sandy beaches all the way southeast and then southwest to the mouth of the São Francisco River and adjacent lagoons.

After visiting the islands at the delta of the Parnaíba River east of the dunes, it's in the dry interior that the jungle explorer will find sites of major interest. Thus you might begin at Ubajara National Park near Sobral, Ceará—an Atlantic forest enclave in the semidesert—and from there proceed west to the nearby sandstone formations at Sete Cidades (seven cities) National Park, a geologist's dream. Then deeper into Piauí state to Serra da Capivara National Park, the site of some of the most ancient human habitation in South America, rich in wall paintings.

On the way there you will cross the caatinga (white brush) semi-desert, the driest and poorest region in eastern South America, which stretches south across Bahia east of the São Francisco. But near Seabra, west of Salvador, you will quite unexpectedly happen upon a lush cliff-mountain oasis with cascading rivers—Chapada Diamantina National Park.

Then it's time to turn back to the coast, which has meanwhile changed: The Serra do Mar (mountains of the sea) have emerged and will be accompanying the coastline all the way down to Brazil's last state, most of it covered in cloud forest called the Atlantic forest. Its most majestic expressions appear at Itaimbezinho and Fortaleza Canyons west of Torres, Rio Grande do Sul, São Joaquim, and Serra do Tabuleiro National Parks in neighboring Santa Catarina and the region of Marumbi behind Paranaguá, state of Paraná, all the higher altitudes in the south embellished by the *Araucaria* pine. A trip by train from the port of Paranaguá to Curitiba up the mountain right alongside the sheer granite cliff edge can be spectacular when the weather is clear. There is also a laid-stone mule trail from the slave days, mostly conserved in the mountains next to scenic Graciosa Road and, a little north, the cave-strewn Ribeira Valley.

To convey an idea of the remoteness still prevalent in many parts of Serra do Mar range, there are Guarani Indians living here who don't speak Portuguese; airplanes have simply vanished (see chapter 18); and people often get lost, so much so that the firemen's corps and military police of coastal states have trained mountain rescue teams. Millions of people crowd the beaches on weekends and holidays, but with the rarest exceptions all these people are afraid of venturing into the abysmal, cloud-enshrouded jungles of the Serra. You step off the bus or train, enter the forest, and might as well have arrived five hundred years ago.

But now it's time to turn inland and head west for Iguazu National Parks by the cataracts, on both the Brazilian and Argentinian sides, with a stopover at Vila Velha sandstone sculptures and sinkholes near Ponta Grossa. The Argentinian Iguazu park is the more beautiful and better managed. One of the park guards, now stationed at Salta, lost a small child to a jaguar at Iguazu.

Proceeding farther west to the Paraguay River basin we come to the great inland sedimentary floodplain, the Swampland—called El Chaco in northern Argentina, Paraguay, and eastern Bolivia, and Pantanal in Brazil—which is most beautiful in the vicinity of Corumbá with vast, open grasslands and lagoons dotted with carandá palm groves and snaking forests. This is the best region in which to watch wildlife in tropical South America. Due to periodic flooding and extremely boggy terrain the best time of the year is the late dry season—July through September.

From Corumbá a visit to the ancient limestone caves and fish-rich, crystal-clear rivers of Bonito in Serra da Bodoquena on the southeastern fringe of the Pantanal recommends itself.

The Swampland extends all the way north to the vicinity of the cliffs and crags of Chapada dos Guimarães National Park northeast of Cuiabá, which separates the River Plate basin to the south from the Amazon to the north.

After Chapada dos Guimarães you might as well head on north to Manaus by the confluence of the Negro and Amazon Rivers, since to the western, Quéchua-speaking, Pacific-minded neighbors—Bolivia, Peru, and Ecuador—the Amazon basin east of the Andes constitutes their less developed backyard.

From Manaus you have before you the beautiful Rio Negro—where there are no mosquitoes—to explore the Amazon forest. And presently you will see, again, rising in the north, the Gurupira Mountains that mark the border with Venezuela.

Permission is necessary to enter or cross private property anywhere, property being characterized by a fence. Where there is no fence or sign you are technically not trespassing, though if there is a dwelling or person in sight you lose nothing by introducing yourself and asking for permission and information concerning the trail.

Of course here you must either know Portuguese or Spanish or be accompanied by someone who does, because people of the hinterland, often illiterate, are unlikely to understand English.

Your motive for seeking permission to enter a private property has to be made clear and understandable to the level of the person in charge, often a primitive. This conversation must be patient and drawn out. That's where time-oriented city dwellers stumble. In rural country you don't just rush up to the farmer and say, "Hey, may I go see such and such a place?" People aren't accustomed to this kind of storming in. You are expected to clap hands at the gate or call a "bom dia" or "buenos dias" if you've been seen, wait until you're asked in, sit down when invited, talk to the people about yourself and about them and their world. Only when a pause appears in the conversation should you tell them what your request is. Backwoods people enjoy these conversations, and you'll learn much from them and make new friends. The foreigner in Brazil, for example, is looked up to, not down upon.

There are, on this continent, a lot of absentee landowners—doctors, industrialists, politicians, and so on—whose ranches are in the hands of a foreman, or capataz. So you'll have to be understanding if this man tells you he is not free to allow a stranger onto the premises. Of course outstanding landmarks usually have a trail leading to them, since everybody wants to see them, and there you will have no difficulty.

Strangers on the property are a delicate matter that goes beyond concern over fire or destruction of installations and livestock. In 1965 a man came very humbly—hat in hand—into the offices at 400,000-hectare (million-acre) Fazenda Bodoquena in the Swampland, saying he was a neighbor on the opposite side of the mountain and wished to obtain permission for some of his employees to camp by a spring on a little-used trail in the hills to hunt some of the jaguars that were devastating his herds.

A month or two later it was discovered that he had already fenced off a large area, was erecting a house and corral, had padlocked the gate, and had posted armed men to make sure no one touched his new fences.

3

WATCHING WILDLIFE

How do you go about watching birds and other wildlife in the tropical jungles?

Where water is scarce, such as in the northeastern semi-arid caatinga and much of ancient limestone Serra da Bodoquena along the Swampland in Mato Grosso do Sul, the best place is naturally where the animals drink and bathe, especially during the dry period—July or August to October—when fountains and water holes reduce to a minimum and the spring mating and nesting season stimulates wildlife to move about and show itself more, the animals' guard being noticeably lowered.

Other options are feeding places like fruit trees and seed grasses, where it's easy to see on the ground whether there has been activity. And try salt licks, or barreiros, where again you will see by the excavations and tooth marks in the clay whether there has been recent action. Barreiros are usually frequented when the ground is moist, such as after a rain, or when located under the overhang of a riverbank.

The river- or creekbank is itself another interesting choice, especially where the accompanying forest or brush narrows down to a thin strip or features an interruption—say, the ramp where cattle descend to drink, or a tongue of meadow. This also goes for the spaces between the tips of two woods and outstanding dead trees, where various birds alight.

In undisturbed areas several animals use regular paths—carreiros—to their drinking and feeding grounds, notably the paca (*Agouti paca*); armadillo or tatu; and peccaries, or queixada and caititu. If tracks are fresh, it's possible to observe them.

Whatever the situation, you must always bear in mind the "rule of S's": Tie up your hammock out of sight, smell, and sound. Don't move, smoke, eat, or go to the toilet in the vicinity.

Movement, on a regular sunny day, involves more than just your changing position. Your shadow on the ground and vegetation also moves. But the most important thing that happens is the change in light reflection from the spots of sun filtering down through the foliage upon your body and clothes. Wild animals, whose life depends on an ever-present consciousness of self-defense, perceive this in the shadows.

Life is never carefree in the jungle. Take a bird, for example: The most dangerous day in its life—assuming its nest is not plundered by a snake, hawk, owl, opossum, monkey, ani, or jay—is the day the fledgling leaves the nest on its first tentative flights. It may fall into the water and drown, or be caught by any one of a dozen predators watching from the sky, brush, or water. In the city snakes, wildcats, and foxes have been replaced by cats, dogs, and automobiles.

Man should stop a moment to reflect on this, and feel ashamed of himself, complaining of this and of that while wallowing in security and comfort, overstuffed with needless food.

BIRD-WATCHING

Bird-watching is one of the major pleasures in walking in the jungle. The veteran bird-watcher will naturally come equipped with books and binoculars and definite objectives; you'll need only the logistics to get to the right places. Thus you may want to penetrate the least accessible gorges of the Serra do Mar cloud forest to try your luck at locating the **black-fronted piping-guan** or jacutinga (*Pipile jacutinga*) and the **solitary tinamou** or macuco (*Tinamus solitarius*)—both threatened with extinction from overhunting. Or look for the rare **ruddy quail-dove** or jurití vermelha (*Geotrygon montana*), which I have seen only once in those mountains. You may also wish to undertake an expedition along the tepuys of the Tumuc Humac and Pacaraima mountain ranges on the northern borders of Brazil in search of the **Guianan cock-of-the-rock**—galo-da-Serra or gallito de las rocas (*Rupicola rupicola*)—one of our most beautiful birds. The canyons of Raso-da-Catarina in the northeastern semi-arid caatinga harbor some survivor **Lear's blue macaw** or arara-azul-de-Lear (*Anodorhynchus leari*).

The present section is for the beginner, who is either entering the tropical jungle for the first time or has only just taken up bird-watching and would like a helping hand identifying the more immediately noticeable species. Since so many birds' names in Tupi-Guarani and Portuguese are onomatopoeic—they attempt to imitate the bird's call—the detail someone coming from an English-speaking country must remember in order to get the sound right is that the *i* is always pronounced as "ee" and the ç as "s."

A FEW CURIOUS TROPICAL SOUTH AMERICAN BIRDS

Top left, the bellbird—araponga (Procnias nudicollis)*—can be heard in the eastern Serra do Mar virgin forests and Iguazu National Park. Top center, the cock-of-the-rock—galo-da-Serra* (Rupicola rupicola)*—famous for its dances, occurs in the mountains dividing Brazil from Venezuela and eastern Bolivia. Top right, the jacamar—Ariramba* (Galbula sp.) *is neither a kingfisher nor a hummingbird, but an insect-eating Galbulidae. Bottom, the hoatzin—Cigana* (Opisthocomus hoazin) *of the Amazon basin is a vegetarian with clawed wings and a strong smell.*

So let's take a stroll together to see what we can find and identify. Bird-watchers must rise early, or they'll miss some species altogether. The ideal sort of day is when the weather is about to change and birds become excited. Or a drizzly day, on which wild animals in general tend to move about more in the weaker light, feeling perhaps better protected, since they don't cast a shadow. You might also try the morning after a rainy period, when birds are eager to procure food. And the best time of the year is spring, from early September on. Besides being the mating season, it's when termites and ants swarm by the millions with the first rains.

The *how-how-how-how* you may have heard during the night was the **barn owl**—coruja suindara or lechuza de campanario (*Tyto alba*)—with which you are likely to be familiar from home since it occurs in many parts of the world. Just before the break of dawn you may also have heard a soft, rapidly ululating call like a child hooting and beating his lips fast with his fingers, which was probably the **tropical screech-owl**—corujinha-do-mato—curucucu (*Otus choliba*). Less common is a *whoo-oh-oh-oh!* like someone crying desperately. That's one of the **potoos**—urutau or mãe-da-lua (*Nyctibius* spp.). This bird is a relative of the **nightjars**—curiangos, bacuraus, or aguaitacaminos—whose red eye reflects a car's headlights on dirt roads. The potoo distinguishes itself by sitting at the end of an upward-bent, broken-off branch, at the same angle as if it were an extension of the branch.

The first glimmer of daylight is barely perceptible when the **thrush**—sabiá or paraulata—begins to sing. Most common are the **creamy-bellied**—sabiá-poca (*Turdus amaurochalinus*)—and **rufous-bellied**—sabiá-laranjeira (*T. rufiventris*). This bird, a slightly larger cousin of the North American robin, is omnipresent throughout the lower Tropics. Though one of the best-camouflaged birds—it's practically invisible among the dry leaves where it scratches for worms—the thrush is nonetheless all attention, and its alarm is heeded by the other small birds. It likes to build its nest of aquatic plants such as duckweed under the eaves or alongside the beams of sheds.

Immediately after *Turdus* it is likely to be the bright yellow, masked **great kiskadee**—bem-te-ví or cristofue (*Pitangus sulphuratus*)—that manifests itself. It usually has its fairly voluminous nest in tall trees near water, where it can watch the minnows, or guarus, it fishes for during the day. *Pitangus* is an aggressive bird that won't hesitate to intercept and persecute hawks. And one morning when I stood by the door convalescing from malaria I saw one catching *Eupetomena macroura*, or beija-flor tesourão (the largest of our hummingbirds), which it only dropped when I rushed out after it. But it does not impress the **green-barred woodpecker**—pica-pau-verde-barrado or carpintero real verde (*Chrysoptilus* spp.)—whose beak is sharp and strong enough to let it ignore the insolent pesterer. Like the sabiá, the bem-te-ví cohabits with man, and you can find it in public city parks and private gardens.

In the Swampland it is the larger birds that you hear first. The **limpkin** or carão (*Aramus guarauna*), looking much like a large rail perched on a bush in the water, may call at intervals right through moonlit nights, a melancholy, chirping call that is the most prevalent sound of the Swampland. But the day in the Pantanal is piped in by the **plumbeous ibis** or curicaca-cinza (*Harpiprion caerulescens*), roosting in twos or fours up in some dry tree, soon to be followed by the noisy, hoarse **chaco chachalaca** or aracuã (*Ortalis canicollis*). Territorial-minded like so many birds, each family occupies a tall tree, where you can see them hopping about. According to folklore, the male calls *quero matar!*—I want to kill!—and the female answers *quero casar!*—I want to marry!

Meanwhile parakeets or periquitos, like the **monk**—caturrita (*Myiopsitta monachus*)—are already actively twittering in the palm trees, where they nest in large colonies.

The next call you hear is another one you will most certainly be familiar with, and it's always reassuring to encounter old friends among strangers: the **common house wren**—corruíra or cucarachero (*Troglodytes aedon*)—a courageous little explorer that, although well camouflaged in russet against aerial observers, is a potential victim of snakes, felines, dogs, toads, and other predators, due to its ground-level search for insects.

Of birds whose call you immediately notice, none makes its presence more readily known than the Amazonian **screaming piha**— quinquió, tropeiro, or minero (*Lipaugus vociferans*)—a uniformly gray, small bird whose sharp whistle is similar to that which a sailor might emit at the passage of a shapely woman. But this bird you normally hear a bit later in the day.

Just outside the door there are likely to be a number of doves waiting to be given a handful of broken rice or corn; if you happen to be in the Swampland, these will be found with red-headed **cardinals** or cardeal (*Paroaria* spp.). The smallest is the **ruddy ground dove**—rolinha-caldo-de-feijão or palomita castaña (*Columbina talpacoti*). Its cousin, the **scaled dove**—rola-fogo-apagou or palomita maraquita (*Scardafella squammata*)—is rather shy and prefers to stay out in the field. Not so the next larger size, the **blue ground-dove**—rola azul or palomita azul (*Claravis pretiosa*)—which has become almost as tame as domestic pigeons. Larger than the blue dove is another shy one, the **white-tipped dove**—juriti or paloma turca (*Leptotila verreauxi*)—which spends most of its day on the ground under orchards and scrub, alone or in pairs, where you can hear its soft, hooting call. Of the larger pigeons, the **plumbeous**—pomba amargosa or paloma plomiza (*Columba plumbea*)—remains distant up in the taller trees of the forests, while the reddish **pale-vented**—pomba pocaçu or paloma colorada (*C. cayennensis*)—can be seen in isolated trees in places like Chapada dos Guimarães. Our largest wild pigeon, on the other hand, the **picazuro**— trocaz or asa-branca (*Columba picazuro*)—has moved into man's vicinity for security reasons: It nests in the larger trees of cities, where it has become quite abundant, while continuing to feed out in the fields. I can hear it calling from the trees in my backyard while writing this passage, together with the mourning of the blue ground-dove.

Another blue bird that spends much of its time close to human dwellings, especially if there's an orchard and water to bathe, is the **sayaca tanager**—sanhaço or azulejo de jardin (*Thraupis sayaca*)—the only one of the large and beautiful Thraupidae family that has taken to living with man. The **palm tanager**—sanhaço-de-coqueiro or azulejo de palmera (*Thraupis palmarum*)—may come as far as the orchard but keeps to itself. Down along the coast at the foot of the Serra do Mar is where you see the most striking tanagers, such as the **green-headed**—saíra-de-sete-cores or tangara azul (*Tangara seledon*); **Brazilian**—sangue-de-boi (*Ramphocelus bresilius*); and **magpie**—tié-tinga or moriche blanco (*Cissopis leveriana*)—to mention only a few. The **burnished-buff**—saíra amarela or tangara monjita (*Tangara cayana*)—and the **orange-headed**—saíra-canário or frutero de sombrero (*Thlypopsis sordida*)—appear here at home in Campinas on occasion, together with the **swallow tanager**—saí-andorinha or azulejo golondrina (*Tersina viridis*)—when the coral magnolia fruits ripen.

One other coral fruit that attracts a particular bird is that of the parasitic mistletoe, or erva-de-passarinho, which forms tufts in tree crowns. It ripens in winter and is especially sought by the now rare **hooded siskin**—pintassilgo or jilguero de Roraima (*Carduelis magellanicus*).

I know when there's a bunch of bananas ripening because of the harsh calls of the **mockingbird**—sabiá-do-campo or calandria (*Mimus* spp.)—which in the Swampland is represented by the very prevalent **tropical mockingbird**—joão-cabral or paraulata llanera (*M. gilvus*)—whose call is a sharp burst of *tautatau!* reminiscent of someone throwing a handful of pebbles into the water. The most beautiful member of this family is the **black-capped mockingthrush**—japacanim or paraulata de água (*Donacobius atricapillus*)—which lives in the reeds of swamps.

If the coast is the tanagers' paradise, Chapada dos Guimarães, where the Amazon and River Plate basins meet, is the realm of the lovely **manakins,** like the **helmeted** or soldadinho (*Antilophia galeata*) with its vast, bright red plume, and the **blue-crowned** or uirapuru-de-chapéu-azul (*Pipra coronata*) with its sky-blue cap. Here you also see the **black-fronted nunbird**—bico-de-brasa (*Monasa nigrifrons*)—along riverine forests. **Toucans** such as **Cuviers**—tucano-de-peito-branco or piapoco de pico curvo (*Ramphastos cuvieri*)—and the largest of all, tucanuçu (*R. toco albogularis*)—are most visible in the savannas. The **chestnut-eared araçari**—araçari castanho or tucan verde y amarillo (*Pteroglossus castanotis*)—is another colorful presence. Other araçaris, such as the **spot-billed toucanet**—araçari-poca (*Selenidera maculirostris*)—are to be found in the Serra do Mar cloud forest, where you hear them groaning like piglets.

But let's move on. Some of the best places to watch birds are where there's scrub, especially alongside water, with perhaps an adjacent open field. Here you are sure to spot the **rufous-collared sparrow**—tico-

tico or correporsuelo (*Zonotrichia capensis*)—which is rarely far from its territorial bushes facing open fields. Occasionally it may come and eat a little broken rice, but it doesn't get addicted and dislikes mixing with the crowd of doves. Another habitual scrub dweller is the **rufous-capped spinetail**—joão-teneném or pijuí de vientre sepia (*Synallaxis ruficapilla*)—twittering in the bushes, a member of the large, generally rufous Furnariidae family, one of whose most interesting species is the **rufous oven-bird**—joão-de-barro (*Furnarius rufus*)—which struts about the ground in a noble posture. It builds its igloo-shaped mud houses in the taller trees or upon the crossbar of lampposts, sometimes two or three together or even one atop the other. When we were building our house in suburban Campinas one came and fetched fresh plaster to construct its own, but after it had made the foundation it found that human "mud" dried too quickly and became too hard to shape. In the Swampland you'll find the **pale-legged hornero** or pedreiro (*Furnarius leucopus*), with a white neck and eyebrows. This entire family builds the most artful nests, many of them enormous structures of twigs ten times the size of the bird, hanging from the tips of branches.

A soft, frequently repeated burst of laughter denotes the presence of the **barred antshrike**—choca barrada or pavita hormiguera (*Thamnophilus doliatus*)—whose male is a gray-and-white-mottled little bird. Another interesting bird you may see in this kind of vegetation in the Swampland and Chapada near water looks much like a large hummingbird or a small kingfisher, but is neither: the insect-eating **rufous-tailed jacamar**—tucuso barranquero or ariramba-de-cauda-castanha (*Galbula ruficauda*). Less common is the **chestnut jacamar** or ariramba vermelho (*Galbalcyrhynchus leucotis*).

Scrub is also the domain of the rain bird, the **striped cuckoo**—saci or saucé (*Tapera naevia*)—which usually calls one or two days before the weather changes. This is a medium-sized, long-tailed bird with beautiful bluish eyes. Another rainbird, this one down in the woods bordering streams and swamps, is the **gray-necked wood rail**—saracura três-potes or chiricote (*Aramides cajanea*)—and some of its smaller cousins. In the Swampland you hear a rather frightening roar issuing from the isolated woods that becomes especially frequent when the weather is about to change. But that's the howler monkey—bugio.

Some more **cuckoos** are frequently present: the quiet, delicate **squirrel cuckoo**—alma-de-gato or piscua (*Piaya cayana*)—soft brown with a long tail, hopping noiselessly from branch to branch or gliding across from one tree to the next. And out in open grasslands you'll find small flocks of **guira cuckoos**—anu-branco or pirincho (*Guira guira*)—light yellow, long tailed, and combing the grass for insects. The black

smooth-billed ani—anu-preto or garrapatero comun (*Chrotophaga ani*)—prefers to accompany cattle and catch the grasshoppers the big animals flush while picking off the occasional horsefly from their legs as well while the polished-metal blue-black **greater ani**—anu coroca or garrapatero hervidor (*Crotophaga major*)—prefers riverside forests, where, in the Amazon, it cohabits with the extraordinary **hoatzin**—cigana or chenchena (*Opisthocomus hoazin*)—a guan-sized, light-colored vegetarian bird and the only member of the Opisthocomidae family.

Performing revolutions in the sky above, you will see **blue-and-white swallows**—andorinha azul-e-branca or golondrina barranquera azul (*Notiochelidon cyanoleuca*). They nest in the chimney of our fireplace and sometimes come out below into the living room when I switch on the light before dawn. By the tallest waterfalls plunging down the cliff walls of Chapada dos Guimarães you'll see a dark **swift**—andorinhão-velho-da-cascata (*Cypseloides senex*)—which nests there.

As you quietly enter the darker, tall forest you are bound to come upon some beautiful and relatively stealthy birds like the **blue-crowned motmot**—udu or pájaro león (*Momotus momota*)—which distinguishes itself from its brothers by a sort of fan on a bare shaft at the end of its tail. Its call is a brief *woo-do-do-do!* Here you are also likely to meet the delicate **collared trogon**—surucuá-de-coleira or sorocuá acollarado (*Trogon collaris*)—whose long drawn-out series of calls and bright colors make it easy to locate on the upper branches. In the Serra do Mar you encounter the **yellow bellied trogon**—surucuá-de-barriga-amarela or sorocuá cola blanca (*T. viridis*)—often together with the **surucua trogon,** or surucuá-de-peito-azul (*T. surrucura*). These are all relatives of the Guatemalan quetzal.

But otherwise being in the twilight down under the tall forest doesn't really allow you to see much. Better hide by a gap in the mantle, such as the passage of a road over a ridge, a clearing between two hills, or a river or swamp that birds must cross in the open. Fishing is also a good way to watch wildlife.

But the first call you are apt to hear in the Serra do Mar, from the longest distance, is that of the **bellbird**—araponga or pájaro campana (*Procnias nudicollis*)—white, with a green face; this is closely followed by another Cotingidae, the **hooded berryeater**—corocoxó or, in German, verrückter-Otto (*Carpornis cucullatus*). Both have had their habitat in the interior of the continent drastically reduced by deforestation. Paraguay has a beautiful melody dedicated to the bellbird—which may soon be all there is left of it in the region. The **black-tailed tityra**—anambé branco or bacaco benedictino (*Tityra cayana*)—is more apparent at Chapada dos Guimarães.

Out in the open fields where there are grass seeds, the most immediately visible birds are the small **grass quits**, especially the **blue-
black**—tiziu or semillero chirri (*Volatinia jacarina*)—which jumps up
from its perch on a post or low branch and describes a circle in the air
each time it calls. Together with it you usually find the **double-collared
seedeater**—coleirinho or corbatita de double collar (*Sporophila
caerulescens*)—as well as the **saffron finch**—canário-da-terra or canario
de tejado (*Sicalis flaveola*)—and the dwarf **blue-winged parrotlet**—
tuim or catita enana (*Forpus xanthopterygius*)—which sometimes nests in
abandoned ovenbirds' igloos.

Farther out, if the sun isn't shining, you are likely to see the **bur-
rowing owl**—coruja-buraqueira or mochuelo de hoyo (*Speotyto cunic-
ularia*)—posted beside its hole in the ground. On the hives of termites
that it feeds on you find the **campo flicker**—pica-pau-do-campo or
carpintero campestre (*Colaptes campestris*). It calls *quick-quick-quick-quick!*
In order to capture its true colors you should seek it in the sandy
Swampland, for in the east of the country it is usually tinted from exca-
vating the red lato soil.

Up in the trees the most easily visible **woodpecker** is the large
lineated—pica-pau-de-banda-branca or carpintero real barbirrayado
(*Dryocopus lineatus*). The smallest is the **white-barred piculet**—pica-
pau-anão-barrado or carpinterito comun (*Picumnus cirratus*). The **green-
barred**—pica-pau-verde-barrado or carpintero real verde (*Colaptes
melanochloros*)—with its mournful call, and the **yellow-throated**—pica-
pau-bufador or carpintero cuelliamarillo (*Piculus flavigula*)—fall in
between. The **blond-crested**—joão-velho or carpintero de cabeza
amarilla (*Celeus flavescens*)—is more easily visible in the coastal Serra do
Mar forests. An extraordinary character is the **white woodpecker**—
birro or carpintero blanco (*Melanerpes candidus*)—which flies in flocks of
five to seven and has a preference for wasp nests, which it peels off layer
after layer to feed on the larvae, indifferent to the insects' reaction. It
nests in wooden lampposts.

Farther down on the tree trunks you are likely to spot one of the
woodcreepers, or arapaçus. There are about two dozen of them, all
basically brown, sharing the woodpecker's habit of hiding behind the
trunk when you approach. One of their distinguishing features is the
size and shape of the bill. Most remarkable in that respect is the **scythe-
bill**—arapaçu-beija-flor or trepador pico de garfio (*Campylorhamphus
trochilirostris*)—that you may see in the Swampland.

The watchman out in the open pasturelands is the **southern lap-
wing**—quero-quero or alcaravan (*Vanellus chilensis*)—a colorful plover
that not only advises when animals or birds of prey approach, but attacks

them as well, for which purpose it carries a respectable spur at the fold of each wing. It lays its eggs out in the open, sometimes at the approach to a gate, and when a herd of cattle rumbles up it valiantly fends them off with outspread wings, making the big brutes open up to one side or the other. It guards the eggs and later the young communally, in threes or fives. I know when a soccer game is being played down in Rio Grande do Sul because of the ever-present lapwings in the field.

Two egrets live out in the open fields: the beautiful, soft grayish **whistling heron**—maria-faceira or garza silbadora (*Syrigma sibilatrix*)—usually in pairs, sometimes near swamps. When not feeding, it spends much of its time up in a tree, preening, scratching, and polishing itself. And wherever there are cattle, horses, buffalo or capybara, you'll find the African **cattle egret**—garça-boiadeira or garcita reznera (*Bubulcus ibis*)—which apparently migrated across the Atlantic to Venezuela in the 1930s. It only seeks the trees by the water to roost, where it gathers by the hundreds together with the **great egret**—garça-branca (*Egretta alba*); the **snowy**—garcinha-branca (*Egretta thula*)—with its bright yellow boots; the lovely, shy **capped heron**—garça-real or garciola real (*Pilherodius pileatus*); and the lonely **white-necked heron**—joão-grande or garza morena (*Ardea cocoi*). The **chestnut-bellied wood heron**—garça-da-mata or garza pechicastaña (*Agamia agami*)—is quite rare.

Other species you normally find in this environment are the common little **striated heron** or socozinho—chicuaco de cuello gris (*Butorides striatus*); the **rufescent tiger-heron**—socó-boi or pájaro vaco (*Tigrisoma lineatum*)—which moos like a cow; and the pretty, bluish **yellow-crowned night heron**—savacu or chicuaco enmascarado (*Nyctanassa violacea*)—whose call, *qua!* you hear as it flies over at night.

Another call coming out of the dark sky, especially in rainy weather, is *iirere!* emitted by the **white-faced whistling duck**—irerê or yagazo cariblanco (*Dendrocygna viduata*). A striking duck in daytime is the relatively small, fast-flying **Brazilian duck**—ananaí or pato brasileño (*Amazonetta brasiliensis*)—usually in one or two pairs, exhibiting flashy greenish blue and white wings with red feet. Largest of the family is the **muscovy duck**—pato-do-mato or pato real (*Cairina moschata*)—whose heavy wingbeat sounds like that of a vulture. The **masked duck**—marreco-cã-cã or patico enmascarado (*Oxyura dominica*)—is less common, whereas the most often found **grebe** is the **white-tufted**—mergulhão-de-orelhas-brancas or macá comun (*Podiceps rolland*)—of a grayish russet coat.

Together with the ducks you are likely to see the **common gallinule**—frango-d'água or gallineta de água (*Gallinula chloropus*)—

which carries a bright red shield upon its face and emits a soft *tuc-tuc-tuc!* call. Along the salt marshes by the coast, where there is scrub to hide, you may see the colorful **purple gallinule**—frango-d'água-azul or gallito azul (*Porphyrula martinica*)—a beauty with a green-and-red beak like the common gallinule but with a light blue spot on its forehead. Only in the Amazon, however, will you be lucky enough to see the **sunbittern**—pavãozinho-do-Pará or tigana (*Eurypyga helias*)—the only species of its family and a study in patterns of brown. There you may also spot one of the **trumpeters**—jacamim or grulla (*Psophia* spp.).

Among the larger aquatic birds, best observed in the Swampland, are the **storks.** The **maguari**—cigueña (*Euxenura maguari*)—looks a lot like the European baby stork. But most impressive is the largest, **jabiru**—tuiuiú in the Swampland, or garzon soldado (*Jabiru mycteria*): As the lagoons and flood channels begin to dry up in late winter, the jabiru rises high into the blue sky in the morning, where you can see it circling together with the **American wood stork**—cabeça-seca or gabán (*Mycteria americana*); **black vultures**—urubus or zamuro (*Coragyps atratus*); and possibly a **king vulture**—urubu-rei or rey zamuro (*Sarcoramphus papa*). The more slender, low-flying **turkey vulture**, however—urubu-cabeça-vermelha or oripopo (*Cathartes aura*)—feeds only on the carrion of wild animals, especially snakes. When the jabiru have selected a pond of the right depth to fish that day, they suddenly swoop down by the dozens, seemingly out of nowhere, and within minutes the water is surrounded by twenty to forty of these noble giants strutting about in their white suits, red neckties, and black heads, or standing still like totem poles.

Once the receding waters turn to mud it's time for the **ibis** to move in. Besides the plumbeous that I've already mentioned piping in the day, there is the **green**—coro-coró (*Mesembrinibis cayennensis*); the smaller, gregarious **bare-faced**—tapicuru or tara (*Phimosus infuscatus*)—that congregates in hundreds and, when it's very cold, beats its wings throughout the night up in its roost; the **scarlet**—guará or corocoró colorado (*Eudocimus ruber*)—found mostly in the Amazon nowadays, as it has disappeared from many coastal swamps; and the **roseate spoonbill**—colhereiro or garza paleta (*Ajaia ajaia*)—usually in small numbers.

In deeper waters fish the abundant, black **neotropic cormorants**—biguás (*Phalacrocorax olivaceus*)—and the solitary **snakebird**—biguá-tinga or viguá vibora (*Anhinga anhinga*)—of a light color.

Returning to the open fields, the largest bird here is, in the midwestern savannas, the **rhea**—ema or ñandu (*Rhea americana*)—often in flocks of about a dozen and lots of young. Since soybeans now cover much of the former savannas, the rhea have likewise adapted to this new reality; you can see them combing the dark green bean fields for insects. Also look for the **crested seriema** (*Cariama cristata*), a bird that looks rather like the North American roadrunner but has longer legs—the size of a female turkey—which you'll see in twos and threes along the edges of scrub, looking for snakes and lizards. From the top of a rock, fence pole, or termite hive it emits a long drawn-out call at sunup and sundown that embodies the savanna the way the limpkin represents the Swampland, and has been recorded in song by Italian-Brazilian accordionist and composer Mario Zan in "Seriema de Mato Grosso."

There are several tinamids out in the open fields and savannas. The **red-winged tinamou**—perdiz or martineta (*Rhynchotus rufescens*)—is the largest of all, whose call, in August and September, is one brief whistle plus three. Then there is the **spotted nothura**—codorna or perdiz chica (*Nothura maculosa*)—of a smaller size that you can hear, on rainy days, piping a lengthy *pi-pi-pi* for several seconds. The **small-billed tinamou**—inhambu-chororó or perdiz de patas rojas (*Crypturellus parvirostris*)—has a call that begins with widely spaced notes drawing closer and ending in three brief, rapid series like a policeman's whistle. Don't expect to see them, for tinamids are ground chickens notoriously difficult to sight except by chance or the patient, able use of bird calls, for which you would need the help of a backwoodsman, or caboclo, who is good at it. Frequent calls during the day signal a change in the weather.

I have already mentioned the rare **solitary tinamou**, or macuco, of the mountainous cloud forest. Its call is one single, brief note. Three or four notes is the call of a smaller relative in the forests and scrub, the **undulated tinamou**—jaó or gallineta ondulada (*Crypturellus undulatus*)—which is widely distributed and easy to attract with your bare lips. Impossible to call without the appropriate bird call and practice is the **brown tinamou**—inhambu-guaçu or poncha montañera (*Crypturellus obsoletus*)—whose trilling call begins like that of the small-billed but extends longer and ends in a series of sharper notes.

Three other birds besides the cattle egret habitually accompany cows, horses, buffalo, and capybara. One is the smooth-billed ani that I've mentioned with the cuckoos. Then there is the lemon-chested **cattle tyrant**—bem-te-vi-do-gado or atrapamoscas jinete (*Machetornis rixosus*)—often seen riding on the backs of animals, also found on lawns, mostly on the ground. And the **yellow-headed caracara**—carrapateiro, pinhé, caricare sabanero (*Milvago chimachima*)—a small hawk that feeds on ticks and grubs off the cattle, plus caterpillars, fish, and animals killed on highways. This hawk is not to be confused with the more common **crested caracara**—caracará or caricare encrestado (*Polyborus* *plancus*)—which is a larger bird with a flat head and reddish face. In my experience the crested caracara is the most intelligent and observant of our birds. At daybreak it flies along highways looking for animals killed during the night, like its yellow-headed cousin. But unlike other hawks and vultures that fly off at the approach of a vehicle, the crested caracara calmly walks over to the road shoulder, for it has perceived that cars don't pass there. In the bygone days when passenger trains crossed the Swampland between Campo Grande and Corumbá, the crested caracaras used to accompany the restaurant car, from which the cook threw them the occasional rejects from steaks, which they caught in the air, to the passengers' amusement.

There are about fifty species of hawks, falcons, and eagles. The smallest and most aggressive is the **American kestrel**—falcão quiriquiri or halcón primito (*Falco sparverius*)—a hunter of bats, birds, small animals, and insects that does not hesitate to dive at people if they happen to approach its nest. Leisurely circling in twos or threes high up in the sky you are likely to spot the mottled **roadside hawk**—gavião-carijó or gavilán habado (*Buteo magnirostris*)—imitating the call of parakeets. But presently they are down among the trees in an attack! Often visible, too, is the **white-tailed kite**—gavião-peneira or gavilán maromero (*Elanus leucurus*)—almost entirely white as seen from below while hovering, or "sifting," stationary in the air. Even more beautiful, though restricted to mountains, is the **swallow-tailed kite**—gavião-tesoura or gavilán tijereta (*Elanoides forficatus*). In mountainous environments like Chapada dos Guimarães you are also likely to see the **white-tailed hawk**—gavião-de-rabo-branco or gavilán tejé (*Buteo albicaudatus*)—large and gray with brown shoulders. My wife and I were climbing one of the tallest cliffs of Chapada along a narrow, backbone-type ridge one morning when presently a couple of them came in a shallow dive out of the heights straight at us . . . I imagined we must have gotten near their nest and was just about to duck for shelter when suddenly they separated, each narrowly sailing along opposite faces of the cliff, until they flushed a swarm of blackbirds, into which they dived.

Here you also meet a little brown bird, the **cliff flycatcher**—joão pires or atrapamoscas de precipicios (*Hirundinea ferruginea*).

The Swampland is a hawks' paradise. I will only mention a handful of the most prominent. In spring you will hear a frequent call like an exasperated *oh come on! come on, come on, come on!* That's the **laughing falcon**—acauã or pájaro guaicurú (*Herpetotheres cachinnans*)—yellowish white chested, wearing a black mask. By the water there is always a **snail-kite**—gavião-caramujeiro or gavilán caracolero (*Rostrhamus sociabilis*)—bluish brown with a very bent, sharp beak, whereas the immature are mottled. It usually alights on fence posts, and calls like beating two polished pebbles against each other. By the water you will also notice the attractive **black-collared hawk**—gavião-velho or gavilán colorado (*Busarellus nigricollis*)—easy to identify in view of its white head and heavy, leather-colored body with long wings and a short tail. It eats fish, as well as insects and aquatic mollusks, and can glide for hours on end. Another quite frequent species here is the **zone-tailed hawk**—gavião-preto or gavilán negro (*Buteo albonotatus*)—black with a yellow face. It flies like a turkey vulture and pounces on small animals.

When you get tired of walking, or it becomes too hot—as it usually does by midmorning in the open fields and savannas—you can enter the tall forest, where it remains cool, especially if there is a stream for a bath. Or you can choose yourself a tall tree, preferably one that has a dry branch or two, or ripe fruit, and hide somewhere in the shade from where you are able to observe most of the scene. Since we've already made a few incursions into the forest while discussing pertinent birds, let's opt for the tree.

That bird with the bright yellow belly up on the tallest dry twig, about the size of a kiskadee but with a smaller gray head that is forever scanning the sky above for insects, is the **tropical kingbird**—suiriri or pitirre chicarrero (*Tyrannus melancholicus*). Tyrannidae are our largest family, with more than 120 species. Let's look at some of the more outstanding individuals. Around September 5 each year the **fork-tailed flycatcher**—tesoura or atrapamoscas tijereta (*Muscivora tyrannus*)—arrives at the tropic of Capricorn from the Amazon, where it spent the winter. Here it breeds and leaves again for the equator with the first cold wave of autumn, when the tails of its young are almost fully grown and they have already learned the basics of the artful aerial maneuvers this bird performs.

Down by the swamps you may be lucky to see another, less common species, the **streamer-tailed tyrant**—tesoura-do-brejo or papamoscas yipiru (*Gubernetes yetapa*). Other attractive tyrants of the waterside include the flashy **vermilion flycatcher**—verão or viudita roja (*Pyrocephalus rubinus*)—flitting about the vegetation; the **white-headed marsh tyrant**—viuvinha or atrapamoscas duende (*Arundinicola leucocephala*)—that makes its nest of the down of the taboa reed (*Typha domingensis*); various **monjitas,** such as the maria-branca (*Xolmis* spp.); and the beautiful **masked water-tyrant**—lavadeira-mascarada (*Fluvicola nengeta*)—white with the softest russet neck, usually on the ground. Here is where you would also expect to find a couple of Icteridae, the **white-browed blackbird**—polícia-inglesa or pechicolorado chico (*Leistes superciliaris*)—immediately noticeable with its red chest and wide, jet-fighter wings; and the **yellow-rumped marsh-bird**—chopim-do-brejo or pechiamarillo grande (*Pseudoleistes guirahuro*)—black fronted with a yellow belly.

You can never be long near water without the passage of a **king-fisher**, largest and noisiest of which is the **ringed**—martim-pescador matraca (*Ceryle torquata*)—especially where there are tall, earthen banks it can breed in. Here you also see the **green**—martim-pescador (*Chloroceryle americana*). But even a completely isolated pool at the foot of Serra da Bodoquena east of the Swampland, containing a small school of shiners, has on occasion been visited by a **pygmy kingfisher**—arirambinha (*Chloroceryle aenea*)—even though it lay a kilometer (0.6 mile) or more from the next water body.

In the appendix, you will find a list of bird books on Brazil and Venezuela.

PART TWO

HEALTH AND SAFETY

4

FIRE AND FLOOD

ESCAPING BRUSHFIRE

Since the best time of the year to visit the Swampland, the Amazon, and the eastern cloud forests is the mostly cooler and dry late autumn, winter, and early spring—May through October—it's no exaggeration at all to foresee your possible involvement in a brushfire, which can turn into a frightening experience if you're unprepared for it.

Horse Sense

In the spring of 1967 three of us were riding across the Swampland on Fazenda Bodoquena, east of Corumbá. With me, the cattle section manager, were the general manager (an agronomist) and the section foreman (a native of the Swampland).

During the entire week in the field we had been encountering lines of flames. They'd begun somewhere along the 100 kilometers (62 miles) of the Noroeste railroad across the ranch (there was no other road then) from live ashes shoveled out of steam locomotives, flying cinders, and cigarette stubs.

And on this particular late afternoon we suddenly found ourselves cut off by the advancing flames from behind, with a deep, dark corixo— a flood channel—ahead of us, so heavily overgrown and entangled with lianas that it would have been dangerous to risk swimming the horses across—any injury or snare might have initiated a piranha attack.

Near us stood an isolated woods, known as a capão in the Pantanal, consisting mostly of carandá palms (*Copernicia alba*) standing deep in dry matter. The general manager proposed, surprisingly, that we enter the woods and wait out the fire there. To this I objected, pointing out that inside this particular capão there was much more dead matter to intensify the flames than out here in the open grass.

The section foreman saved the day by resorting to lore. He suggested we give our horses the reins and let the animals decide. Confirming what is known as horse sense, the three pantaneiros did not hesitate: They took off at a gallop straight for the advancing flames, chose a spot where the vegetation was thinner, and sailed across the line of fire, after which they had mostly ashes under their hooves.

Should you have the experience, while out walking, of finding yourself cornered by advancing brushfires, the first thing is not to panic, bearing in mind that tropical fires are nowhere near as intense as those in temperate zones.

Here are the procedures to follow:

If there is water, mud, sand, or a sufficiently large clearing in which to wait out the fire, get busy lighting counterfires to reduce the fuel available to the advancing flames around you, thus deadening their intensity and broadening your breathing space (see Fire Against Fire, below). Be sure to have on hand some sturdy palm leaf or other green branch with which to control the direction of your counterfire before lighting it.

In the event that there is nowhere to make such a stand, and the height of the vegetation or wind conditions are unfavorable for a safe counterfire, then here is what you must do:

1. Take your plastic raincoat out of your companion bag (see chapter 13) and put it on, including the hood, and have your pruning shears handy. If possible tie a wet handkerchief across your nose and mouth to filter the smoke.

2. Select a spot where the flames are (or will be when they reach it) less intense. If there is wind, then the line of fire advancing upwind (against the wind) will be milder.

3. Do as our horses did: Crash through the line of fire and keep on moving until you're out of the smoke, so that you can breathe freely, cutting any eventual crisscrossing creepers out of the way with your shears as you go.

But do not stampede, as this is no time or place to risk a debilitating accident, such as stepping into an armadillo hole and breaking your leg or foot.

Both the Swampland and cerrados, or savannas, have frequent sandy spots, trails and erosions, or water where you can either wait out a fire or make an unimpeded retreat.

If you are on a mountain and find fires coming up the slopes, it's advisable to study the terrain and the wind, then make your exit early, before the whole place gets enveloped in smoke and heat. Here you can perish in any of three ways if you procrastinate: heat, carbon monoxide poisoning, and asphyxiation when the flames consume your oxygen.

UNDERSTANDING BRUSHFIRE

There are three important things to know about brushfires in the Tropics:

1. No resinous wood. Here we don't have those heavily resinous conifers of temperate forests, which burn like pyres all the way up to the crown. With rare exceptions, tropical fires move along the underbrush, close to the ground. So they are not that risky to break through. Which is not to suggest climbing a tree to wait for the fire to pass, because heat rises, and the smoke does with it!

2. A line of fire. The flames usually move in an irregular line according to available fuel, mostly leaving dead ashes behind, except for the odd smoldering stump. So once you are through, the danger has mostly stayed behind, except for residual smoke.

3. High- and low-intensity periods. A tropical brushfire has a high-intensity burning period, which lasts from about 9 or 10 A.M.—when the sun has dried up the dew—until after sundown. The low-intensity period starts when dew sets in around the middle of the night and lasts until sunup. That's when the fire, in a windless night, becomes almost dormant, and large stretches go out altogether.

Wind, on the other hand, will keep a fire going, like a bellows, and turn any attempts at control in higher places into a nightmare, pushing the smoke ahead just where you would have to tackle it. Any work in such weather would have to be restricted to the bottom of the lower valleys, which are more protected from the wind.

So if you must either cross a line of fire or put it out, but are not under pressure to do so immediately, then the predawn and earliest daytime hours are the best time to move.

FIGHTING A BRUSHFIRE

Fire Against Fire

If you are forced to stand and fight an approaching fire, as when it threatens valuable property that cannot be evacuated, or it happens to be a breakaway fire from your own camp for which you are responsible, then the best procedure is to counter fire with fire, as mentioned above. Arm yourself with some green, stiff palm leaves, branches or bundles of vegetation, water, and a shovel (if available), using these to beat out the flames going where you don't want them to go. Like any military commander preparing for a battle, choose the best terrain—in this case the cleanest, where there is the sparsest fuel; then start a counterfire to meet and kill the undesirable one. Try to keep this counterfire under control so that animals retreating ahead of the flames you propose to combat are not trapped between the two fires. Also, you want to keep your own fire from turning around on you. The best way to start a counterfire is to light a bundle of dry matter and run or walk along your proposed line of defense for 5 to 10 meters (yards) at a time, then turn back to control the lighted stretch before moving on.

Patrolling the Firebreak

This line, once it has been extended as far as necessary, must then be patrolled preventively. You want to make sure no new fires spark up with a breeze, or a burning leaf is levitated by the hot air and lands across the firebreak, or a dry, burning trunk collapses across the firebreak.

Don't Lose Your Head

The most important thing is not to panic. Then follow the instructions herein.

Fire must be dealt with like a battle, with tactics and an overall strategy. So think as a commander: Is this a case for attack, defense, or retreat? Where and when is the "enemy" most vulnerable? Above all, your information (lookout) system must remain alert throughout the operation to avoid getting yourself corralled by fire coming in from the rear or flanks to cut off your route of retreat.

Keep your eyes, ears, and nose open for smoke, telltale crackling, or fleeing animals. Once the presence of fire has been verified, check the wind to know which way it's moving. In mountainous terrain a fire will eat its way up the slopes and cliffs, spurred on by the wind its own rising hot air generates. Memorize water and clearings along your passage to fall back on if necessary. Observe the density and dryness of the vegetation. When possible, go and look at the fire—spy on it—while your rear is safely open to retreat. Study a fire's behavior in order to identify its weak spots.

FLOOD

The risk of a flash flood must be imprinted on a jungle camper's mind like second nature. It should always be his first consideration in selecting a site to camp.

Look for telltale signs in the vegetation—driftwood up in the tree branches, scrub bent downriver, bark sheared off by rocks, debris lodged in nooks and crevices—to evaluate how high the water can get. Avoid gullies, especially below the line where the rocks are bare, and valley bottoms. In the Swampland you should opt for the isolated islands of forest out in the field, where the ground is 2 or 3 meters (7 to 10 feet) higher than the surrounding swamps. It must be remembered that alluvial ground on riverbanks, high as it may be, was deposited there by floods that rose even higher.

When I built bridges on the opening trans-Amazon highway along the foothills of Serra dos Carajás in the state of Pará, our free-span quota (the free-flowing space for the river under the beams and bridge floor) was 7 meters, or 23 feet, above dry-season levels. And that was just barely enough. While fishing from high, sandy beaches by the Xingu River Falls below Altamira, it was sobering to look up into the tree crowns above and find swaths of flood debris and driftwood lodged there.

Once my wife, Maria, and I stopped our jeep on the bank of a creek at the foot of the Serra do Mar range near Ubatuba in the northeast of São Paulo state in a broad, forested valley. After exploring the surroundings we tied our hammocks—one above the other, under a single tarpaulin—to two trees on the creekbank. Typically, it poured with rain until about midnight, when Maria—who occupied the lower hammock—woke me to say she was in the water! Looking out, a pale moon shone placidly on a sea of water surrounding us. There was nothing else for her to do but climb up into my hammock. The car keys, which lay on the bottom of our joint, zippered mosquito net, were safe; but one of her boots, which had remained on the outside, was gone. In the morning we had to light a little fire under the motor to get the car started.

5

JUNGLE INSECTS AND ARACHNIDS

PARASITES

Cattle Grubs or Bernes (*Dermatobia hominis*)

Jungle parasites are generally tiny and hard to see, and usually manifest their presence only when they have already begun to cause trouble: either exploding in their semifinal, larval form, as is the case with cattle grubs, chiggers, *Larva migrans*, maggots, and intestinal worms, or when biting themselves fast, like ticks and leeches. Therefore the utmost care must be given to a study of what to expect and the corresponding preventive measures to be taken, which boil down to dressing properly, sterilizing drinking water, applying tick repellent where necessary, and performing body inspections when bathing.

When I was a cavalry sergeant serving on the border with Paraguay at Ponta Porã in the late 1950s, I made friends with two American oil engineers who had come down from Aruba to plant coffee in the Paraguayan Chiriguelo region, together with a lot of other foreigners swindled into a deal too big to describe here. Every now and then John Morgenthaler and Paul Ruhther met with me in town over lunch to swap news.

One day they arrived at my room with John looking rather distressed. He took off his shirt to reveal a reddish lump on his shoulder. Inside, he said, there seemed to be something moving. A visiting American doctor had been pressing it, to no avail—or rather, to aggravate the condition, for he didn't know what it was.

"Watch the procedure, boys," I told them, "in case it happens again. Tomorrow you'll laugh at how simple it is!" I cleaned the spot with alcohol while Paul watched, and pointed out to him the tiny hole in the middle of the lump, through which the intruder breathes. Then I flat-

41

tened a piece of adhesive tape about 2.5 centimeters (1 inch) square over the area, making sure there was no air pocket. "Don't touch the place, protect it from water during your shower, and come back tomorrow!"

The next day I slowly raised the tape with one hand while with the other I pressed gently behind the lump, that is to say, between the lump and the body. Thus the dead worm came out, its head stuck to the tape where it had tried to reach air. Then all we had to do was cover the hole with a Band-Aid.

A berne is the larva of the fly *Dermatobia hominis*. The wiggling worms travel attached to a host fly, which in turn deposits them either on a leaf that mammals might touch or directly on the bare skin. They penetrate the skin and develop underneath.

To know whether the insect occurs in a given region you need only look on the backs of cattle and dogs for oozing lumps. People get them occasionally in exposed areas of the skin, mainly the shoulders, neck, and head, usually in mountainous country, and always singly.

If you happen to get one on the head, you need to shave the spot in order for the tape to adhere properly; no air must be allowed to penetrate. No attempt should be made to press out the *live* grub. Its body is not only much larger than the hole in your skin, but also corrugated and bristly as an adult. Moreover, the pain of trying to press it out alive is the lesser evil: It may also burst inside with the effort, producing a first-class infection that might require surgery to clean out.

Some locals attach a cube of bacon in place of the tape, so that the grub climbs out of the skin and into the bacon in its search for air.

Maggot Flies or Varejeira (*Cochliomya macellaria* and others)

This insect must be guarded against at all times—not only with regard to any open, exposed wound, but also with meats and fish for the table. When handling these, avoid touching your ears or nose with an unwashed finger; the smell alone is sufficient to attract the fly to you when unawares, such as when you are taking a nap in an unscreened hammock. Should the larvae manage to enter your ear or nose, you are in for terrible suffering and possibly death.

Though there are several maggot flies, the most common and widely distributed is *Cochliomya macellaria*—a large, shiny blue-green fly that has the habit of hovering in midair, when you can easily hear its humming, similar to a honeybee's. It is viviparous, depositing its whitish larvae—which look like grated cheese—directly upon or as near as possible to a wound. At this stage they can be scraped off with a knife. From here they start eating their way into the wound within hours, doubling their size each day up to about 2.5 centimeters (1 inch). Once inside, they are best extracted individually with tweezers and patience, followed by adequate protection to avoid reinfestation.

Protection consists in maintaining good hygiene and covering dry wounds with insect repellent salve such as hipoglós or wet ones with Anaseptil dust or bandages. Meats and fish must be either sealed in plastic (for short periods) or thoroughly salted and preferably screened.

Chiggers, Bicho-do-pé, or Nígua (*Sarcopsylla* or *Pulex penetrans*)

In your emergency kit there must always be two or three well-honed and -polished, stainless sewing needles—preferably so sharp that if you touch the tip with your finger, it penetrates before you know it!

If you are bothered by an itch under your toenail, the indispensable magnifying glass in your companion bag (good also for lighting fires in sunny weather) will show you the bicho-do-pé or nígua in the form of a dark brown dot, a bit larger than the period printed by a typewriter, in the middle of a small sac of pus. This you lance with your sharp needle and scoop out, sac and all. Disinfect the site, and always wear shoes and socks thereafter. You pick them up from walking barefoot on beaches and sandy riverside trails. Germans call them "sand fleas," Brazilians "foot-animals."

Larva Migrans or Bicho Geográfico

When an intense itch appears—generally under the foot but sometimes also on the belly, buttocks, and other parts of the body if you've been in contact with the sands of beaches polluted by feces of capybara or dogs—search the area through your magnifying glass, after washing, for reddish "geographic designs" that look like rivers under the skin.

No use scratching. That's the bicho geográfico (*Larva migrans*), and now is the time to use your tube of Foldan ointment (tiabendazol—whatever it is, it works). Apply the ointment twice or more times a day for *five* days, on and around the affected area—which moves, mind you!

Not long ago I had an infestation that began around my belt line. As I applied the medicine, the fleeing worms moved up along my side and across my chest so that I could see the channels advancing before my eyes while I spread the ointment practically every hour. They passed under my armpit to the shoulder, on top of which they finally died. It was an experience!

Wearing sneakers and sitting on newspaper or something when on the beach or fishing from a sandy shore should prevent the problem. Although flip-flops are better than nothing, they often sink into the sand and the strap snaps.

Ticks, Carrapatos, or Garrapata
(*Amblyomma cayennense* and others)

There are three basics about ticks, whether they are at the stage of the tiny pin dots spreading in a brown circle of thousands on your trousers as you follow a cattle or game trail across low brush in the early dry season, or the pinhead size in their dozens toward the end, or finally the odd individual adult carrapato estrela.

1. They should be scraped off your clothes with a knife or machete or else beaten off with a short stick, which rids you of most of them. This has to be repeated as you detect more. But that's not enough. Every day you must scrub your body energetically with a natural dishcloth gourd (bucha) or other coarse sponge, and soap. This is best done during lunch break, when you can see well, and again in the evening, before they have time to bite themselves tight.

2. After bathing and while drying yourself you need to wash your clothes as well if you are allergic to the insect's bite. While these are drying make a complete examination of all parts and folds of your body, with the help of the mirror in your companion bag and your sense of touch, to pick off the survivors. These should either be cracked between your fingernails or dropped into the water, where they drown easily—if the shiners, or lambarís, don't get them first. As long as this procedure is followed you should not feel any major discomfort, which can be anything from a mere itch in the case of nonallergic people all the way to a rash with fever, as was the case with my sister-in-law's husband, who had to see a doctor. Fenergan ointment is a good antidote for this and other insect bites.

3. Pay attention—what in North America is known as Rocky Mountain spotted fever is called in Brazil febre maculosa do carrapato and in Spanish, fiebre maculosa del garrapata. Red spots appear around the wrists and other joints, together with fever. My wife and I had a mild attack from but a few immature specimens in the Chapada dos Guimarães National Park mountains east of Cuiabá, Mato Grosso, in the very center of South America, which lasted for a little over a week. My daughter, who got one or two ticks from us in the car, had an even milder manifestation. But to some it can be lethal.

What can be done to prevent ticks? Well, my maternal grandfather, who was a painter and spent most of his life out in nature, used to spray turpentine—which he needed for mixing his paints—on his clothes. Any repellent with a lasting, strong smell will do, but beware of fire! If you are staying longer, much as with malaria prevention, you cannot keep passing insect repellent on your skin day after day, because our skin has pores that absorb the poison, so that in the end the repellent does more harm than good. Whenever you are given the choice between a chemical and a mechanical solution, by all means opt for the latter. Anything moving on your skin is to be checked, for it may be an estrela tick, which should be removed before it has the chance to bite itself tight. Or you can choose to visit in the appropriate time of the year, the rainy season—late September to early March—when ticks have mostly vanished.

Left, the conenose or kissing bug—barbeiro (Triatoma geniculata)*—is a transmitter of* Trypanosoma cruzi, *which causes Chagas' disease. Right, the* Anopheles *mosquito (note its characteristic sitting posture, at an angle to the body) transmits malaria, though not in the Swampland.*

Leeches, Sanguessugas, or Sanguijuela (*Haementeria ghilianii* and others)

Only once have I found one of these bloodsuckers on myself, when I was a boy, in a swamp near Pitangueiras in the north of São Paulo state. Take some salt from your food bag, spread a few grains upon the leech, and it will drop off your body by itself. They are inhabitants of moist places like swamps, but some also live on land. In the Amazon they reach an impressive size.

If I had to wade around in waters harboring leeches I would either order a pair of waist-high fly fisherman's boots (not available locally), or else have strong elastic sewn into the hems of my trousers to close tightly around boot leggings. Temperature permitting, this is also a good idea for protection against ticks and other insects. And I would never drink directly from a body of water, for leeches may dash up and enter the stomach.

ANTS
Correição Army Ant (*Eciton praedator*)

You perceive the approach of this medium-sized black army ant by the rustling and fluttering of fleeing insects and small animals ahead of these troops of Huns, which leave nothing alive, entering every nook and cranny and climbing every tree in their path. The presence of birds such as antshrikes (*Formicariidae* spp.) and tyrants feasting on the fleeing fauna may be another indication.

There is no need to panic if you wish to observe these interesting soldiers in action, as long as you wear boots and pants with elastic-lined hems, maintain an open line of retreat, and leave no edibles within their reach. The bite of a correição is not particularly painful on an individual basis, but this is an army of *thousands*.

The other day I was watching them climbing a sheer, brittle, sandy wall. Those carrying insects and larvae could not get a sufficiently firm hold and would fall back down. So they lined their zigzag path up the bank with a soft wall of thousands of their fellows on each side. Slipping carrier ants then dropped only a short distance back against either one of these propping walls, and proceeded from there.

A live wall of thousands of army ants (Eciton praedator) marches up a vertical, brittle sand bank that shortens and cushions the frequent fall of companions loaded with prey.

Should they invade your camp when there is

no condition or time to rescue things, you might apply kerosene or repellent to the ropes connecting your hammock to the trees, get inside, zip the mosquito net shut and raise it off the ground, then lie back and wait out their passage.

Lavapés Fire Ant (*Solenopsis saevissima*)

This is the smallest of the fire ants and the most common. It builds its mounds of soil on lawns, in pastures, and the edges of trails, usually during the rainy season. And the moment you tread on one, thousands of little reddish combatants swarm out over your foot and attack, causing intense itching.

When you happen to be near water, the best remedy is to step into the liquid with a bar of soap and sponge and wash off the aggressive devils. That's where their name comes from: *Lavapes* means "wash the feet." In case there is no water, rub them off energetically, then apply Fenergan ointment.

The itch doesn't last long. Scrubbing with sponge and soap alleviates it more rapidly. Wearing shoes and socks is the best preventive measure—and watching where you tread.

Novato Fire Ant or Taxí (*Pseudomyrma* spp.)

A beautiful, cone-shaped tree in the Pantanal has large leaves and dark pink flowers; when it drops its seeds they come down like little helicopters. Stay away from it! The name of this tree is pau de novato, which means "greenhorn tree" (*Triplaris formicosa*), because only an outsider would be foolish enough to touch it.

Fire ants live inside the tree, which is hollow, and the moment you touch it they emerge from little holes under the joints of branches and leaves by the hundreds and simply fall upon you, stinging as they go, so that in a few minutes you will be all tattooed and burning. It hurts! It hurts for hours afterward, like wasp stings.

In parts of the Amazon there is a similar tree, *Taxia guianensis*.

Saúva Cutter Ant (*Atta* spp.)

The largest colonies of ants found in tropical South America are the various atta cutter ants, whose dwellings can be the size of a basement and are easily recognized by the mounds of earth brought up from deep down, of a distinctly lighter color than the organic surface soil, and the clean-cut trails leading to them, which their legions occupy after sundown to go cut and bring home the leaves to farm the fungi on which they live.

A saúva army consists of reddish brown workers and soldiers, the latter immediately recognizable by their large, bright red heads with powerful pincers. Unlike correição army ants, saúva follow their clearly marked trails and won't fight you unless you happen to block their passage, when the warriors can produce nasty, scissorlike cuts. They are, however, attracted by salt.

Many years ago, as a soldier, I was camping by a brook in the Serra do Mar cloud forest southwest of Santos with a companion. We had climbed up from the railroad station by the seaside for the better part of the afternoon. When I washed my underwear, handkerchief, and socks that evening so that they would dry by the fire and be fresh and clean to put on in the morning, I forgot a white, sweat-soaked T-shirt, which remained on the rock, unwashed, a little apart.

When I went over to pick it up the next day, a neat half-moon the size of my fingertips came off in my hand—and this continued to happen in every place where I tried to lift the shirt. Searching for the salt from my sweat, the saúva had cut up the entire garment into little half-moons!

In the Amazon the saúva's trails are impressive 30-centimeter (1-foot) highways, with one lane to go, another to return. The ants look from a distance like an anaconda crossing the road!

Tocandira Stinging Ant (*Paraponera clavata*)

This large, sturdy black ant is usually a loner minding its own business, so long as you don't touch it. The trouble is, the tocandira is a common ant found almost anywhere walking about. So care must be taken at all times before touching anything at all—your own rucksack, firewood, a bromelia. Always tap and shake your shoes before slipping your feet inside.

Indians use this stinging ant in the rituals young men undergo to reach adulthood and become warriors.

One night I was climbing a tree near a salt lick by the Apa River on the border with Paraguay below Bela Vista, Mato Grosso do Sul, with hopes that some animal might come to the lick. To reach the branch where I intended to tie up my hammock, I had to climb past a rather voluminous bromelia in one of the forks. There was a tocandira nest in the bromelia, and three or four of these ants stung me in the arm. I gave up on my hunt.

Other Ants

In a tropical jungle there are simply so many varieties and sheer numbers of ants that a sloppily managed camp becomes a gold mine with hordes of "prospectors" descending upon it. But food—especially sugar—is not all that attracts them: Shoes, a shirt hanging from a chair, clothes on a line, hats become infested; every now and then there's an ant biting you for no apparent reason, mostly causing only an inconvenient itch or burn. There are large black ants that you rarely notice walking about, yet within twenty-four hours they've got a nest with dozens of individuals in your clothes!

OTHER AGGRESSIVE INSECTS

Bees, Abelhas, or Abejas (*Apis mellifera adansonii* and others)

In the Swampland you may be surprised by a piece of advice that runs more or less like this: "If you happen upon a fierce-looking bull, jaguar, alligator, or anaconda, stand perfectly still until it has moved off. But see that woods over there? Don't go near it, because there's *bees* in there!"

Across the vast sedimentary plain of the Mato Grosso Pantanal or Spanish Chaco, where no pesticides are used and there are trees, shrubs, vines, grasses, or aquatic plants in bloom year-round, the greatest health hazard—potentially fatal—is the European honeybee (*Apis mellifera*), sometimes Africanized.

The Swampland is the honeybee's paradise. Alongside the many varieties of wild bees—which are harmless—you find the European bees' nests hanging from branches, inside hollow trunks, in abandoned termite hives and armadillo holes, under overhanging riverbanks, and in the roofs of houses and barns.

Besides these established colonies there are always migrating swarms around separatist queens hanging on the tips of branches or suddenly buzzing overhead. These won't bother you unless you collide with them.

The victims of bees are often fishermen, who come in large numbers from the industrial east after the dorado (*Salminus maxillosus*), pintando (*Pseudoplatystoma* spp.), and pacu (*Colossoma mitrei*), make a lot of irritating noise with their outboard motors, and pay little attention to the riverside vegetation.

But not only outsiders are hit: An ex-student of mine from Corumbá, born and brought up in the Pantanal, died when he and his companions were easing their boat in among the sarã vegetation (*Sapium haematospermum*) in order to tie it up, and the bees fell upon them. With nowhere else to go they dived overboard to seek refuge in the water. But this young man had already been stung by too many. He suffered heart and respiratory failure and drowned.

In such a case the boat should be promptly overturned and everybody dive in underneath; forget about lost gear. Push the canoe out and let the current carry it away.

Other targets are noisy parties crashing through the brush, wielding machetes, for the sounds and smells of cut vegetation and sweat irritate the insects, as do brushfires. Riding parties of tourists, although better equipped to outrun the bees, are on the other hand exposed to the double danger of stampeding horses throwing, dragging, or trampling inexperienced riders. It is therefore a must to be accompanied by a local cowboy guide.

If you are a nature-watcher interested in zoology and botanics, keep your party small and observe the "S" recommendation—no sound, smell, or speed; stay out of sight—and keep absolutely still in the face of potential danger, always paying special attention to the telltale buzz of bees. You should as a rule have no trouble, even though you may occasionally find yourself facing a hive at little more than arm's length. Wait until the insects have calmed down and gone back to their normal activities, then retreat slowly, being careful not to snap any branches underfoot, always watching the bees. One or two scouts may fly out to inspect you; remain immobile until they've gone. The procedure is the same when you find a snake in your path.

A piece of important advice, though: Keep your body and clothes clean! Many Northern Europeans, especially young people, are unaccustomed to bathing and washing their clothes every day, walking around in smelly, sweaty T-shirts, jeans, and socks for the duration of their trip. You may get away with lax hygiene in cold winters up in the temperate regions, but here in the Tropics where warm temperatures exacerbate sweating and smells, you must wash your clothes every day and, when walking out in the jungle, bathe twice a day: at lunch break and at the end of the day's excursion. When it comes to bees, a strong-smelling body becomes, in itself, a health hazard.

Do not under any circumstances whack scouting bees or beat about you, even if they should alight on you: The smell of a squashed bee may bring the whole colony upon you. And if that happens, you are in serious trouble . . . you cannot outrun them, and if you jump into the nearest water *while flailing about unnaturally*, you are inviting the piranhas to join the party, as has happened on occasion.

What to do, then?

You stand the best chance if you are on horseback. Give your mount the reins and hang on for dear life, for a horse will outrun the bees. But remember: You won't. So where there is water, dive in—naturally, without beating about lest the piranhas get the wrong idea—and swim underwater as far as you can, preferably to come up in the shelter of some vegetation. So long as you swim or dive normally and there's no blood you needn't worry about piranhas.

Where there is no water, one of the few things you can do is to dive into the densest vegetation and move under its cover where the insects have difficulty following; if there is nowhere to go, lie still and wait out the attack. There being no cover nearby, get under the plastic raincoat from your companion bag to reduce the exposed areas. Don't bother about the odd bee that may have gotten inside, because each bee stings only once. Or set the grass on fire and move away in the smoke. Whatever you do, remember that after the attack has begun it's a life-and-death battle for both you and the bees, which die after stinging.

Someone allergic to bees should not run the risk of a sting in the first place, for it may mean death. Remember: The honeybee is the most dangerous animal in the Swampland! Even if you are not allergic and can take anywhere from one to two dozen stings without major conse-quence, the poison is cumulative. We all have a breaking point some-where along the line at which our immune system succumbs.

In the case of a party of people under attack, each individual should run in a different direction—without slapping at the bees—in order to break down the pursuing colony into fewer attackers. If a wooded area is not available for shelter, resort to fire with plenty of smoke. (Don't for-get to advise the rancher as soon as possible if you are unable to put the fire out yourself.)

The time of the day is important with bees. Early in the morning, when it's cool, they are seldom aggressive; on sweltering, stuffy after-noons preceding storms, however, they are most irritable. As soon as they've become accustomed to your presence they are unlikely to molest you, though when there's fire or vibrating noise (say, from a chain saw or motor) in the vicinity you must be on guard.

Bees out working will only sting if you touch them. Sometimes in the late dry season (September) in the Swampland you'll find tens of thousands around the edges of the few remaining pools of water, or floating on them in mats, like duckweed. Herds of cattle approach, blow aside the buoyant rafts of insects, and drink unmolested. Bees only attack to defend their queen and nest, and it's a kamikaze attack.

Native Tropical South American Bees

Though there are close to fifty kinds of native bees, these should not scare you because, except for the large and well-known bumblebee, native bees do not sting, are mostly smaller, have naked eyes as compared to the furry eyes of the dangerous Africanized European bee, and do not swarm like the latter.

Some, such as the black irapuá (*Trigona fulviventris*), whose large, dark nest looks like a tree termites', will go for your hair if you get too close, from where their sticky bodies require patience to disentangle. Lambe-olhos—eye licker (*Nannotrigona duckey*)—is, with all of its 2-millimeter length, the world's smallest bee, and may sometimes bother your eyes in search of humidity, but this bee is not to be confused with a tiny fly of the same popular name (*Hippelates* spp.), quite a pest on sweltering days in the savanna and open grasslands.

Others, like the small (4-millimeter) yellow jataí (*Trigona jaty*), which nests in cracks among rocks and in tree trunks, produce delicious, medicinal honey. Many are very beautiful, among them the northeastern Brazilian uruçu (*Melipona* x *scutellaris*) with its black, laterally white-striped abdomen, head, and thorax of a bright, tawny fur. Some are social, living in colonies, while others are solitary.

Beetles, Besouros, or Abejorros

The burrico rove beetle or potó (*Paederus* spp.) is a small, lead-colored beetle that secretes a caustic liquid that produces skin lesions such as erythema and ulceration resistant to treatment; if an eye is struck, it can cause blindness. The most dangerous areas are near bright lights on spring and summer evenings, such as open-air cafés in places by the Swampland like Corumbá or in the Amazon.

Your protection consists in keeping away from bright lights. With that you will also be free of another rather frightening though harmless insect, the giant water bug—baratão d'água (*Lethocerus grandis*). That can reach a good 7.5 centimeters (3 inches) and circles the lights at such high speed that if it should accidentally collide with your head it may knock you out cold. It's so tough that if it's crawling across the street and a car rolls over it, it may continue on its way unabated.

Caterpillars, Taturanas, or Orugas

It was the first time I was taken along on a wild pigeon hunt with my uncle and older brother. I was all excited as we clambered through the brush at daybreak, following an overgrown trail that lead toward a stand of caruru (*Amaranthus* spp.), whose dark berries were much sought after by these shy birds. I was about five years old.

Right after brushing past some leaves—probably guava—I felt a rapidly growing pain in my arm that rose up to the neck and down my flank with such intensity that I was soon howling.

We had nothing better than tobacco and soap to rub on in those days, and that simply had to do. But our backwoods caboclos (as the

South American hill-billy is called) say the best antidote is to squash the caterpillar and spread the mass from its bowels across the affected area. I haven't had an opportunity to try that.

When my daughter Jaci was between two and three, one day she presented a similar clinical picture. Remembering my experience as a child, I went out into the garden where she had been playing, and indeed located the culprit on the trunk of our guava tree: a caterpillar about 7 centimeters (2.8 inches) long of the flannel moth, known as lagarta de fogo, or fire caterpillar. It has a smooth, silvery mane of long hairs the color of a puma and rising in the middle

Only long sleeves and pants will shield the jungle walker from poisonous caterpillars such as this megalopygidae (Podalia *spp.), positioned under the leaf, where it is not visible but will severely burn any exposed part of the body brushing past, causing intense generalized pain.*

like the back of an angry dog. It is on these hairs that it carries its defensive venom.

Several other caterpillars have hairs or barbs of varying toxicity. The main problem with these insects is their perfect camouflage against tree trunks or the underside of branches and leaves, where they hide during the day from birds such as the papa-lagarta—the dark-billed cuckoo or cuclillo grisáceo (*Coccyzus melacoryphus*). But nature has a way of giving one the weapon and the other the protection against it: The inner surface of our hands and feet is practically immune to caterpillar hairs (though not to penetrating barbs). Thus the pain occurs when you touch them with another part of the body.

There is something going on in southern Brazil at this moment that may become known as a momentous event in biological evolution: A caterpillar appears to have replaced its traditional venom with a more potent formula! So much so that it is now called the killer caterpillar.

The larva of a moth (*Hylesia* spp.), it has been occuring in the most heavily farmed regions of Rio Grande do Sul and Santa Catarina states. These are the areas most intensely subjected to agrotoxic poisoning.

This may well be an early manifestation of Mother Nature's endeavor to rearm her children more adequately in the face of the array of poisons—against weeds, against insects, against fungi, against nematodes—with which humans have been raping their environment.

The sobering fact for us, in this guide to walking the jungle, is that this caterpillar's new poison has already killed several people through generalized hemorrhage.

So how can you protect yourself?

Tropical vegetation is full of beautiful butterflies by day and exotic moths by night. This means lots and lots of caterpillars of all sorts, of which only a few are poisonous. Just to give you an idea of the numbers, during a recent trip to Bahia in the early-summer month of December I traveled ten full days with orange, yellow, and lemon butterflies of the genus *Pieridae* heading north almost without pause. I had already witnessed the same phenomenon along the trans-Amazon highway, likewise in December. Millions of them.

The best protection—as recommended repeatedly in this guide— is dressing fully, including gloves. This is especially important when touching plants, climbing trees, and so on, when you cannot always see where you are placing your hands.

Cockroaches, Baratas, or Cucarachas (*Periplaneta americana* and *Blatella germanica*)

This is an insect to beware of not so much out in the wild but rather close to human habitations: in manioc flour sheds, abandoned or uninhabited houses, or shabby hotel rooms close to kitchen or bathrooms.

I have been bitten by cockroaches in all these places. At health posts in poorer regions it's also common to come across infants bitten by these pests.

One memorable experience happened during the opening of the trans-Amazon highway. The road-building company for which we were constructing one of our bridges near Tucuruí in Pará was having money problems and thus lagged behind in the delivery of cement for the pillar bases and road ramparts. When the rainy season set in, there was nothing to do but pack up in a hurry and leave before we found ourselves cut off by floods.

All afternoon and far into the night we fought the effects of the first heavy rains: sanding slippery gradients; lining mud holes with branches; wading slowly across inundated flats, followed by the truck, to make sure the road and temporary bridges were still there; filling erosions with trunks and stones for the heavily loaded vehicle to get across; pushing and shoveling every so often.

It was midnight by the time we rolled into the village of Repartimento on the main Marabá–Altamira trunk. Wet, mud spattered, and tired as hell, we headed straight for the empty mess hall of a construction company that had moved on some three months earlier.

The only thing the boys wanted was to tie their hammocks and go to sleep. Some didn't even bother to rig up their mosquito nets, despite the place being a malaria hole. Soon it was quiet.

But after what seemed only minutes we were all wide awake: There appeared to be some kind of poltergeist on a rampage. Shoes were being dragged about, there were squeaks and rustlings all over the place, people were cursing and slapping about in the dark. Even the ropes of my hammock were vibrating!

I switched on my rather weakened flashlight, and the scene I saw was straight out of Steven Spielberg. Outside my mosquito net there were two or three rats gnawing away at the ropes. The wooden walls had a rafter halfway up and all around to reinforce the vertical plank structure, which was now packed tight with rats, one next to the other, their eyes shining like a city street. And everywhere—on the mosquito nets, walls, floor, clothes, everything—there were dark oval shapes flitting about: cockroaches. Hundreds of them!

There was but one thing we could do that night: We gathered our things and beat a hasty retreat back out onto the damp and dirty truck bed, spread an old canvas tarpaulin over us for some protection, and spent the night there.

As the next day broke we prepared to counterattack. From the local pharmacy we got an 18-liter can of strong disinfectant, which was mixed into a 200-liter drum of water. Everybody armed themselves with sticks, brooms, tool handles, and buckets, and then we attacked with a vengeance. Rats that made it out of reach of the brooms up to the roof I shot down with a little .410-bore insert barrel in my 12-bore shotgun. The remainder were beaten to death after they emerged from their flooded holes together with all the cockroaches. Even medieval war devices such as ladders were brought into battle to make sure none of the vermin remained up under the roof. A sizable hole had to be dug to accommodate the piles of beasts.

Manioc flour sheds are very common throughout tropical America and consist of an isolated room outside the residence, housing the oven and equipment to prepare farinha or harina, the staple food in the region. These are cockroach-breeding nurseries. Travelers seeking shelter for the night are often asked to tie up their hammocks in the manioc flour shed. Thus the hammock mosquito net is an indispensable item wherever you go, entirely closed and with a zipper at the bottom. More on this under part 3, Equipment.

Fleas and Lice, Pulga e Piolho, or Piojo

These you don't get out in the jungle, either. You get them from humans living in substandard hygiene. Fleas are found on the floor of abandoned dwellings and in unclean beds, together with lice, which also transfer through direct physical contact.

By sleeping out in the wilds in your car or hammock, and taking a close, preliminary look at any potential sex partner's hair and general cleanliness, you will remain free of these pests.

FLIES

Borrachudo Gnats (*Simulium* spp.)

These small biting flies can drive you mad along the rivers where they occur, usually fast, rocky mountain streams such as those cascading down the Serra do Mar and the headwaters of some of the Amazon tributaries, especially in the cloudy, foggy weather of the rainy season. They are called borrachudo (rubbery) because of their flexible resistance to slapping with the hand. Where other mosquitoes drop crushed to the ground, the borrachudo—called pium in the north—may finish sucking up its blood and fly away, no worse for the slap.

Some people are allergic and develop swellings and sores. But even if you are not allergic you will have to use repellent (Autan in Brazil) because the body has a limit. We reached it at the Caripé River bridge works near Tucuruí, Pará, in October 1972, when the infestation got so bad we couldn't go to the toilet without getting our backsides all bitten! That was too much. We moved our camp to the Pucuruizinho, a slow-flowing stream no more than 30 kilometers (just over 18 miles) away, where there were none.

Along the seacoast and Chapada dos Guimarães Mountains there is a very small borrachudo—called maruim or pólvora, because it's the size and shape of a black-powder grain—that bites on right into the night, with a preference for the hairy parts. My worst experience with this hellish little Chironomidae happened on the way to Mérida in Yucatán during a motorcycle trip in 1960. There had been a hurricane, and the ferryboats weren't operating at El Carmen Island due to strong residual surf. Consequently the motorists, mostly truck drivers, had been waiting for several days, their heads covered in blankets and T-shirts to try to ward off the daylong clouds of millions of these tiny bloodsuckers, which found their way into ears, nose, and eyes . . . people slapping themselves continuously and to no avail. Then something typically Mexican happened: A black Mercedes drew up and a hard-faced man stepped out, a .45 pistol handy in his belt. "Que pasa?" he asked, dryly. "Que?" he exclaimed, his eyes narrowing as he marched resolutely to the shed where the ferry operators were idling. In a matter of minutes the engines sprang to life and transport was resumed. Once the man was out of earshot, having crossed on the first ferry, there was a generalized burst of laughter among the motorists.

Mutuca Horseflies (*Tabanidae* spp.)

These bloodsuckers are present in all tropical American jungles. The smallest are mottled fellows barely larger than the common housefly that keep circling your head in small swarms of three to six and bite you in the ears and neck if you don't kill them; the largest, a few moth-sized, dark giants of nearly 4 centimeters (1.5 inches) that make you jump when they bite your legs even through the pants. There are several sizes in between. You have to keep on the lookout for them. The small head-circling ones are the easiest to perceive, and the way to kill them is to hold your hand up over your head horizontally, palm turned down, while continuing to walk. You will feel when they alight. Then you bring your hand slowly down in front of you—without stopping—and whack them with the other hand. Soon you will have eliminated the lot and be free for a while. If you stop, they won't alight on your hand. The larger ones, which are present in the Serra do Mar cloud forest, require a powerful slap or you won't kill them. If you plan to fish, save them in a plastic container for bait.

The most intensive attack I can remember happened in the savanna at Chapada dos Guimarães northeast of Cuiabá in central South America one warm, hazy summer morning. Since I expected the trail I was exploring to be relatively clean, I risked going in shorts. I must have easily slapped 150 of the bloodsuckers off my legs! As a matter of fact, I was able to concentrate on little else but slapping horseflies. Their rate of success was low—1 or 2 percent—since I could feel them alighting. But every few steps a new swarm of from four to ten would swoop in, and persist until the last one fell!

Savanna Flies

When camping on sandy ground in the savanna in summer you may be surprised to find that during rainy spells there will be more wild flies inside than outside your screens, especially a blue variety with a coral head. These flies breed in the ground, and all they want to do is get outside. You'll have to raise your screens on forks for the insects to get out; otherwise they'll swarm around your head the moment you put on a light at night, although they won't bite.

Wasps, Vespas, or Marimbondos

Unlike bees, wasps use their sting professionally for either killing and eating or else anesthetizing their prey for later consumption by their larvae. There are a number of interesting species worth knowing something about.

A Tame Wasp

When my uncle Eric was a schoolboy in the southern Brazilian state of Santa Catarina, his colleagues were mostly the children of German immigrants, like himself. Some of them had a lot of creativity.

We have a brown wasp in South America nearly 4 centimeters (1.6 inches) long—the marimbondo caboclo (*Polistes canadensis*). It builds a pendent nest that looks like a honeycomb, mostly under house eaves.

One boy had the idea of opening the lid of one of the breeding capsules and giving that single larva extra food, to see what would happen. Not only did this wasp grow to an extraordinary size, but it became attached to its benefactor, too, riding about on the boy's shoulder, even to school. In the end it had to be killed there when it attacked other kids.

An Intelligent Wasp

Another incident with the same species happened to us. My wife, Maria, had some maidenhair growing from a fern vase on the veranda. One day we detected a few small green caterpillars on the leaves. Remembering that our caboclo wasps were always on the aquatic plants in the garden pond, I took one there, found a wasp, and gave it the caterpillar. It was immediately devoured.

Maria found another one that was likewise eaten. But when she turned around and went back to the veranda, the wasp flew after her and into the maidenhair, where it proceeded to hunt down some more! From the smell or taste of the caterpillars the wasp must have recognized what plant they were feeding on.

Watch Wasps

That wasps are much like dogs was suggested on another occasion. When our daughter Jaci was about five years old, she used to spend most of her time playing in the garden and orchard. In the lemon tree there was a wasp nest about the size and shape of a kettle, hanging from a low inside branch. It was well concealed from marauding parties of white woodpeckers (*Leuconerpes candidus*). Like most of the fauna we share our home with, this small, black wasp never bothered us.

But one day Jaci was playing with the neighbor's boy. She ran past under the wasp nest; nothing happened. The moment the boy did likewise, however, he was stung by nearly a dozen!

Another noteworthy species is vespa tatu (*Syboeca* spp.). *Tatu* is the armadillo, and these wasps got their name because of their nests, which look just like an armadillo—including the transversal bands—built against smooth trunks. This is a metallic-blue wasp the size of the caboclo and usually very aggressive because urchins are fond of stoning its house, when it comes out bristling in large numbers with a crackling sound like crumpling paper.

Where it has had experience with kids' provocations it may attack first and ask questions later as you approach. Be more careful closer to human habitation, because its sting is very painful.

By far the largest and most interesting wasp to watch at work is marimbondo caçador of the Pompilídae family, known in the American West as a "tarantula hawk." It is most commonly all metallic blue, though some have a reddish backside, and grows to an impressive 7.5 centimeters (3 inches). Despite its frightening size, this is—except for colonies in coastal sand dunes—a lone insect that goes about its business. An accident will only occur if you happen to tread on one barefoot, since it spends most of its time on the ground hunting spiders, grasshoppers, and such.

When in doubt, remember the standard procedure, which applies to this as well as to practically all animals: Remain absolutely still—while taking the opportunity to observe it in action—until it has moved on.

A Thorough Job

I once stood in my backyard, watching a marimbondo caçador hunting. Scouting the ground this way and that, it came close to my feet. From here it unexpectedly took off, rising straight toward my face . . . but two-thirds of the way up it dived under a large castor bean leaf, from where it dropped back to the ground grappling a grasshopper nearly twice its size.

Having anesthetized its prey, the wasp got busy digging a hole in the ground. It had to give up on its first site because it hit upon a brick.

The second site turned out to be satisfactory, and eventually the hopper was dragged over and pushed down into it after receiving a small supplementary dose of anesthesia. The necessary enlargements were diligently excavated in the hole in order for the voluminous insect to fit entirely, which required pulling it out again two or three times for additional work.

As soon as the locust fit snugly inside the hole, an egg was laid on top. After this the hole was neatly closed, first with tiny twigs and pebbles to ensure adequate ventilation, then with sand to cover the top, smoothing and pressing the cover here and there the way a caring nurse would adjust sheets and blankets over a patient.

The wasp's work took more than an hour, and I was amazed at the insect's diligence and neatness. No professional human could have worked more objectively or done a more thorough job.

A Near Miss

While driving across Mato Grosso, my family and I were by chance spared a potentially serious accident with one of these giants. The three of us—my youngest daughter, Jaci, my wife, and I—sat on the front seat of a Volkswagen microbus, going at about 80 kilometers (50 miles) per hour, when one of these wasps hit the windshield on my side at an angle, pieces of the insect raining all over us. Fortunately. For if it had missed the windshield and been hurled inside, as failed to happen by a hair, at least one of us would have been stung in the neck or face.

Motorcyclists are especially susceptible to being stung in the neck by wasps and bees they collide with on country roads.

For all these reasons I treat wasps with respect. Yet white woodpeckers—pica-pau-branco or carpintero blanco—gaily attack wasps' nests in small swarms of four to seven individuals, expertly detaching layer after layer of the nest walls and gorging themselves on the larvae, with apparent indifference to the insects' counterattacks.

SPIDERS

Tarantulas or Aranha Caranguejeira (*Theraphosa* and *Acanthoscuria* spp.)

I start with this gigantic arachnid here to dispel fallacies; for, contrary to popular belief, this spider (*Theraphosa blondi*)—which along the northern fringes of the Amazon basin reaches the size of a human's hand—is not one of our most venomous spiders. Still, it has been known to burn down houses . . .

That happens when people are foolish enough to throw alcohol on the spider, followed by a match. The little animal makes a last desperate dash for its hole under the house, where it burns to death and in the process ignites the wood. Serves such heartless people right!

The Swampland tarantula (*Acanthoscuria* spp.) has another natural enemy besides the giant wasp, tailored to measure: On the spacious patio of Fazenda Bodoquena we used to see the buff-necked ibis—curicaca or tautaco (*Theristicus caudatus*)—stick its long, scythe-shaped beak into the spider's hole in the ground, then dance around this axis until the beak aligned with the downward curve and the bird was able to tweeze the spider in its chamber and drag it out.

According to Butantã Institute sources, there is no record of a fatal accident caused by a caranguejeira in Brazil.

Banana Spider or Aranha Armadeira (*Phoneutria* spp.)

Be careful not to mistake this spider for a tarantula, as it may also grow quite large. Unlike the actual tarantula, however, the banana spider is responsible for most serious accidents. As a matter of fact it has been called the most dangerous spider in the world; its Latin name means "fierce killer."

Stay clear! Poised in its unmistakable posture to jump-strike, the banana spider—armadeira (Phoneutria nigriventer)—*which has thorns instead of hairs on its legs and clawlike fangs, is responsible for most spider accidents.*

But before I even describe it I must warn you to get no nearer than 1 meter (1 yard) from it, because its characteristic mode of attack is to jump at you—like those cute little fly-catching fellows you see on garden furniture. You're bitten before you know it!

The armadeira is of a lighter brown than the caranguejeira (which is almost black) tending toward gray. It does not have the hairy body and legs of the tarantula, but has scattered black barbs instead, which it bristles when irritated. Its black, horizontal, inward-curving fangs are clearly visible in front of its mouth, surrounded by fire-colored fur. And it will "cock" itself to strike, like the hammer of a gun, by raising its front legs and sitting back. This is where it derives its popular name.

Black Widow or Viúva Negra (*Latrodectus* spp.)

More widely known is this small, 1-centimeter (0.4-inch) black spider with red dots, or gray with yellow dots, on a perfectly round body. It's the only one among our venomous spiders that weaves large, communal webs, where it lives by the dozen or hundred. When disturbed, it drops to the ground and pretends to be dead.

These spiders are rare—so much so that I cannot be sure I've ever encountered them out in the wilds.

Field treatment for black widow accidents consists of inducing intense sweating, so as to eliminate the poison through the pores of the skin.

Gray Lycosa or Aranha de Grama

There are two more arachnids to beware. First is the gray-and-brown grass wolf spider or aranha de grama (*Lycosa* spp.). I trod on one of these one night as a child, with no other consequences than a lot of pain in the foot and a swelling for some days. In graver cases, however, it can cause local necrosis. This spider occurs everywhere, even in high altitudes, but serious accidents are few.

Brown Loxosceles or Aranha Marrom

Much more poisonous is a small brown spider of comparatively slender build and long legs—aranha marrom. This spider occurs from the southern United States throughout Latin America, and is especially prevalent in desert and semidesert conditions in Chile and Peru. *Read this carefully:* The brown spider's venom is the worst of them all—including snakes—with a potential to jeopardize kidneys, lungs, and other organs.

Although it isn't aggressive, the brown spider bites when it feels threatened through physical contact, such as if it has gotten inside your clothes or shoes during the night. Since this is also a habit of other arachnids, insects, and even snakes, be sure to hang your clothes from your hammock inside the mosquito net while you sleep. Also, each item taken from your rucksack or clothesline should be shaken and examined inside out before putting on.

Shoes and boots that are usually kept outside and underneath the mosquito net in order not to dirty it with mud must always be handled carefully. Knock them out well before putting them on.

SCORPIONS

Scorpions, or escorpioes, are nocturnal, as is the centipede. They spend their day hiding in dark corners behind rocks or logs and inside cracks, from which they emerge at night to hunt, especially for cockroaches. Always assume their presence when you pick up a rock or piece of firewood, or climb a tree. Scorpions do not attack; they only defend themselves. So it's mostly the insufficiently careful who are stung. Use caution especially toward the end of an operation such as, say, removing stones or wood from a pile: The scorpion will fall back as long as it has places to hide, so that when you pick up the very last pieces it is likely to be behind them.

Tityus and *Rhopalurus* spp.

In Brazil only these two genera are considered dangerous. *Tityus serrulatus* is 7 centimeters (close to 3 inches) long, tea colored or light yellowish brown with a serrated ridge atop the last joints of its tail when extended. *Tityus bahiensis*, of the same length as *T. serrulatus*, is however distinctly darker and stockier.

Rhopalurus, of the semi-arid northeast, is even lighter, without a tail ridge.

Like spiders and many snakes, scorpions can cause moderate to grave accidents depending on the amount of venom in relation to a victim's weight, as well as the victim's health.

A Minor Accident

The Caripé River near Tucuruí in Pará had been rising fast throughout the rainy day. When we knocked off at dusk it was no longer easy to find a place to bathe that did not have either muddy banks or a dangerous current.

The top of a rock emerging just above the waves in a cove seemed an attractive and safe base from which to wash myself in peace, so I blithely sprang out onto it—and was immediately stung in the foot by a scorpion, which then scurried down the side of the rock and disappeared underwater. My foot was painful enough to keep me awake until close to midnight. Then it began to abate, and by next morning it was nothing more than just uncomfortable.

CENTIPEDES

The centipede or lacraia (*Scolopendra viridicornis*) is a fast, nocturnal arthropod capable of killing nothing much larger than a rat, although it must always be remembered that small children are more susceptible to all these poisons due to their reduced relative weight. A centipede sting requires only local treatment to reduce the pain.

TREATMENT

Although there exist several specific serums, it is enough to carry just the soro antiaracnideo polivalente in your emergency kit. This covers *Tityus* scorpions and *Phoneutra*, *Loxosceles*, and *Lycosa* spiders.

Latrodectus, the black widow, is as mentioned above treated by subjecting the victim to intense sweating. This can be done both externally—via sun and fire—and internally, by drinking a lot of liquid.

6

SNAKES

THE DANGER

"I realize now what it is: It's the suddenness!" said my Texan friend Billy Pate. We were in the process of detouring around one of the beautiful Xingu River's waterfalls through the Amazon forest below Altamira, Pará, and had just frozen in our tracks as a green jararaca verde (*Bothrops bilineata*) materialized in the foliage ahead at chest level. A snake facing you at eye level is like a tennis ball hitting the center service line: You don't see it easily.

And that is the essence of snake danger: Suddenly you are upon one! When you spot a snake *before* you step on or near it—which will come naturally as you acquire a trained eye—and you possess the necessary self-control to stop absolutely still until it seems safe to either move on or retreat in slow motion, about 95 percent of the danger will have passed, because the serpent is normally unlikely to attack you unmolested.

My mother once lay down under a peach tree in the farm garden in Santa Catarina, to read. Then she fell asleep. When she woke up she found a coral snake halfway across her belly. There was only one thing to do, and that was to remain perfectly still until the ophidian had moved on.

In most of my hundreds of snake encounters I have found the creature immobile, either asleep or watchful. And I remember a few extreme cases. In one, I squatted in the forest to relieve myself—almost on top of a jararaca, or yarará. And in another, I unscrewed a generator from its wooden base by our Caripé River bridge works because we needed it more urgently at another site. This required fumbling around with a wrench and both hands in the dark space under the motor inside a straw shed. One of the screws needed extra effort to loosen. Then the boys moved in to pick up the generator, tied to a rod across their backs, and carry it out to a waiting truck.

They had barely begun to raise the load when they swiftly dropped it and scampered out: a jararaca—fer-de-lance—lay curled up right where I'd been fumbling with my hands.

I do, however, allow for the 5 percent of snakes that show exceptional aggressiveness. And I have experienced this with the urutu (*Bothrops alternata*), the *Bothrops jararacussu*, and the bushmaster (*Lachesis muta*), all much feared for this characteristic.

SNAKE PRECAUTIONS

Although the typical caboclo (backwoodsman) of the Amazon spends his day in the jungle wearing nothing more than flip-flops, shorts, and a narrow-brimmed hat, while carrying a machete, a shotgun, and a game basket, or paneiro—you, as an outsider, lack his trained eye to instinctively identify and avoid dangers, and his thick, well-adapted skin.

Therefore you must wear the necessary accessories to protect yourself: boots or sneakers, long jeans or soft, well-tanned leather chaps, gloves, a cool, long-sleeved shirt, and a hat or cap. This is especially important in the evening, around camp or the farmhouse, when snakes, spiders, and scorpions are out hunting.

These clothes will also protect you against *Larva migrans*, chiggers, cattle grubs, toxic plants, and, to a degree, various biting and stinging insects and thorns, not to mention sunburn.

Once, walking across dense scrub as a teenager in the region of Capão Bonito in the south of São Paulo state, I found a coral snake hanging from my trousers by its short fangs. Fortunately I was wearing boots underneath.

And later, near New Haven, Connecticut (of all places!), I was polishing my boots after a fishing trip when something like glass splinters protruding from the thick leather attracted my curiosity. It was the broken-off fangs of a snake, which had apparently struck while I was walking through the thicket around a pond, casting for largemouth bass. Its teeth got stuck in the leather, and I must have kicked it off against some trunk or stone. Again I was saved by appropriate footwear.

Snake by the Lake

As with bees, spiders, and other inhabitants of my world, I was initiated to snakes early in life. In those days prior to pollution there was a great variety of native fish in the stream crossing our farm near Cotia, São

Paulo. This brook was dammed, forming a sizable lake partly covered in water hyacinths—aguapés—from which a channel led to the mill. The public road passed over the dam and alongside the channel.

On the opposite side rose a hill with some forest. If you cleared a swath among the hyacinths on that side, where the sun could shine down into the deep, dark water, the larger traíras (*Hopplias malabaricus*)—carnivorous fish of habits similar to the northern pike's—would, after a few days, begin to rise close to the surface, where they'd lie, well camouflaged among the plants, to sun themselves.

Armed with a scythe, or foice, I'd approach the place on tiptoe, sometimes with my older brother, Rolf, with the intention of capturing a fish by hacking it behind the head while it slept.

I was six years old when, on one such raid, I suddenly felt a sharp, penetrating pain on my bare foot. Looking down, a jararaca was slowly slithering away.

We ran home, about a kilometer (0.6 mile), where my grandfather placed a piece of carbonized deer antler on the bite, to suck out some of the poison while my mother changed clothes. Then I walked with her to the main road, another kilometer, where we hitched a ride on a charcoal-hauling truck into São Paulo and somehow reached the Butantã snake farm and research institute.

There we looked at snakes until the doctor arrived, when I was given a large injection behind the shoulder. My foot was by now swollen and bluish, though there was no unbearable pain or other immediate consequence.

But some two or three days later we went down to Santos, on the coast, a drop in altitude of some 800 meters (2,600 feet), and I was almost immediately in the grips of a most violent and generalized allergic rection. My whole body became an uninterrupted sea of itching lumps. Lips, nose, ears, and penis were swollen out of all proportion. A pharmacist came and gave me a small anti-allergic shot, after which I began to improve, and was practically well when we went back up to São Paulo and Cotia some days later.

The moment we were up the mountain the allergic reaction struck again! Fortunately it was now milder, and soon receded. That was the first manifestation of my sensitivity to altitude, which was to manifest itself again later in life with malaria.

I was lucky, though, for only one of the snake's fangs had sunk into my small toe, thus injecting just half of the regular dose of poison. And I was then less than two hours away from Butantã Institute. Others have been a lot less fortunate.

Green Snake

In the 1960s Fazenda Bodoquena occupied about 400,000 hectares (1 million acres) in the Swampland and adjacent foothills. The Noroeste (Brazil–Bolivia) railroad—the only year-round transportation overland in those days—ran 100 kilometers (62 miles) through the farm and had seven stations within it. Fazenda Bodoquena raised exclusively beef cattle and was divided into four sections and twenty-one outposts. At each outpost lived a herdsman and an assistant, who were responsible for areas equivalent to large ranches, with several thousand head of cattle in each.

At the Porto Rodrigo outpost by the Miranda River, 12 kilometers (7.5 miles) from the Guaicurus ranch headquarters, the assistant herdsman's house had stood empty for a couple of years when a young family from mountainous Minas Gerais arrived and occupied it. They had a four-month-old baby boy and one or two older children.

The new environment was so foreign to these people that—like myself the first time I entered the Swampland—they didn't even have mosquito nets. From a distance the baby looked like he had a healthy, rosy color. But on close examination the strong color came from millions of mosquito bites, one beside the other, more than a hundred to the square inch! But a harsher fate was reserved for this child . . .

Unknown to the new tenants, a green *Philodryas viridissimus*—mboi oby to the Guarani Indians—was living in the house, where it hunted tree frogs and mice. One morning while the house was quiet this snake climbed up the cot and, seeing the baby's toe protruding from under a flimsy sheet, took it for some little animal and pounced upon it. The father, who was in the paddock when he heard the child shriek, found the serpent attached to his toe. He killed it, saddled his horse, and rode for ranch headquarters . . . leaving behind both the baby and the snake!

The first 3 kilometers (nearly 2 miles) he rode through thigh-deep water, for this was the rainy season, yet it never dawned on him that his horse was the only means of crossing the swamps at this time of the year.

It was thus nearly 11 A.M. when the man arrived at Guaicurus—only to be told to turn back immediately and fetch the baby and the snake. I was sent after him by car with syringe and serum. The driver was said to be the farm's most experienced. And I—having just recently arrived—was urged to leave to him the decision of whether or not to risk crossing the innundated area.

The jeep got irretrievably bogged down and I proceeded on foot across the flooded plains. It was about 3 P.M. when I waded out of the water onto the higher ground of the outpost, just as the herdsman's assistant was again leaving for headquarters.

This was one of those episodes in life I would rather erase, if I could; but it keeps coming back with the same force and clarity of the first impact that afternoon at the edge of the swamps. In a can tied to the saddle the man had a dead green snake with all the appearance of a nonpoisonous species. But it possessed *rear* fangs.

In his arm lay the wimpering baby. He folded aside the cloth the infant was wrapped in, and I saw that the little creature was literally disintegrating, his tissue breaking apart in fissures all the way up the leg, thigh, and trunk, body serum oozing out.

No use even attempting to give the child antisnakebite serum, because the active principle of this medication is to prevent, not cure, the process that had already evolved. Besides, it only covered fer-de-lances and rattlesnakes. I could only urge the man to ride on ahead, in the hope that he might reach Guaicurus in time for the plane to fly the child to a hospital. He didn't make it. We arrived back at midnight, after a tractor pulled the jeep free and then got stuck too. The baby had died at 11 P.M.

Bitten Inside the Car!

One of our pickup jeeps in the bridge-building firm I worked for during the opening of the trans-Amazon highway had been involved in an accident: It had tumbled down a 50-meter (165-foot) bank and crashed onto the giant trunk of a felled Brazil nut tree, where it remained, suspended about 3 meters (10 feet) above the ground for approximately a month.

The extraordinary thing about this mishap, which occurred late at night with the car full of half-drunk people when it overturned in the air and landed on the large trunk with such an impact that its frame bent into a V, was that the most serious injury turned out to be a broken collarbone! Even the windshield remained intact, although out of place.

When we concluded the 105-meter (340-foot) Tuerê River bridge at Kilometer 282 west of Marabá, the boys were paid, treated to a barbecue, and then loaded onto the truck for the trip to Marabá. From there, those who had families would take the bus to Carolina or Imperatriz in Maranhão state for a two-week vacation, while the ones who were single or lived too far stayed in town and spent their money locally.

On the way, the expedition stopped at the site of the accident and, with the coupled steel cables of two Tirfor hand winches, hauled the wreck back up the bank and onto the truck bed, to be given a ride as far as our workshop by the Cajazeiras River at Kilometer 67 from Marabá.

Two or three of the men made themselves precariously comfortable inside the pickup cabin, including one of the master carpenters. "First class!" they joked. The seat had partly collapsed in the accident, so that the fellows sat like half-open jackknives.

When we stopped at the only settlement along the way—Repartimento—at dusk for something to eat, the carpenter in the jeep cabin found that his wallet had slipped from his rear pocket and fallen behind the seat. So he lay down on the cabin floor and reached under the bench, groping about in the dark.

There was a yell and everybody swung round as the deathly pale companion backed out of the cabin with a 1-meter (3-foot) fer-de-lance dangling from his arm, where it had bitten itself fast.

He was lucky, though. The serpent was promptly killed by his comrades and the carpenter conducted to the pharmacy only a few steps away, where he was given the specific serum on the spot. There were no aftereffects, because this happened to be one of those rare accidents to occur under ideal conditions, when the serum did 100 percent of what it is meant to do: prevent the action of the snake venom.

Where People Are Bitten

Since snakes obtain their food by stalking or lying in wait for their prey, it follows that either they are well camouflaged—like the eighteen known species of *Bothrops* or fer-de-lances, the one or two rattlesnakes, and the bushmaster—or else they have exquisitely bright designs to attract the unwary, like all but one of our eleven deadly *Micrurus* corals.

While revising this book in the jungle of central South America north of Cuiabá, Brazil, I happened upon a 1.2-meter (4-foot) *Bothrops atrox* fer-de-lance that lay—in theory—easily visible on dry leaves under the forest, yet with all my sixty-six years' experience I was made aware of its presence only a couple of steps ahead of me by its sudden movement. Slowly it slid down to the river, a beautiful specimen and one of the largest of its species that I've ever met. There it considered swimming across, but since I wasn't pursuing it opted to wait out my passage under a tree stump in the water. As I had come down to bathe and wash clothes only a few steps downriver, I did so rather warily, I must admit, keeping one eye on the stump.

The following statistics speak for themselves: About 72 percent of snakebites occur in the foot and lower leg, 15 percent in the hand and forearm, and the rest in the backside, face, neck, and shoulders. Neck and shoulder bites occur mostly in the Amazon basin, because of *Bothrops bilineata* and *B. castelnaudi*, which climb trees (see below).

What does this tell us? That people are hit when placing their foot (walking), their hand (sticking it into holes or picking things up), or their buttocks (sitting down) on or near a snake . . . because they failed to see it! For the same reason you may be bitten in the face, because the head of a serpent pointed straight at your nose is very difficult to see.

Though the majority of poisonous serpents in tropical South America don't climb trees, thus allowing us to concentrate most of our attention on the ground, stumps, and fallen trunks, some accidents do occur around the upper body—the shoulders, neck, and head.

That's because four of our fer-de-lances do climb. The jararaca ilhoa (*Bothrops insularis*) lives exclusively on Queimada Grande Island off the coast of São Paulo. It probably washed ashore there originally on some floating tree brought down a river in a flood; the snake then had to adapt itself to an island where there is nothing but birds to feed on. The jararaca boca-de-sapo (*Bothrops neuwieldi*) lives in the Swampland, due to seasonal flooding. And two inhabit the Amazon basin: the jararaca verde or cobra-papagaio (*Bothrops bilineata*), a beautiful, yellow-streaked emerald green; and the less common gray jararaca cinza (*Bothrops castelnaudi*).

MEET THE BUSHMASTER

This Amazon basin viper—also known as the surucucu (*Lachesis muta*)—commands special respect. Not only is it a huge snake, the size of a boa constrictor, armed with 2.5-centimeter (1-inch) fangs and correspondingly large poison sacs, but it's known for bouts of temper as well. It may, for instance, attack a campfire and everybody around it in the middle of the night quite unexpectedly. For this reason it is also called surucucu de fogo.

I had two encounters with this creature while building bridges along the new trans-Amazon highway in the early 1970s. One night I was driving in a rainstorm just above the junction of the Tocantins and Araguaia Rivers when a bushmaster between 3 and 4 meters (10 to 13 feet) long appeared in the headlights, crossing the road. I stopped the car long enough for it to reach the shoulder. The snake was in its rightful place, I was not threatened by it, and there seemed to be no residents in the vicinity, so I had no business attacking it and thereby exposing myself unnecessarily.

But my next meeting with a surucucu was quite different. One beautiful, star-rich night sparked off and on by distant summer lightning, I was fishing from a canoe anchored off the lower tip of an island in the Cajazeiras River. A tree frog—perereca—on a nearby branch protruding from the island above me had been croaking rhythmically for hours, only silencing momentarily whenever I stirred to check my bait.

Sometime past midnight I was alerted by a sudden silence: The perereca had ceased croaking. I had not moved, but something had, somewhere. Across the fine mists rising from the slowly swirling waters I perceived, from the corner of the eye, a faint S-movement. I stood up noiselessly, flashlight and double 12-gauge coach gun ready. I switched on the light—the large serpent was coming alongside, its head raised high. Upon the impact of the shot it sank for a moment under a geyser of water, then hung motionless from the river surface as it began to drift with the current. I allowed myself a minute to make sure it was really dead while I reloaded, then pulled in the line and anchor and set out after the snake.

At first I tried hoisting it on board with the oar, but the heavy, arm-thick corpse kept slipping off the blade back into the water. By now I could see that half the head had been shot away and the spine was broken; so I lifted it in with my hands, feeling the roughness of its scales, reminding me of a pineapple or jackfruit, which is why it is also called the surucucu pico-de-jaca.

The next interesting thing in this snake's anatomy was its sharp, bony, dart-tipped tail, where a *Crotalus* has its rattle. All my life I had been hearing stories told by our caboclos of a large serpent with a dart (ferrão) in its tail, dragonlike, and here it was! Having no venom, its purpose must be for fighting.

WHICH SNAKES ARE MOST POISONOUS?

Although *Bothrops*—fer-de-lances—are mentioned frequently in this text, because they constitute the largest family throughout tropical South America and are therefore responsible for most accidents, the jararacas, urutus, caiçacas, and cotiaras are not our deadliest snakes; their fatality rate is no more than 15 percent. Be aware, though, that children—being smaller in proportion to the amount of venom—are naturally more susceptible. And so are horses, whose principal killer in the Swampland is the boca-de-sapo (*Bothrops neuwieldi*). This is because horses graze throughout the night, whereas cattle congregate in large herds on clean ground, where they stand or lie and chew their cud.

Not being killed, though, doesn't mean coming out unscathed! Ask the countless caboclos whose limbs have had to be amputated. At the mouth of the Cajazeiras River, where it meets the Tocantins, I came across a diamond prospector whose leg was slowly, inexorably rotting away from the bite of a bushmaster.

My grandmother was bitten by a jararaca as a young German immigrant in the southern state of Santa Catarina. She lay agonizing between life and death for a number of days.

The real killers are the rattlesnake or cascavel (*Crotalus duríssus*), and the eleven known species of corals (*Micrurus* spp.), all very beautiful and deadly, with fatality rates in the upper 80 percent.

The fangs of corals are short, though, and their bright colors make them easily visible. But they are, as their name in Guarani says, ibiboca—underground dwelling—and therefore apt to appear in the cleanest yards and verandas, surfacing from termite or ant holes, which makes them especially dangerous to children.

All accidents with *Micrurus* are considered *grave*.

TREATING SNAKEBITE

Don't ever underestimate the snake!

As we have seen, snake venom has terrible effects upon body tissue. Amputation is often inevitable due to advancing necrosis, since more often than not a snakebite occurs somewhere out in the wilds, requiring hours or days to get the stricken to medical assistance.

Antisnakebite Serum

It must be well understood that antisnakebite serum counteracts and neutralizes the active agents in the serpent's poison—it does not cure! After the venom has had a field day in the victim's tissue—as in the case of the Fazenda Bodoquena baby—the damage is irreparable, and there is no further sense in applying the serum. An American farmer by the name of Cole gave a native Paraguayan woman thirteen injections on his ranch near the border town of Pedro Juan Caballero, for instance; she died just the same. A hospital is then the only hope, and all it can do is attend to specific symptoms. Depending on the kind of venom, these may involve neurotoxic action—toxic to the nervous system; hemolitic—destructive to the red blood globules, possibly leading to a collapse of the kidneys; diffusing—increasing tissue permeability, causing generalized hemorrhage; hipotensor—leading to a decline in blood pressure; and more.

This doesn't say it all: The rattlesnake's crotalic poison blinds the victim a few minutes after the accident, so you don't know where you're going or what you're doing, and can't read any instructions. You can still call for help, however—but not if you've been hit by a coral! This snake's elapidic poison takes away both sight and speech, so that you can't describe what occurred if you happen to be found.

Thus if your activity in the field is of a nature that exposes you or those with you to the risk of snakebite, it becomes indispensable that you carry the necessary antisnakebite serum, or soro antiofídico, along with needles and syringes.

There are five kinds. Polivalente (crotalic and bothropic only) is used when you aren't sure whether a bite came from a rattlesnake or one of the fer-de-lances. The other four have specific actions: Anticrotálico is used for the rattlesnake (cascavel); anti-botrópico for the fer-de-lances (jararacas, urutus, caiçacas, and cotiaras); anti-elapídico for corals (corais); and anti-laquético for the bushmaster (surucucu).

Note that the two latter snakebites are not covered by the polivalente serum. Nor are any of the opistoglyphous or rear-fanged serpent poisons, since accidents with these are rare.

It follows, then, that you must be able to identify the aggressor in order to apply the appropriate serum. It's unlikely that you will have a manual on the subject handy when and where the accident occurs—and even if you do, you may be too stressed to consult it while precious time ticks by. It's something you have to know by heart, in order to act promptly. Thus it's worth making a good preliminary study, including a visit to a serpentarium (usually inside a zoo) in the city where you land.

Butantã Institute

If your destination is Brazil, you'll probably land in São Paulo before proceeding to the interior. Here it is a must—and you won't regret it—to reserve one full day for an unhurried visit to Butantã Institute, one of the world's most respected centers of snake and insect venom study, treatment, and antidote development.

Butantã is comprised of the research center, the Vital Brazil hospital, a serpentarium, and a museum on spacious, pleasant grounds with eating and resting facilities. The museum includes a section on the effects of snake venom displaying a series of necrosed, amputated limbs; a visit here is a sobering experience worth having.

In Rio and other major cities a similar place to visit would be the zoo—and in Belém, the Emílio Goeldi museum and zoo. But all you will see there is the snakes themselves, which is better than nothing but not comparable to Butantã.

However, identification for the purpose of applying the specific serum antidote isn't difficult if you bear these simple instructions in mind:

Recognition Through Fang Marks

If you didn't see the snake and have only fang marks to work from, you can make a rough identification based on the following details:

- Coral snakes have very small heads, like nonpoisonous snakes, so their fang marks are less than 1 centimeter (0.3 inch) apart. That's half the distance between the marks of the average rattlesnake's or fer-de-lance's fangs. This is not a foolproof identification method—you may have been bitten by an immature specimen of the latter—but serves as an early warning of what to prepare for. Then go by the Symptoms below.

• The surucucu has not been found south of the Amazon basin and, along the coast, Rio de Janeiro state. Thus a bite in the south or southwest of central South America showing fang marks more than 1 centimeter apart came from either a fer-de-lance or a rattlesnake, so the polivalente serum can be applied without delay.

• A U-crown of small, fairly uniform tooth marks, no larger canines, is the bite of a nonpoisonous snake and can be disregarded.

Recognition Through Snakebite Symptoms

• **Bothropic Group (jararacas and company).** Watch for pain, increasing progressively, on the spot where the snake hit, with gradual swelling and the appearance of reddish or bluish spots. Then come blisters, with or without blood inside. With the intensification of local reactions, fever sets in, and frequently secondary infection. In graver cases there may occur vomiting, either colorless, bloody, or biliary (greenish yellow), followed by prostration, sweating, and fainting. When heavy doses of poison have been injected, such as by a jararacuçu— the largest of the group—there may occur hemorrhage through the nose, gums, fingernails, and hair, and in the urine.

In milder cases blood remains coagulable, but in graver ones it breaks down after thirty minutes to an hour, with consequent drop in circulation and pressure. The patient becomes pale, with cold skin and heavy sweating.

Important: Noncoagulating blood is indicative of a grave case.

• **Crotalic Group (rattlesnake).** There's generally either mild or no pain at all on the bitten spot, which remains normal or swells a bit, accompanied by formication—a sensation of ants crawling over the skin. Thirty minutes to an hour after the bite, muscle pains arise in various parts of the body, particularly at the neck, together with clouding, reduction, or loss of sight, eyelids fallen or semiclosed (neurotoxic facies),

dizziness, double vision, reduced cola-colored urine, sometimes vomiting, and possible kidney failure.

Important: The so-called neurotoxic facies indicates a grave case.

• **Elapidic Group (corals).** These symptoms are very similar to those of a crotalic bite, all the way up to neurotoxic
facies. Here is the difference, however: There may occur thick
salivation, as well as difficulty in swallowing and pronouncing
words. Death may come early through respiratory paralysis.

Important: All bites from *Micrurus* corals are considered grave.

• **Lachetic Group (bushmasters).** Look for very much the
same symptoms as with the bothropic group, though there
may occur alterations in eyesight. The poison itself appears to
be less active than that of the fer-de-lances, but you must
remember that this most feared snake can reach 4 meters (13
feet) in length and close to 50 centimeters (over 19 inches) in
circumference, weighing more than a dozen kilos (26 pounds).
It has 2.5-centimeter (1-inch) fangs with poison sacs that permit it to inject around 10 milliliters of venom. It can strike
from a distance of 2 meters (6.5 feet) and a height of 1 meter
(3 feet). So here it is the quantity of venom, and the depth that
it is injected, that count.

Recognition Through Snake Identification

If you're bitten, the first step is to kill the offending snake. But be cool and
methodical, so as not to expose yourself or others to a second accident in
the process. The correct way to kill a snake is to whack it energetically
across the neck with your slightly bent walking stick. Should you, in an
emergency, be forced to make use of a cutting tool, such as a scythe (foice)
or machete, always hit with the *blunt* side. If you cut a snake's head with
a sharp blade it may fly off and bite itself fast on somebody, or be lost and
jeopardize the identification process. Take the snake along when seeking
medical assistance in order to avoid time-consuming doubts.

My uncle Eric was hit by a rattlesnake near Embu, south of São
Paulo city, and was just about blind by the time he'd walked home.
Taken to hospital—sightless, dizzy, suffering muscular pain, his blood
pressure decreasing, shivering—he still had to argue with doctors to
convince them beyond doubt that he knew for sure it had been a cascavel. The doctors had a point, of course: Most people nowadays don't
know snakes well enough.

• The coral snake, soro anti-elapídico (*Micrurus* spp.) has a small head—some so small they look like they don't even have one! It is neither by its head or its colors that you will recognize a coral verdadeira, but rather by its tail, which ends abruptly, similar to that of other venomous snakes. The tail is therefore the only quick distinction between a true and a false coral. Do not attempt identification by color, for *Micrurus fischeri* (venomous) and *Pseudoboa trigemina* (nonpoisonous) are very similar, and so are *Micrurus filiformis* (venomous) and *Erythrolamprus aesculapii* (nonpoisonous). Relatively knowledgeable people have died mistaking one for the other.

Though the trained eye will spot a difference in the heads, at first glance in the jungle only the thin, gradually tapering tail distinguishes this false coral (Pseudoboa trigemina) from its deadly look-alike below, Micrurus fischeri, of Serra da Mantiqueira in southeastern Brazil.

• The rattlesnake, cascavel, soro anti-crotálico (*Crotalus durissus*) is the easiest to identify because of its rattle—guizo—although this does not always vibrate in warning. Rattlers occur in rocky, arid, hilly, scrub, and savanna country. Therefore they're unlikely to be found in the lower Amazon forests, although stray specimens may occasionally drift down from the higher, drier fringes of the basin on uprooted trees or flotsam caught in drifting islands of hyacinths. Thus they have been found on Marajó Island at the mouth of the Amazon. These snakes can go for months without eating, which makes them exceptionally fit for survival by giving them time to adapt their skills to the requirements of their new environment, as was the case with the tree-climbing jararaca ilhoa on Queimada Grande Island. Except for its tail, the South American rattlesnake looks and acts much like any of the jararacas—but is deadlier!

• The bushmaster, surucucu, soro anti-laquético (*Lachesis muta*) is found from the north of Rio de Janeiro state up through the coastal rain forest and in all the Amazon basin. Its distinctive marks include the horny dart in its tail tip, where a *Crotalus* has its rattle, and clean-cut, dark brown triangles, their bases joining at the ridge of an otherwise spotless ocher body.

• The fer-de-lances, soro anti-botrópico (*Bothrops* spp.)— jararaca, caiçaca, cotiara, and urutu—comprise all the rest of poisonous biting snakes. If the offending viper was none of the above, then it was one of these. The most distinctive among *Bothrops* are the aggressive urutu (*B. alternata*) with its horseshoe design; the green jararaca verde or cobra-papagaio (*B. bilineata*) with yellow lateral dashes and a prehensile tail; and the exceptionally large (up to 2 meters, or 6.5 feet) jararacuçu (*B. jararacussu*) with very dark, often black triangular or lance-tip designs. The remainder of the family all display various triangular, rectangular, or trapezoid markings, some with smaller spots in between, generally from the lightest to the darkest shades of brown. And the gray jararaca cinza (*B. castelnaudi*) has brownish rings and a prehensile tail, this being another tree climber.

• Opistoglyphous or rear-fanged serpents. There are about fifty species of snakes in tropical South America with poisonous fangs in the back of the mouth, of all colors and shapes, including false corals. They are not capable of striking, but once they succeed in getting a prey's limb or head into their mouth, the poison can be as deadly as that of striking vipers. It was one of these that caused the fatal accident at Fazenda Bodoquena. There is nothing to distinguish opistoglyphous snakes from their nonpoisonous cousins. Thus you must never play around with a snake that is to all appearances nonvenomous without first conducting the check below, behind its half-moon of small teeth as well as in front. There is no serum for the bites of these snakes.

FER-DE-LANCES

Some of the outstanding members of the poisonous Bothrops *clan. Top: Two manifestations of the widely distributed B. atrox, ranging from the southernmost reaches of tropical South America, where it is called jararaca, through the northeast—caiçaca—and Guianas— fer-de-lance—to Central America; it is responsible for most accidents. Center, right: The aggressive and feared urutu (B. alternata), easily identified by its strong horseshoe pattern. Center, left: The largest, B. jararacussu, of a darker coloring, may reach 2 meters (7 feet). Bottom, two that never meet: At right, the parrot snake or green jararaca (B. bilineata) of the Amazon basin is a tree climber with a slightly bent, prehensile tail like a monkey's; and left, B. cotiara of the southeastern Araucaria-pine-forested mountains.*

Is It Poisonous?

If you aren't safely familiar with tropical American snakes, or if the tooth marks on the stricken person or animal are not clear-cut, then you must establish—*before* grabbing for serum and syringe—whether the serpent was indeed venomous. Some of our nonpoisonous snakes can look, act, and bite very mean! (See Nonpoisonous but Aggressive, below).

A wound containing one to four (though normally two) deep indentations means poisonous. A half-moon or U of small tooth marks, with no large ones behind, means nonpoisonous. If the victim is an animal, you may have to shave the spot in order to see the tooth marks.

With the exception of corals, our venomous serpents have a large, triangular or heart-shaped head, with visible nasal cavities, a relatively compact body, thin neck, and short, abruptly tapering tail.

Corals, on the other hand, have very small heads; their bodies are no different from those of false corals *except for the tail*, which is distinctly shorter. And all except *Micrurus albicinctus*—which has thin white rings on a dark body—exhibit black, white, or yellow and red rings in various arrangements just like some of the false corals. This is why color patterns should not be used for identification, as I've noted.

These characteristics may, however, at times be insufficient to firmly establish whether a snake is venomous. You should then immobilize the ophidian at the throat with a forked stick and insert a twig crosswise in its mouth, as far back as it will go, then push it forward along the roof of the mouth. If the snake has fangs, these will now emerge from their sheaths, looking much like bent needles or fishhooks, either behind or in front of smaller teeth.

MEANWHILE, A SNAKE APPROACHES . . .

In the jungle you must be constantly alert, like the birds that never stop looking in all directions; for, as Texan Billy Pate noted, "It's the suddenness!" of snakes that will get you when you least expect it.

Let's look at this hypothesis: A snake is slithering toward you at an average speed of 600 meters (or 2,000 feet) an hour. Slow, isn't it? But that's 10 meters (33 feet) a minute! As you look around in the jungle you can see the ground reasonably clearly for about half that distance, with luck. Just half a minute later, there might be a snake next to you! In other words, the fact that you've just examined your surroundings is no basis at all for assuming that you can now sit down or move about at ease without constantly repeated searches. It's much like driving your vehicle in the city. How long did it take that bushmaster to close in alongside the canoe after I had first spotted its suspect S-movement out there on the Cajazeiras River? Fifteen seconds perhaps. Just barely enough time for me to silently pick up my flashlight and weapon and stand up without destabilizing the boat.

With time and experience, though, you will receive help from a precious ally: your subconscious or instinct, which will warn you when a shape, movement, or color pattern to look out for appears . . . mostly. But then look at this incident:

While writing this book in October 2001 I was sitting on a platform above the Rio Claro in Mato Grosso. The river flowed wide and shallow from my left, forming a deep pool on a bend below my position and then another shallow rapids, where some friends of mine were bathing. Something drifted past that looked just like an upright piece of branch, with only a small tip appearing above the surface. Probably some old, partly waterlogged piece of wood that had been hung up somewhere and now drifted upright, eventually to sink. I gave it no more than a passing glance. But as it got to the bathers, one woman called out to the others, "See if that isn't a snake, drifting toward you!" The first to look said no, it was a stick. But then someone cried, "It's not a stick, it *is* a snake!" and people rushed out of the water to let the perfectly camouflaged ophidian pass. Later the caretaker told me that this snake had already been sighted by several people, always in a vertical posture, letting the current carry it.

NONPOISONOUS BUT AGGRESSIVE

Some nonvenomous snakes are, as I've mentioned, capable of putting up a bluff show impressive enough to make anyone flee, including natives. Notable among these is our only toad-devouring species, the boipeva (*Xenodon merremii*), which carries a whole lot of popular names related to its defensive flattening. And the jararacuçu-do-brejo (*Mastigodryas bifossatus*), another swamp dweller, reaches close to 1.8 meters (2 yards). Many of these species, such as *Tropidophis*, *Helicops*, and *Atractus*, look very much like poisonous snakes, whereas *Pseustes* and *Spilotes* resemble Indian cobras.

The most important group of nonpoisonous but aggressive snakes, however, is the constrictors. There are about half a dozen species in tropical South America of these very large serpents that kill their prey by constriction or suffocation. Although nonpoisonous, they should not be provoked, for they have sharklike, inward-curving teeth on which there may be decomposing remains of past kills that could cause blood poisoning. Also, anyone firmly in the grip of their teeth may be dragged down underwater—especially children.

Anaconda or Sucurí (*Eunectes murinus* and *E. notaeus*)

This is of course the most impressive of tropical American snakes. *Eunectes murinus* has been given an exceptional length of 10 to 12 meters (33 to 40 feet). Eight-and-a-half meters—28 feet—is the largest I have seen, and I tell you, it's quite big enough!

Its coloring covers various shades of olive green, gray, and black. The male has a curious appendage for securing copulation: a pair of shiny, dark brown claws, concentrically curved, one on each side of the sex organ.

Both *E. murinus* and *E. notaeus*—described below—are commonly encountered during a day's ride in the field or crossing the roads in the

Pantanal or Chaco, where they receive no more than an identifying glance from local cowboys. When stopping along the road to take pictures of a sucurí, you are in much graver danger of being run over by some idiot shooting past at over 100 kilometers an hour in his car than anything else.

At the Caripé River bridge I was bitten by a sucurí while removing driftwood piling up against the bridge scaffolding. It did not drag me underwater, though, as its size was hilarious: about 15 centimeters (6 inches)! The little fellow must have been born the previous night.

The *Eunectes notaeus* anaconda reaches about 7 meters (23 feet) and distinguishes itself from the previous species by its dark spots upon an ocher background. It seems to occur only in the Swampland and lower Paraná basin.

The extraordinary thing about these large animals is their capacity to hide in small spaces where you wouldn't expect them. In the Pantanal one of my cowboys clearing an overgrown trail in the region of Carandasal, near the northern tip of Serra da Bodoquena, flipped aside a dry, fan-shaped leaf of the carandá palm on the ground. Perfectly rolled up underneath lay a 4-meter (13-foot) sucurí.

And on the plateau near Paranatinga, Mato Grosso, just south of Xingu National Park and Indian reservation, whose springs lead to four large river basins—where my daughter Adriana was a judge—one of the farm dogs accompanying cowboys stopped by a small water hole in the open field, to drink.

Presently the dog cried out, and when the people rode up it was already being dragged under. There ensued a pulling contest, each side holding on to one end of the miserable dog. The sucurí's strength was such, however, that they had to resort to the revolver to save the dog.

No wonder. When the snake was finally dragged out of this improbably small compound, it was found to measure close to 6 meters (nearly 20 feet).

Another feature of this snake is its capacity to stealthily sneak up close to the farm. While I was managing a cattle ranch west of Barretos, São Paulo, back in 1965 an employee killed a sucurí inside our fowl pen, where it had already swallowed a number of ducklings.

One morning a few years ago I was sitting with a friend on a bench under an open, thatch-covered shed at Fazenda Santa Clara ranch and inn north of the Miranda River in the Swampland, waiting for her companions to finish getting ready in order for us to go out on a tour. Everybody wanted to see a sucurí, and we had not yet met one.

Then a ranch hand dashed past us and, wading into a small pond behind our backs, grabbed hold of a half-submerged white duck. He proceeded to dispute with something underwater that tenaciously held on to the domestic bird . . . An anaconda had just noiselessly drowned the duck while we sat there talking, no more than 10 meters (33 feet) behind us, with people and vehicles moving about in the patio. We never heard a sound from that duck, or perhaps our subconscious minds disregarded its wingbeats—if it was caught on the surface—as something ducks habitually do when stretching their wings. But there you are. It was like someone drowning right in front of a crowd sunning themselves around the pool.

Boa Constrictors or Jibóias

These boas are distinct from all other constrictors in that they prefer dry, open country of somewhat higher altitude, such as savannas, or cerrados. There are two. One has striking, very distinct, large dark brown designs on a light brown background (*Boa constrictor constrictor*), whereas the other has somewhat smaller patterns on a gray to light olive-green background (*B. c. amarali*). Both have double ridges on the back, giving them a square, rather than round, appearance.

Their maximum size is given as 5 meters (over 16 feet), though I saw a skin at the Porto Velho, Rondonia state, Indian museum of 6.5 meters (21 feet)—an exceptional size.

These are peaceful animals, sometimes maintained in jungle homes as pets to control rats—although I would not leave a baby or dog near one. This is the snake exhibitionists like to show wrapped around their necks.

Deer Snakes, Cobras-de-Veado, or Salamantas (*Epicrates cenchria crassus* and *E. c. cenchria*)

These boas are less well known. My workers captured a specimen near the Valentim River bridge site some 90 kilometers (56 miles) west of Marabá on the trans-Amazon road measuring 4.5 meters (close to 15 feet). It distinguishes itself from other South American snakes in that it has light-colored dots on a purple and noticeably sturdy body, with a prehensile tail.

This particular individual was not difficult to catch—though heavy to carry—because it had a large, bulging belly from a mateiro or wood deer (*Mazama americana*) that it had swallowed. The serpent was presented to the local chief of the National Highway Department (DNER), who had it placed in a wire-mesh cage in the center of the department's spacious, babaçu-palm-shaded patio atop the high left bank of the Itacaiúnas River, overlooking the city of Marabá.

I had expressed concern that the snake might escape through a gap between the top of the wire mesh and the zinc roof of the cage, but was laughed at by the worker in charge, who pointed at the snake's big belly. "Not with this bulge she won't!" he stated, looking around at the small assembly of highway officials, who had brought their families over to see the unusual boa.

The next morning when I dropped by, a strong stench of carrion pervaded the area, and someone was emptying a sack of lime into the cage. During the night the salamanta—another name it is known by—had regurgitated the half-digested deer and slipped out through the gap, disappearing down the riverbank, never to be found again. That snake knew just what it had to do, and when. Talk of animals acting only on instinct . . .

7

OTHER DANGEROUS ANIMALS

CROCODILES AND ALLIGATORS

In the Amazon basin lives the jacaré-açu (*Melanosuchus niger*). Naturalist Henry Bates wrote that while he was in the Rio Negro region north of the basin with his colleague Alfred Wallace in the mid-1800s, he came across a specimen measuring 6 meters (more than 19 feet). This length was also given by German botanist Phillip von Martius, who traveled the Amazon in 1819 with his companion Dr. Johann Baptist von Spix. More recent authors admit no more than 5 meters. Both are probably right, as fossils found east of the Andes in Peru and Bolivia and in the south of Venezuela give evidence that in prehistoric times these saurians were much larger. Overhunted, the jacaré-açu has become rare, and apparently smaller, just like the anaconda.

Our other alligators are distinctly shorter. In the Swampland you'll rarely see a specimen much larger than 2.5 meters (8 feet).

Although during the day these animals are normally found peacefully sunning themselves on riverbanks or beaches, diving into the water when disturbed, *after dark* they are on the prowl, and you can hear snapping, thrashing, churning, and roaring going on all night long.

One of your most important safety measures should be not to leave any food in camp that might attract alligators, such as fish, meat, or live animals, for they will come up the beach and are able to upset things quite thoroughly while trying to get at food. Like the one that visited our camp by the Apa River below Bela Vista on the Paraguay–Brazil border one night: It entered one of the tents, passed under somebody's camp bed and made it collapse, came out the other side dragging a game bag it had entangled itself in, and made off down the bank and back into the river, bag and all.

Dogs must remain loose, not tied up.

Another Danger

In the late 1950s when I was an army sergeant I was strolling along the edge of a corixo or flood channel near Fort Coimbra on Brazil's border with the Paraguayan and Bolivian Chaco, a day's travel by boat down-river from Corumbá.

I was moving quietly, examining the tracks in the sand between the clear water of the flood channel and a bank taller than myself, behind which rose the jungle. Presently there was a crash, and a torpedo of an adult alligator shot over my shoulder, just barely missing my head! With a spectacular splash it disappeared in the deep, leaving me dumbfound-ed at my narrow escape from being knocked clear out of my senses and into the piranha-infested water. This jacaré had been sunning itself upon the high bank and, when it heard some sound I must have made, hurled itself toward the water—its protective element—probably as surprised as myself at finding me standing in between.

In the late dry season—August and September, sometimes October—the shallower corixos and baías (lagoons) dry up in the Swampland. Then the alligators, sometimes stranded in their hundreds, set out across the fields toward other waters. Away from its element, the jacaré knows only one form of defense: attack! This is when it's most dangerous, for it may hurl itself at anything approaching, including the horse you are riding. The gravity of the attack is thus multiplied by its unexpectedness: You are ambling along at ease, watching nature, when all of a sudden your mount rears or shies sideways, throwing you liter-ally into the saurian's teeth . . . It's important always to sit correctly in the saddle, with your toes firm in the stirrups and reins held trim so as to be ready to control the horse in an emergency.

Should such an attack succeed, your best defense—when possi-ble—consists in pressing your fingers upon the alligator's eyes, thus clos-ing off its view. It will usually let go.

FELINES

Jaguars or Onça Pintada (*Panthera onca*)

Just a few years ago at the Carajás mining community southwest of Marabá, Pará, a child was carried away by a jaguar and eaten. A similar tragedy happened with an Argentinian park guard at Iguazu. Children in or near the jungle must always be supervised by an alert adult, because they remind jaguars (and other animals) of the monkeys they are accustomed to hunting.

Jaguars are, of course, to be given a wide berth when accompanied by young. But then, what mother isn't? Even a small anteater (*Tamandua tetradactyla*) reared to give me battle when I happened upon her one night in the Swampland, several tiny eyes peering fearfully from behind her back.

Only rarely do you hear of someone attacked by a feline, and then it is usually a crippled or old animal no longer able to hunt. Most accidents in the past used to happen during jaguar hunts, which are now forbidden. One North American big-game hunter was killed in the Swampland by a jaguar *with a rifle!* One blow of its powerful paw sent the nearest man's gun flying like a spear straight into this visitor's belly.

Jaguars can also claw you quite nastily *postmortem.* Swampland rancher Chico de Barros, of Corumbá, showed me a single deep scar on his hand. "And didn't it strike you anywhere else?" I asked, imagining a close-quarters battle at the mouth of some cave, based on scars I had seen on others.

"No, because I stopped and disentangled it!" he said, then explained: "You see, I was walking in the rear of a general store with my arms full of merchandise I'd selected, when I was hooked by this claw from a skin hanging among ponchos and saddles and gear . . ."

The small-spot jaguar or malha miúda (*Panthera onca palustris*) is our largest jaguar, often found measuring about 2.7 meters (9 feet) from tip to tip. Still, I once had the opportunity to see an exceptionally large skin in Aquidauana, Mato Grosso do Sul, nearing 3 meters (10 feet).

In the north and east of tropical South America roams the slightly smaller malha larga—broad-spot—which science curiously does not distinguish despite its striking characteristic of having occasional black cubs, a pigmentation phenomenon opposite to albinism, which malha miúda doesn't exhibit.

A Close Encounter

I myself met an impressive malha miúda on a bend inside a gully we were both taking, unknowingly, on a collision course. And the ensuing battle—just the two of us in the wild—was so close that for my third shot with a rather inappropriate .22 Hornet rifle I had to shove the muzzle into the feline's mouth to fend it off, at which point it was not at all clear yet whose skin was going to hang on whose wall.

That happened back in 1967 at Fazenda Bodoquena, when I was half my present age. It was a great event. If it happened today I'd just stand absolutely still—though ready—and wait. The animal would probably end up slipping into the thicket.

Puma, Onça Parda, or Suçuarana (*Felis concolor*)

This is the same cougar or mountain lion widely distributed throughout the Americas. Its overall length is quite comparable to that of malha

larga, although the puma is a more slender animal with a smaller head
and paws. The backwoodsman distinguishes two varieties: one a light
brick-red or ocher, while the lombo preto—black ridge—is a beautiful
silvery gray, tending toward white on the chest to compensate for its
dark back.

WILD HOGS

White-Lipped Peccary or Queixada (*Tayassu pecari*)

The white-lipped peccary normally roams in herds of from one to
three dozen individuals, rooting as they go and generally minding their
own lives. People living in the jungle are, however, unanimously afraid
of this combat-prone animal, but that's because they are always accompanied by dogs. I've already mentioned the danger created by having a
dog with you.

What can arouse the queixada to a collective attack is the dog's
barking. As a matter of fact, hounds that have survived queixada attacks
don't bark when the hogs are around if they know what's good for
them, and stay close to their owner's feet, tails between their legs, in evident and justified fear.

So your very first measure must be to make the dog shut up by
closing your hand over its mouth. Next, climb upon a fallen tree stump,
rock, or branch that needn't be more than 90 centimeters (3 feet) above
the ground, and there wait until the pigs' rumbling has faded away—so
long as the dog remains silent. If it barks or snarls, the queixada will
remain milling around below you for hours.

Such an encounter can easily become a tragedy if you are caught
with your family and dogs where there is nowhere to climb in a hurry.
Thus I'll repeat my previous recommendation: Don't take a dog where
there are queixada.

Otherwise the white-lipped peccary is unlikely to attack a pedes-
trian. Back in 1968 I was bathing in a natural pool at the top edge of
Serra da Bodoquena's western cliff overlooking the Swampland one
hot, windless afternoon when I perceived a rumbling and clacking, like
a brushfire in the nearby taboca (*Guadua* spp.)—a low, thorny, tangled
bamboo—getting louder.

Behind me stood a short, stocky acurí palm (*Scheelea phalerata*)
whose long leaves curved down low over my head, partly hiding me. I
could climb the acurí in a couple of leaps if necessary, so I sat still where
I was, with water up to my chest, and waited.

The rumbling had ceased, and presently, quietly, the pigs began to
file out of the taboca thicket and into the water some 10 meters (33

feet) above me. Soon the pool was black with hogs drinking and wallowing about.

Two rooting sows kept coming in my direction. Then there was a brief gust of wind. A roar went up as the animals sensed my presence, and in one body they stampeded out of the pool to vanish in the taboca. Five minutes later they were all back in the water again!

In the enchanting region of limestone caves and crystal-clear streams full of fish around Bonito, farther south in the same Bodoquena mountains, a rancher took up feeding the queixada whenever they called at his farm, and this daily event has turned into a major tourist attraction. This man wisely built sturdy elevated paths for people to watch the animals from, for this is a primitive, feral creature that you can never come to trust. I have seen some ugly wounds inflicted by queixada, which do not lag behind the work of a shark.

Near Corumbá lives a middle-aged Portuguese man who raised a female queixada piglet, which he kept free in his yard with other domestic animals. After four years this pet suddenly turned on the man, and would have killed him as she gouged slivers of flesh and tendons out of his thighs and buttocks, had it not been for his wife's firm intervention. He very nearly had his leg amputated.

Jungle dwellers generally claim that this is the one animal the jaguar respects, being careful to attack only strays or the last comer in a herd. Still, in the spring of 1967, while opening a new cattle-breeding section in a formerly virgin part of the Swampland along the Jaguaretê flood channel (corixo) crossing from the Miranda to the Paraguay River, I came upon an isolated paratudo tree (*Tabebuia aurea*) whose first branch stretched out horizontally at a height of about 7 meters (23 feet) above a well-beaten queixada trail across the grass.

The tree's thick, deeply corrugated bark was profusely streaked by the claws of a frequently visiting jaguar. Around the tree lay the skulls of several peccaries the shrewd feline had slaughtered. What seemed amazing was that even the steepest possible angle required a 9- to 10-meter (30- to 33-foot) pounce upon the pig. A very convenient arrangement, incidentally, for in case the queixada turned in an attack the jaguar could always bound back to the paratudo and up out of their reach.

Collared Peccary or Caititu (*Tayassu tajacu*)

This smaller hog is a shyer animal, living in families of about half a dozen in hollow trunks and shallow caves. But individual for individual it can be defensively as ferocious as its larger cousins. A group of friends of mine on a hunt in the Mato Grosso do Sul region of Bela Vista were made to feel this when a wounded sow took them on—dogs and all—

and managed to deeply gouge the booted legs of two of them, plus several dogs.

Every now and then you'll come across "tame" caititu on a ranch that were picked up young and raised, like the queixada noted above. It is a natural temptation to be kind to these animals nowadays and see them through Walt Disney's optics, perhaps handing them a bite to eat. But this should only be done with due precaution, accompanied by the farm supervisor, for you can never be sure. You may carry on your pants the scent of a dog or other animal and arouse the pigs' suspicion, or the peccary may be entering rutting season, normally in spring.

As a rule all these wild animals must be returned to their native jungle at the first sign of change in attitude as they approach adulthood.

Feral Boar or Porco Monteiro (*Sus scrofa*)

This animal inhabiting the Swampland region of Nhecolândia north of the Miranda River in large numbers was originally a domestic pig gone wild. Some can be as large and frightening as a jaguar when they come at you with their protruding, bent tusks.

My friend Giorge O'Brien of Corumbá and I had such an experience when, back in 1970, our dogs precariously held a huge boar at bay inside the thicket of a swamp. The moment we spotted the animal facing us some 8 meters (26 feet) off, the brute cocked its head and came on in a straight line. The plan had been for Giorge to fire with his 20-gauge shotgun loaded with an appropriate, heavy, rifled slug, while I was to cover us with a Colt .38 revolver.

Now, Giorge is the kind of person whose things are perennially out of order: His door locks don't turn, the plumbing leaks, the furniture is wobbly, hinges hang loose, inflatable mattresses are punctured, the doors and windows at his hotel rooms are either stuck open or stuck shut . . . The only thing Giorge is systematic about is his bills: They are never paid. Yet—as long as you have no financial business with him—you could not hope for a better, nicer, and more helpful companion and friend than Giorge.

The problem, of course, was that as the heavy boar stormed upon us, Giorge's gun failed. I fired all six chambers as the animal rushed in, and it literally collapsed on our feet, senseless but not dead, with five of the bullets in its forehead and mouth, none having penetrated the carapace to the brain. We had to quickly bleed it with a machete.

Monteiro hogs don't normally attack people, but then there's always the rutting season, when boars are known to come out of the jungle and break into farm pigsties after a sow in heat—at which point you should just get out of their way! Besides, there are sows with young out in the brush.

Occasionally you'll hear of European wild boars appearing in the interior of Brazil's southernmost state, Rio Grande do Sul, where they've come across from Argentina, but there have been no accidents as yet.

MORE DANGEROUS CREATURES

Giant Otter or Ariranha (*Pteronura brasiliensis*)

At the Brasília zoo some years ago a boy fell into the ariranhas' compound. An army sergeant jumped in after him and managed to save the kid. But he himself was killed by the otters.

Out in the wild I don't know of any otter incidents with people. But the ariranha is a social animal that lives in packs and will promptly attack and destroy dogs swimming across the river (see the recommendations concerning dogs in the introduction).

SOME INTERESTING TROPICAL SOUTH AMERICAN ANIMALS
Top left, the paca (Agouti paca) *is the first to disappear with the arrival of man due to over-hunting for its meat. Top right, the tayra—irara* (Eira barbara)—*loves honey. Center left, the giant anteater—tamandua bandeira* (Myrmecophaga tridactyla)—*walks on the back of its hands. Center right, the howler monkey—bugio* (Alouatta *spp.*)—*is red in the south of Brazil* (A. fusca), *black in the Swampland* (A. caraya). *Bottom, the mane wolf—lobo guara* (Chrysocyon brachyurus)—*eats fruit in addition to small animals, and takes long steps.*

Howler Monkey, Bugio, or Guariba (*Alouatta* spp.)

This bearded simian, largest of our South American monkeys, is capable of frightening newcomers quite thoroughly with its powerful, howling roar at sunup and during the day when the weather is about to change.

In the Swampland you hear them in the morning calling from the various isolated woods, or capões, and through binoculars you can spot them in the tallest trees. But don't stand directly underneath, for they may urinate and defecate upon you, and throw branches.

This is another animal that dislikes dogs and may, at times, come all the way down to the ground to fight them. On the other hand, I was driving along a trail in the Swampland with my family some ten years ago, the path consisting of two deep ruts made by the wheels, with grass in between. Ahead of us walked a howler in the right-hand rut, when in the left-hand one came a dog. They passed each other, neither animal having perceived the other.

Sometimes you come upon howlers out in the open, if there's fruit in the low scrub or the family is crossing from one woods to the other. Then the male may camouflage himself as a tree termite hive while the females quietly slip away.

The bugio is not known to attack people, though here again you should not leave small children wandering about on their own. As a matter of fact, in the tourist city of Serra Negra, about 170 kilometers (just over 100 miles) north of São Paulo, lives a howler who has "adopted" man of his own initiative, coming out of the forest for regular strolls downtown, where Chico—as he has been named—accepts the occasional banana or other fruit he fancies from passersby. Here I am writing about walking in the jungle, and along comes a monkey walking in the city!

Harpy Eagle or Gavião Real (*Harpia harpyia*)

With a wingspan spread of 2 meters (6.5 feet) and claws 7.5 centimeters (3 inches) long, this is the world's most powerful bird of prey, feeding on—among other animals—dogs, goats, calves, and monkeys.

The harpy eagle is rare, though. As a matter of fact, I have never knowingly seen one out in the wild. I'm referring to a bird that has alighted, for in flight the harpy isn't easy to recognize up there.

But while building the Tuerê River bridge in 1973 I was driving our pickup down the mountain one morning, loaded with peons and freshly cut rods for scaffolding, when we spotted a man staggering down the road: a short, young, bare-chested mulatto, the back of his head and neck streaked with blood.

He was recognized as a new settler who had only just arrived a week or so before from the northeast of the country with his wife.

On closer examination he revealed several deep furrows from the neck up to the top of his head, made by talons that had very nearly scalped him. We helped the feverish man into the car, and while we drove to camp for first-aid treatment before dispatching him to the field hospital, he told us that he'd stood resting in the doorway of his hut under construction when something swooped down out of the trees from behind and hit him so violently that he was thrown forward on his face, while the "large, hawklike bird" flew out the other side of the hut and vanished up in the trees.

Apparently the eagle had not seen the whole man—whom it evidently took for a monkey in the shadows—or had misjudged his size, and upon realizing its mistake let go of his head.

This was such an extraordinary experience that the man had to repeat the account time and again as groups of peons came in from work to see him.

Cattle, Gado, or Ganado

The Swampland, a huge floodplain of grasslands, savanna, channels, and lagoons dotted with slightly elevated "islands" of forest, is cattle-breeding country. That's the only large-scale economic activity there besides tourism, and it's compatible with the preservation of nature since the poor, sedimentary soil cannot be machined. Thus practically all grazing occurs on native grasses, periodically submerged.

So what you see mostly while in the Swampland is East Indian Brahma cattle, nearly all of them light gray Nelore, whereas the bulls, at a proportion of one to every fifteen or twenty cows, are often of the darker Guzerath lineage, which fight—and break—each other less than the Nelore.

These bulls are impressive animals weighing around 700 kilos (more than 1,500 pounds) that can scare the newcomer by approaching in a "mean" posture, their sharp horns full of debris from "battling" termite hives, and emitting short, gruff snorts very much like the jaguar's, especially when they happen by your camp at night.

But this should not worry you. Just quietly give them the right-of-way and detour or stand still until they've passed. Of course, if they happen to be fighting each other you don't want to stay inside your tent, lest you find yourself underneath a ton and a half of battling muscle, hooves, and horns.

An isolated cow is to be guarded against more circumspectly. The calving season—June to October—coincides with the dry, tourist season. A cow by herself, away from the herd—unless it's a rainy day, when cattle tend to scatter—most likely has a calf hidden nearby, which you may be approaching unknowingly. And she's going to defend it. So she may charge you before you know what's happening, if you happen to be on foot. A horse she doesn't mind.

In such a case you've got to run, because she's after you specifically as an imagined threat to her baby. These are usually short dashes; as
soon as she's satisfied you're on the run she'll want to return to her calf.

Prevention thus consists in keeping an alert eye open for isolated
cows and giving them a wide berth.

Coatí (*Nasua nasua*)

This cute little tree bear is neither large nor aggressive. On the contrary,
it is quite easily tamed. At Iguazu National Park by the great falls whole
families come out of the woods to beg tourists for morsels.

But they must not be touched or hand-fed, for the coatí has
extremely sharp teeth that may draw blood even if the animal is only
playing. A friend who had one as a pet in Bela Vista had to have the den-
tist dull its canines to protect his children.

Bats, Morcegos, or Murciélagos

Although the ordinary citizen may not be aware of it, there are bats
practically everywhere in the Tropics. At dusk you can see them performing elaborate maneuvers up in the sky after insects, like swallows.
Underneath our mango tree in Campinas I often find partially eaten
fruit and seeds that don't belong there, such as of Malabar almond—
chapéu-de-sol, palm nut, or coquinhos—and loquats or nêspera, which
they bring to eat in the protection of the tree's dark crown, thus consti-
tuting an important step in nature's process for distributing and planting
larger-seed trees. Just the other evening I was walking along a fence
when I came upon a wild fig tree—figueira (*Ficus* spp.)—crowded with
bats eating the small berries.

But those are all harmless. Now, in the limestone regions rich in
caves and crevices such as the Ribeira River Valley in São Paulo state and
Serra da Bodoquena bordering the eastern edge of the Swampland in
Mato Grosso do Sul, there are vampires, or vampiros. These bloodsuckers are especially harmful to horses but will also attack other mammals,
including people. Every now and then there is a report in the papers
about children—mainly—being bitten.

The bite itself is not painful, though multiple or repeated attacks
may seriously deplete the victim of blood. During one journey up the
Cajazeiras River we slept at a caboclo's home above the mouth of a long
stretch of whitewater.

A puppy, perhaps two months old, slept against my mosquito net.
During the night it whimpered several times, which I supposed was
from fleas bothering it. At daybreak, however, the little animal could

barely stand up, and where it had lain my mosquito net was red from the bloodsuckers' feast.

But another, graver danger with these bats is that they are potential transmitters of rabies, or raiva. Cases of people getting rabies are extremely rare in Brazil, so much so that preventive vaccination is not justified.

Much simpler is to always use the proper mosquito net—in which the hammock swings free without touching the net (see chapter 11)—or screen-fringed tarpaulin (chapter 14) when sleeping in the car or a well-screened tent. See also Rabies in chapter 9.

ANIMALS YOU DON'T NEED TO FEAR

Mane Wolf or Lobo Guará (*Chrysocyon brachyurus*)

This is a beautiful, lone, shy animal that feeds on fruit and small game inhabiting the savanna. Its tracks look like those of a large dog, except that the distance between footprints is considerably bigger because of the wolf's exceptionally long legs. The guará is a curious, snoopy animal, and that's where it might give you a shock: It has a habit of jumping up into the air in order to be able to look over the tall grass and see what's going on. Unfortunately that is also where it has lost many a companion to trigger-happy individuals.

At Chapada dos Guimarães National Park around 1996 my wife and I had been walking an abandoned trail every morning in hopes of spotting a guará, whose tracks and feces were evident. There was an old garbage deposit where small animals gathered, and we approached carefully in case the wolf was on the prowl. It was: Presently my wife turned around, and there it stood, some 15 meters (50 feet) back on the trail we had just walked, observing us.

Tapir or Anta (*Tapirus terrestris*)

Here is a gentle, easily domesticated large animal that once roamed much of the planet's surface but is nowadays restricted to Latin America and Malaysia. A vegetarian, it has no defenses other than force, which is why it has died out elsewhere.

Giant Anteater or Tamanduá Bandeira (*Myrmecophaga tridactyla*)

The tamanduá is a curious-looking bear with a long, thin head and tongue and a large horse's tail. It possesses enormously powerful claws for breaking open termite hives, but it will only fight defensively. Slow and poor of sight, it's a frequent victim of felines and speeding vehicles.

One morning I was walking along a cattle trail by the big quick-sand swamp of Agua Verde near the mouth of the Salobra River flowing out of the Bodoquena range west of Miranda, Mato Grosso do Sul. I was looking for jaguar tracks when I heard a scratching noise such as a stiff broom might make. I stood back off the trail and waited. Minutes later a tamanduá ambled along, stopped to sniff my boots, then moved on slightly faster, sensing that something was not quite right!

8

FISH

Sharks, Tubarão, or Tiburón

Just the briefest warning is needed here, since sharks occur only on the very edge of our area of interest. Still, along South America's sunny northeastern coast swimmers and surfers are periodically attacked, especially around Pernambuco.

Candiru (*Vandellia cirrhosa*)

This small, milky-colored catfish, which grows no longer than about 8 centimeters (just over 3 inches), occurs in some rivers of the Amazon and Orinoco basins and has the habit, when young, of entering human orifices, such as the vagina and urethra, where it then bristles or expands its razor-sharp fins, locking itself in place and thereby causing its host excruciating agony, hemorrhage, and, when surgery is not available, even death, for the slightest movement deepens the cuts.

Thus no nude bathing, for either women or men. Always wear a regular bathing suit or tightly fitting bikini of a single, inconspicuous color; and when washing yourself stand up in shallow water and use a bucket or pan.

Although I have not heard of facial penetrations, it stands to reason that if the fish slips into the orifices of the lower body, there is no assurance that it won't enter your mouth, nostrils, or ears if given the opportunity. So it's better to avoid bare-headed diving, too.

Electric Eel or Poraquê (*Electrophorus electricus*)

Here is another interesting—and dangerous—inhabitant of the Amazon basin. Unlike the candiru, the poraquê grows to an impressive size. My blacksmith on the trans-Amazon highway, Domingos, caught one in the

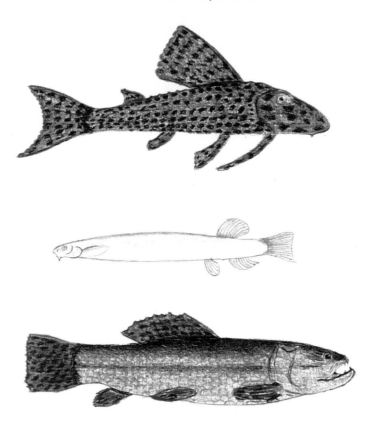

FISH OF TROPICAL SOUTH AMERICAN WATERS
Top, the cascudo (Hypostomus *spp.*) *is a primitive, delicious fish that can be caught by hand among the rocks of rapids or falls late at night. Center, the dangerous candiru* (Vandellia cirrhosa) *of the Amazon basin has the habit of penetrating the vagina and urethra, where it opens its razor-sharp fins. Bottom, the traíra* (Hoplias *spp.*) *is an impulsive carnivore usually found at the mouths of rapids and among aquatic plants, where it is fished by beating the surface with a metal lure or bait. Its teeth are needle sharp.*

Cajazeiras River about 2 meters (more than 6 feet) long, which is the largest I've ever seen of any kind of eel.

A friend from the Brazilian Indian-protection foundation FUNAI, stationed at the Pucuruí River outpost near one of our bridge-construction sites—now at the bottom of the Tucuruí hydroelectric reservoir—told me of two significant experiences with this extraordinary fish, capable of an initial discharge of 300 volts. In one that he personally witnessed, an Indian had suffered a discharge while bathing, and drowned. In the other the agent himself, upon squatting down one evening beside a creek and dipping his hands in to wash, took an appreciable shock. Since he was sure he hadn't touched anything, he shone his flashlight into the water, and there, on the bottom, a good 0.5 meter (1.5 feet) down, lay a poraquê.

These eels are nocturnal and spend the day inside holes and crevices among rocks. Accident prevention consists in not entering water at night other than the shallowest, and well lighted with a flashlight. And in the quite frequent case where you happen to hook one while fishing, cut the line. Do not reel in a poraquê alongside an aluminium boat!

Piranhas (*Serrasalmus and Pygocentrus* spp.)

The piranha—scissor fish to the Indians—occurs in all major South American river systems in some or all of its half a dozen species.

During the construction of the trans-Amazon highway we had only one accident: While at the Tuerê River site I was aroused in the middle of the night by the sound of excited voices approaching. Moments later one of our professional fishermen, who was from São Paulo, was brought into the halo of light from a kerosene lamp. His arm was a dark, bloody mess with a piece of skin and muscle dangling, half bitten off. He and his partner had been checking their paternoster fishing line—espinhel—stretched across the river, when they hauled in what looked like a pacu-caranha (*Colossoma mitrei*) but turned out to be a black piranha—piranha preta (*Pygocentrus piraya*). These grow especially large: I caught one in the Cajazeiras River that weighed close to 3 kilos (6 pounds) and was so old that it had already lost two of its teeth. This fish is here completely dark, though in some regions it may be yellowish.

The predominant piranha in the Swampland, where it causes great damage, is *Pygocentrus nattereri*. Smaller than the black Amazon species just mentioned, it reaches nearly 2 kilos (4 pounds) and is dark gray on the back, bright yellow-to-red around the belly.

On the right-hand bank of the Paraguay River, just above the Campo Grande–Corumbá highway crossing, there is a fishermen's lodge at a site called Morrinho (hillock). On this elevation stand two white crosses facing the river. Lodge employees used to take the garbage in drums out in a rowboat and dump it in the river as chum for fish, the owner told my friend Giorge and me. One day their boat overturned in the process, and piranha made no distinction between food and feeders.

Along the rivers (corixos or baías) across the Swampland I have met several women who lost a finger or two, while washing clothes, to piranhas rising in the foam. An Englishman who worked for Fazenda

Bodoquena before me, Thomas Horton, tried to drink directly from a corixo by lowering his head to the water, and had the tip of his nose clipped clean off.

I once hooked a dorado of about 5 kilos (11 pounds) on a Daredevil lure in a corixo entering the Miranda River. I was reeling in the fighting fish slowly when it got entangled in the branches of a dead tree. I was just beginning to wade in when there arose a splatter, like heavy rain; within seconds all I had left on my hook was the dorado's jawbone.

Every year a number of healthy young Swampland cows in the prime of their productive life have to be shipped off to slaughterhouses because they have lost their teats to piranha and can no longer nurse a calf.

While washing our horses one evening in the Miranda River after a long day's ride, one of my cowboys had his heel clipped off in a single, isolated bite.

There are piranhas everywhere in the Swampland—even in ranch wells, which they enter during floods!

The term used in Brazil for "scapegoat" is *boi de piranha*, which refers to a steer that is sacrificed above a river crossing so that the rest of the herd may swim across unmolested while the piranhas concentrate on this single individual.

Does all of this mean you can't even go near water? Not at all. You can bathe quite safely where local people tell you it's all right. Nevertheless, precautions must be taken: Wear a bathing suit like that recommended regarding the candiru (page 97)—no exposed penis, scrotum, or nipples—and remove all those bright little ornaments that enhance you to fellow humans, such as earrings, bracelets, watches, rings, and necklaces. Even if you aren't fond of fishing, you must have already seen some of those lures fishermen use—metallic spoons and the like—that reflect the sun and attract the curiosity of aggressive species. That's what your ornaments do, too . . .

It's common while fishing to get your lure or baited hook caught on a branch or rock. As a good fisherman you will want to recover it, especially if you're out in the wilds where you can't get replacements. Just keep in mind what that lure was made for in the first place, and always use a forked stick, never your bare hands. When I was fishing with my friend Billy Pate by the Xingu River waterfalls below Altamira, his lure got caught on a rock in shallow water, and I swam out to release it with my foot. It was only when I had the bright, flickering piece caught on my toe that I realized the danger I had unthinkingly exposed myself to.

Other practices to avoid are unnatural movements, like splashing with hands, feet, or objects; wrestling; or pretending you're drowning— as young people in groups are fond of doing. All these vibrations may be interpreted by piranhas as coming from an injured animal or fish, struggling.

I have ridden or swum my horses across hundreds of corixos without incident. But should the animal's legs get snared in submerged vines or fences—the Swampland cowboy's nightmare—then you may be in real trouble. Only swimming immediately back to firm ground and cutting loose the fence wires with your hunting knife may save the horse. Fence wires in the Swampland are smooth, not barbed, and run through holes in the posts, tied to a stretcher or moorage post every 100 meters (330 feet) or so.

Crossing a channel on your own anywhere other than by a clearly visible cattle ford is risky. And if your horse is reluctant to enter, don't insist; give it the reins and let it find the crossing it knows.

The peril multiplies with the advancing dry season. Water in the corixos shrinks, increasing the density of the fish population. That is when the piranha become most aggressive, hitting anything within jumping reach. Cattle lose parts of their snout, ears, teats, or scrotum; hunting dogs are lacerated; other fish that cannot seek refuge in the shallowest water, as catfish do, are wiped out.

Stingrays or Arraia (*Paratrygon* spp.)

People are so concerned with piranhas that this other dangerous inhabitant of tropical rivers is often overlooked. This fish, which is sometimes the size of a car tire but more often smaller, is armed with one or two barbed darts, the longest of which may be about 10 centimeters (4 inches), located on top of its tail.

These are covered by a black, gelatinous film that facilitates penetration and is said to be the poison.

When stepped on, the ray will lash out with this formidable weapon in an inward-curving arc—as opposed to a scorpion, which stings in an outward curve—driving the sting or stings into the foot or lower leg all the way to the bone. The pain manifests itself within five to ten minutes. I myself have never had the experience, but have been told by people with scars on their legs that the suffering is so excruciating a man will howl for twenty-four hours. Besides which, it may spark a piranha attack.

So an accident of this kind requires a potent painkiller in the emergency kit or, where possible, hospitalization for symptomatic treatment. But it is best avoided: When wading across any body of water, do not lift your feet! Push them, instead, along the bottom. That way you cannot tread on the fish, and should you touch it laterally it will go away. Do not trust your eyes in clear water, for the stingray's camouflage is perfectly matched to the river bottom: It may be mottled in shades of gray, brown, and green among rocks and pebbles, or else it may burrow in the sand and you see nothing.

If, however, you do get hit by a stingray and have no recourse at hand other than a woman companion, you may try an expedient that Swampland caboclos of Indian ancestry claim will alleviate the pain: The woman spreads apart her genital labia and sits with her vulva pressed directly upon the wound.

Most men's first inclination is probably to laugh this off with comments like, "Well, it should at least distract the victim, if the woman is nice!" But I don't take it lightly: It makes sense that Mother Nature, who as a rule provides the means to every end, should have been especially attentive in furnishing this most wonderful and sensitive laboratory of conception, development, and birth with the antiseptic, antigenic, and analgesic qualities necessary to protect both mother and child, and facilitate the baby's safe entry into the world.

The same people who recommend the above procedure also affirm that the first saliva in the morning, before ingesting food, has healing powers; this I also believe. I rub my eyes lightly with saliva when I have an itch, and it ceases without causing irritation.

I would not, however, dare apply the above system against caterpillar burn, because the residual venom or hairs on the surface may act upon the woman, too.

Traíra (*Hoplias* spp.)

This carnivorous fish, which enjoys sunning itself camouflaged among plants and debris, or burrows in the mud, can reach the impressive size of more than a meter (over 3 feet) in some rivers of the Amazon basin. It strikes the lure or bait aggressively in rocky places such as the mouth and base of rapids or, in the evening, along the edge of water hyacinths or reeds. The traíra is to be handled with care, for its body is very slippery, and even the smallest specimen of but 7 centimeters (3 inches) can sink its needlelike teeth into your finger in no uncertain terms, as has happened to me. Imagine what one of the big ones can do! It does not, otherwise, constitute any danger.

When I was in junior high school in São Paulo I had a German classmate, Hans Aumann, who sometimes spent the weekend with us on the farm, and was somewhat overeager. Once he jumped onto a branch, Tarzan-like, without noticing that it was rotten, and plunged with the branch and a colony of ants into the river, shiners jumping all around him after the ants' eggs. Another time I hooked a 20-centimeter (8 inch) traíra and hurled it onto the pasture behind me. Hans threw himself upon the fish and, like a film played in reverse, backed off with equal speed, his hand already bleeding profusely.

Mandís (*Rhamdella, Pimelodus,* and *Parapimelodus* spp.)

Likewise, there are about twenty species of small catfish, generally called bagres or mandís, some of them armed with extremely sharp and painful stings on their dorsal and pectoral fins. When fishing these must be handled with care, either by slipping your fingers from behind in among the fins around the body, or using pliers.

Dogfish or Peixe-Cachorro (*Raphiodon vulpinus*)

This fish, which can reach more than 5 kilos (11 pounds), has an impressive denture. Its long canines may eventually protrude above its upper jaw, giving it a fierce-looking, wild boar's mouth. But it is in reality quite harmless. Often hooked near the surface while fishing for dorado in agitated waters, the cachorra—as it is better known in some regions—puts up a sporty fight, but is easy to hold and generally lies quite still while you remove the hook. Rarely eaten due to excessive bones, it is best returned to the river so that others may enjoy the fun of battling it on light gear.

9

DISEASES

Prevention is the best medicine in the jungle. We are going to talk about all this in detail. At this point I'm only going over things briefly, since you want to know what shots and medicines you may need.

DISEASES TO BE AWARE OF

Chagas' Disease

This is a serious, incurable disease. It can be acute, when it ends in death after just two to four weeks; or chronic, affecting the heart, esophagus, muscles, nervous system, and more, when it is possible to live with it. Charles Darwin is said to have died of it at age seventy-three, some forty-five years after being infected. An aunt of my wife's was informed she had Chagas' disease about twelve years ago and has been able to lead a more or less normal life thanks to medicine, including surgery to enlarge her esophagus.

Although this aunt got the disease through a blood transfusion, doença de Chagas, caused by a protozoan (*Trypanosoma cruzi*), is trans-mitted principally by a weevil, barbeiro (*Triatoma* spp.), in the following manner: In the quiet and dark of night the barbeiro—which alights with a *zzup!* sound—sucks itself full of blood, after which it may defecate nearby. The *Trypanosoma* are in the feces.

On an unclean body, such as that of some of our caboclos and a lot of water-shy Europeans, the site will eventually itch, inducing the vic-tim to scratch himself. In so doing he brings the bug's excrement in contact with the hole in his skin by which the insect sucked up its meal, thus "vaccinating" himself with the protozoan, which enters the blood-stream through the hole.

A hygiene-conscious person who examines and washes himself instead of scratching greatly reduces the danger. But through the simple expedient of always sleeping within a fully enclosing mosquito net you are totally free of the barbeiro. A tent, even when well screened and kept closed at all times, has a weak point: Where the zippers meet there usually remains a hole through which all kinds of creatures—even a snake—can enter. This must always be fully sealed, either with something soft like a handkerchief or, better still, by fitting it with a magnetic "ear" of the press–pull kind that camera cases and some clothes now come with (see chapter 11).

Not that all droppings of barbeiros contain *Trypanosoma*. The insect is but a vector. Transmission requires the host. In the Pantanal or Chaco, for instance, the disease is said not to occur at all, due to a very low demographic density and the fact that everybody has to use mosquito nets due to literal clouds of mosquitoes; there are plenty of barbeiros. One night I was in my hammock up a tree in the Swampland east of Corumbá, waiting for pumas. There were few mosquitoes, so I didn't bother with rigging up the net; also, I wanted to see better. During the night I kept hearing the telltale *zzup!* of barbeiros alighting. In the morning there were about a dozen in the hammock, several of them full of blood.

But this insect is not the only means of transmission. Besides blood transfusions—always risky in principle in the Third World—the consumption of improperly cooked meat of host animals, mainly armadillos, can also transmit Chagas' disease.

Cholera

This potentially deadly epidemic pops up occasionally here and there, and is characterized by a continual flow of murky, waterlike stools, vomiting, and muscular cramps. It requires prompt, no–nonsense action: *Buckets* of serous fluid (see Diarrhea, below) must be drunk, cup after cup, to make up for the rapid loss of water, since the liquid runs practically through the body and out. You can also use Bactrin-F 500 as recommended in the instructions.

From mild diarrhea up to the gravest condition, cholera, the causes are basically the same, and avoidable: spoiled or contaminated food or water.

Here, as everywhere else throughout the pages of this manual, *prevention* is the watchword. If you prepare your own food, wash fruit and vegetables in chlorinated or vinegar water, choose and cook your meat well, and don't try to save money by reusing perishable leftovers, you should have no problems. See also chapter 12.

Dengue Fever

This is an infectious, virulent, tropical and subtropical epidemic disease transmitted by the *Aedes aegypti*, a dark, spotted mosquito whose trademark is that it bites in daylight. The symptoms are fever, rash, and severe pains in the joints. The hemorrhagic form of the disease is potentially fatal. Otherwise it will pass after about a week.

Diarrhea

This debilitating and dehydrating disease is the scourge of travelers. Yet it needn't be. It's a form of rebellion of the stomach intended—like the often accompanying nausea—to expulse spoiled or contaminated food. A cleansing of the system, in its milder manifestations.

For this reason it should be allowed to run its course without attempts to stop or combat the condition for the first day or two—unless it's something virulent, like cholera. You must be careful, especially when hiking, to use the toilet tissue's absorbence rather than friction, washing with neutral soap such as coconut soap when possible, so as not to aggravate things by irritating the anal region. You don't want to trigger a hemorrhoidal thrombosis on top of a diarrhea . . . out in the middle of nowhere.

For the first twelve hours do nothing at all, camping if necessary and resting or reducing exertions if you feel low. Lie in all positions so as to help the intestinal system clean itself out as completely as possible.

After twelve hours, and no matter whether the condition has improved or persists, it's time to start replacing lost body liquids by drinking a serous fluid, soro fisiológico. You can buy this in dry packages to add to water, or prepare it yourself by boiling local water for five minutes and then adding, to each liter or quart, 1 level teaspoon of salt and 2 of sugar. Simple enough. Drink as much as you can.

Eat nothing at all as long as you don't feel hungry. Give your stomach time to cure itself unhindered by the extra workload of digesting food. Drink sugar-sweetened tea instead. Hunger will tell you when it's time to start eating something. Begin with a few dry crackers or some stale bread. Bread and water, that age-old diet of the jailbird in solitary confinement, is your best friend in this condition. Cooked oatmeal with nothing but a little salt is okay, too. As your condition normalizes you may add a banana to your bread and oatmeal. But keep food to a minimum. Bear in mind that naturalist John Muir lived on nothing but tea and bread for long periods back there in the Yosemite Valley and sequoia forests 120 years ago.

In case of a more serious infection, with stools containing blood and pus and unrelenting after forty-eight hours, it's time to add a measure of Bactrin-F 500 every twelve hours. This is a good oral antibiotic, specific for these kinds of conditions, including cholera and lung infection.

One day a canoe beached near our bridge works at the Cajazeiras River, brought in by two caboclos coming down from the Carajás jungles. In it lay an extremely thin white man, consumed by malaria and diarrhea. He was taken in a truck to a nearby pharmacy, where I presumed people would do what was necessary.

But the owners of a sawmill across the river, on hearing of the incident, felt it their duty to follow up the case, in order to make sure something was in fact being done. They discovered the man lying in a shed. With a Samaritan effort they took him in to Marabá hospital, but there he died that same night.

Hantavirus

This is the interesting disease that appeared at a Navajo Indian reservation in the American Southwest in the 1990s, where primitive and modern medicine came face to face, the former emerging victorious: The Navajo medicine man said the disease was brought by the wild rats. There had been more rain in the past years, which lead to an increase in pinecones and consequently a proliferation of the rats that feed on them.

It took modern medical researchers a long time to come to the same conclusion by scientific means, based on a similar precedent during the Korean War, when American servicemen contracted the disease in the region of the Hantan River, thus its name.

Carried by rodents, it causes epidemic hemorrhagic fever and severe respiratory infections in humans.

Hantavirus has been detected in the *Araucaria angustifolia* pine regions of the southern state of Paraná, Brazil, especially in the area of Guarapuava. This means you must be on guard in the entire *Araucaria* pine region, from the Mantiqueira mountain range in eastern Minas Gerais south to Rio Grande do Sul. Be especially careful during the edible pine seed—pinhão—harvesting season in April and May; hygiene is, once again, your best bet. Wear a dust mask on windy days. Curiously, the disease has also been detected in Mato Grosso, where there are no pines, probably brought by migrants.

Leptospirosis

My friend Frank Rough died from this disease.

Leptospirosis is caused by screw-shaped bacteria that enter the bloodstream and settle in the organs, such as the liver and kidneys. It is found in rats, mice, cattle, dogs, and pigs, and is acquired when water contaminated by the urine of these animals, principally rats, comes into contact with the skin, more often in poorer city suburbs than out in the wild.

Symptoms are high fever, pains, headache, nausea, shivers. Milder cases are overcome in seven to ten days. But the more virulent form, Weil's disease, caused by the *Leptospira icterohemorragias*, leads to wide-spread bleeding and finally kidney breakdown followed by generalized collapse if not promptly treated with specific antibiotics and blood replacement.

Malaria

When you are just traveling through a potentially malaria-endemic region such as the Amazon basin, or spending a few weeks there, you can take preventive pills against the disease. This preventive treatment should be started a couple of weeks *before entering* the region and ended a fortnight *after leaving*. This is in addition to the use of a well-closed *fine-mesh* mosquito net and repellents when you notice the presence of the *Anopheles* mosquito. It sits at a characteristic and easily identifiable angle to the body instead of parallel to it like other mosquitoes.

Of these measures, the mosquito net is by far the most important; the pills don't entirely prevent malaria, they just neutralize the intensity of the attack. Notice that I emphasized *fine-mesh*. That's because the *Anopheles*, due to the unusual angle at which it sits, has comparative facility climbing in through larger mesh.

A few years ago I accompanied a group of Germans across the Pantanal swamps. They had brought some last-generation, superlight and practical tents with telescopic nylon or carbon fiber rods that permitted instant assembly and blah blah blah . . . Luckily we had stopped by Aquidauana, at the entrance to the Swampland, to buy some good old-fashioned hammock mosquito nets, which we then had to throw over these newfangled tents because the *Anopheles* simply swarmed right through their improperly large mesh.

There is no malaria in the Swampland, though there are enough mosquitoes—also called pernilongos, carapanã (in the Amazon basin), and muriçoca (in the northeast)—to carry you away.

If you have to remain in a malaria-infested zone for a longer period of time, such as was our case during the construction of the trans-Amazon highway, you cannot keep on taking preventive pills every other day for months or years on end. Quinine, taken over a long period of time, may do you more harm than good, eventually affecting kidneys, liver, eyesight, and hearing.

Neither can you indefinitely spray insect repellent on your skin, for the obvious reason that it's toxic.

In our case we couldn't even dress in more than shorts, shirts, cap, and flip-flops, because our bridge-building work was mostly by or in water. Add regular night shifts till 11 P.M. whenever the weather permitted—there was nothing else to do in the jungle but work, no women being allowed in camp—and the result could not have been different: All of us got malaria.

The first attacks were the most intense: headache, high fever, shivers, hallucinations, nightmares, loss of appetite. A cup of red wine at mealtimes helped me to eat. The attacks last for about a week, recurring every afternoon. But the disease stays in your blood. For a while even abrupt changes in altitude brought me new eruptions. Nowadays, twenty-five years later, I get only mild manifestations of intense shivering when I catch cold or rain. Then I have to dive under several blankets in a hurry and stay warm for about an hour. A hypothermic sensitivity is what it has come down to.

Rabies, Raiva, Rábia, or Hidrofobia

If you happen to be bitten by a suspected rabid animal, you must seek a hospital without delay for the appropriate antidote, which consists of a number of injections. Rabid animals act strangely, have a detached, hunted look, do not react to summons or a whistle, are unable to drink, and will bite defensively. Some may have signs of foam around the mouth. I have only seen two rabid dogs in all my life, one of which I was called to shoot. That's another reason for that pistol in my pocket.

Schistosomiasis

This disease is endemic to regions of high population density and primitive sanitation, such as agglomerations of poor people with low levels of education and no treated, piped water.

In the semi-arid Brazilian northeast, where the disease is widespread, the above conditions are aggravated by a natural shortage of rain and running water. As a result all water-dependent activities are often concentrated around a single pool, where cattle drink and defecate while people wash clothes, bathe, and drink directly.

Schistosomiasis is caused by a 1.27-centimeter (0.5-inch) worm (*Schistosoma mansoni*), the eggs of which, expelled through human feces, are washed into rivers and ponds. There they infect snails as intermediary hosts, from which they return to the water to penetrate the skin of bathing humans. This is why it's also called the "snail disease."

They travel through the bloodstream to lodge in the intestines, liver, and spleen. Eggs of adult females are furthermore transported to the bladder and other organs, with destructive effects.

I made a 4,000-kilometer (2,500-mile) overland trip through the northeast in December 1998, and solved the water problem by carrying two containers: one of 5 liters (quarts) for drinking water, replenished along the way with bottled water of known brands bought at service-station shops; and the jeep's 20-liter reserve-fuel container, flushed out and filled with water for washing, replenished from ponds and streams by the roadside and disinfected with chlorine.

In the Swampland—Pantanal or Chaco—there is an abundance of snails, just like most other forms of life, but no schistosomiasis, for the same reason that there are none of the other diseases: an extremely low population density, due to all-encompassing and long-lasting seasonal floods that impede the establishment of villages, with a yearly dry season in between, and the single economic activity in the region, other than tourism: beef-cattle breeding, which employs few hands. A typical 20,000-hectare (50,000-acre) cattle ranch is run by no more than half a dozen cowboys, of whom only one or two have a family, and breeds a maximum of three thousand head of cattle on the fragile, sandy soil, with a production that rarely exceeds 37 percent per year.

In case of contamination there are specific medicines that eliminate the *Schistosoma* from the blood when treated early. But after the liver, lungs, and heart have been affected, there is no way of regenerating them; transplants are required.

Spotted Fever or Febre Maculosa do Carrapato

This disease has been briefly mentioned under Ticks (see chapter 5), which cause it in some mountainous regions. Here again we see the influence of altitude on disease—so much so that in North America it is called Rocky Mountain spotted fever. In Brazil it occurs in some areas like Pedreira, approximately 150 kilometers (93 miles) north of São Paulo, and Chapada dos Guimarães, some 60 kilometers (38 miles) east of Cuiabá, Mato Grosso, where my wife and I caught it.

Spotted fever is mainly transmitted by carrapato estrela (*Amblyomma cayennense*), a relative of the American lone star tick (*A. americanum*). These ticks have various stages of evolution, from brown lumps of thousands the size of pinpricks, to dozens of red pinheads, and finally to the occasional adult, about 7 millimeters (just under 0.25 inch), gray with black markings. It can also be transmitted by immature ticks of other species.

The disease is easy to recognize because of the spots in its name, which appear as red dots a bit larger than mosquito bites around the wrists, ankles, hands, and footsoles together with headache, fever, shivers, and pains in the muscles and joints. In severe cases these spots are said to spread over the whole body; there may be involvement of the lungs, liver, and kidneys as well as heart failure. In our case the spots spread to the beltline but no farther, and eight to ten days later the symptoms had disappeared.

See Ticks for protective measures.

Yellow Fever, Febre Amarela, or Fiebre Amarilla

After decades without a case, when it was thought to be gone for good, this potentially deadly viral disease—transmitted by the same daytime-biting *Aedes aegypti* mosquito that spreads dengue fever (above)—has reappeared in rural zones of the central Brazilian states of Goiás and Minas Gerais. Thus vaccination is necessary.

10

PREVENTION IS THE BEST CURE

The best way to protect yourself in the Tropics from sunburn, caterpillars, cattle grubs, chiggers, *Larva migrans*, snakes, spiders, scorpions, thorns, and allergies from poison webs, ivy, and other plants is simple, as you will no doubt have concluded from reading these pages: It's by wearing proper clothes—head, hand, and foot coverings included. You need a hat or cap, ventilated; light but long-sleeved cotton shirt; light leather gloves; and long jeans or soft, well-tanned leather chaps. Under the chaps you need only light bermudas in order to keep your legs cool and ventilated. Weight is decisive in choosing chaps for walking, as they are normally intended for riding and therefore rather heavy. And don't forget boots. With light pants you need taller boots or shoes with leggings (perneiras) because of snakes, whereas with chaps the ordinary cowboy wears only elastic-sided half boots.

Resist the temptation to "go native"—shirtless, in shorts and flip-flops—because you are not a native. After a long-enough time living in a given region, when you have acquired experience and your built-in computer is able to recognize the conditions that constitute danger, you may do without this or that item at times, as I often do. But if I went to Africa—a continent I don't know—I would definitely wear full dress and take all recommended precautions.

In the caatinga of the semi-arid northeast you need leather clothes from head to foot to ward off the aggressive, thorny plants. Such clothes are best acquired on the local market, made of various leathers.

HYGIENE

You also need to take good care of yourself physically and mentally. Sleeping well in the jungle is essential to keep your head in place and your senses alert. If you are familiar with military tactics, you will appreciate that keeping the enemy awake is intended to disrupt his capacity to think.

In order to sleep well, besides a good mosquito net and sufficient darkness, you need to keep clean. For me the best time to take care of hygiene in the jungle is during lunch break, when the sun is straight above. It is then that I interrupt my walk in some spot of mixed shade and sun by the water, remove my clothes, and wash them—shirt, underpants, socks, handkerchief (pants when necessary), everything—with neutral coconut soap, then hang them up on branches or spread them out on rocks to dry; branches are preferable, for ventilation. Then I wash myself, with the same natural dishcloth gourd and coconut soap. Avoid beautiful, bright-colored toilet soaps, because of allergy-causing ingredients in the pigments. Skin with scratches and cuts is more sensitive than usual.

While these dry I watch birds, butterflies, and fish, examine plants and rocks, look for diamonds and gold—which I've never found—in the sand. And I carefully examine myself for ticks, athlete's foot, chiggers, skin rashes, thorns, and cuts, taking advantage of the day's best light.

This is also the time to check equipment and mend things. Then I have my snack, sharing the crumbs with the fish, after which my clothes will be dry and feel good on the body, while I feel refreshed and reenergized to carry on until evening.

When it's raining, socks and underwear must be washed in camp and dried over the embers of the fire, together with all wet or moist items on a line or rod tied across under the tarpaulin.

Shoes are all-important. Once they have dried, they must be greased for impermeability and flexibility with any lubricant on hand: cooking oil, margarine, sardine oil, motor oil, tallow, what have you. You cannot walk in the jungle without lovingly cared-for shoes or boots. Of course sneakers, made mostly of rubber and cloth, should not be oiled.

DANGEROUS COMPANIONS

When you find yourself in a mixed group, it is wise to establish one thing very clearly before you start out: Who is in charge?

Once I was hired by a group of young university professors and other professionals from São Paulo—all colleagues—to lead a tour of the Swampland.

One of these fellows was considered superintelligent and treated somewhat deferentially. Well, this idiot did nothing but one irresponsibly dangerous thing after the other, to show off.

To begin with, he had brought a concealed shotgun along, which was fortunately discovered in time to warn him it could not be carried. He hooked a tame alligator that was accustomed to being fed . . . In the inn restaurant he'd pull his machete out of its sheath and wield it in the aisle where people tried to pass with their food . . . During an evening walk he sneaked around behind a herd of cattle and stampeded them upon the rest of the group, causing a young woman who didn't know what those charging animals were the shock of her life . . . And so on.

With an individual of this kind running loose in a group you don't need snakes or bees or piranhas, for he alone is sure to cause an accident sooner or later. It didn't happen that time only because we had a serious talk.

Another fellow from the same group kept playing around in the water with a short stick, despite my repeated warnings to guard against rising piranhas . . . until there was a splash, and he was left staring at the stump of his stick in his hand—which could just as easily have been the stump of his finger!

Don't assume that someone who's good at one thing is also automatically as good at another. Exceptionally bright people in a given area may reveal themselves abysmally stupid elsewhere. And this is a detail that must be foreseen and guarded against when entering the jungle.

Other human dangers may await you in the Amazon region. When, after serving for three years at Ponta Porã I was once again promoted and transferred to the Tenth Cavalry Regiment at Bela Vista, some 120 kilometers (75 miles) farther west on the same border with Paraguay, I shared a rather isolated house with two other bachelor sergeants and a corporal. This house had a rather large yard around it with mango and orange trees, and there was a swamp across the street. Each of us had a room to himself.

My window opened upon a small hedge of fence roses. One night I lay reading, the place silent, when I became aware of a movement in the hedge just outside the open window: One of the rose vines was slowly *rising* . . . I drew the .45 Colt pistol from under my pillow, and the moment a head of hair emerged I fired, convinced that whoever was sneaking up out there in the dark of night could only have criminal intentions.

There was a scream of fright, followed by agitated, muffled voices. I switched off the light and, picking up my flashlight, dashed to the window. Outside sat two girls on the ground, one very pale and feeling her head where the heavy bullet had burned a hole through her hair. Fortunately nothing more.

This incident, which by a hair did not result in a tragedy, is to me a permanent reminder that however much something may seem to be what you fear, it may not be, after all. It turned out that these naive girls had come to see the corporal, but were not sure which was his room. Instead of announcing themselves at the door and asking, they had opted to take a secret peep into the one window where there was a light on.

You may also be dealing with someone who is drunk, or drugged, and doesn't know what he's doing. On Christmas Eve 1972 I was driving a pickup from the Caripé River bridge works near Tucuruí to Marabá, Pará, with about eight workers on board, nearly all ill with malaria. They had received their wages and were going to proceed to their hometowns in Maranhão state by bus from Marabá on.

It had rained nonstop for about thirty-four hours and the trans-Amazon highway, still under construction, was a quagmire where only the two central tracks for the wheels of one vehicle were at all passable. Any attempt to overtake another car by detouring out toward the shoulders would have ended either in the car nosing into the soft dirt and getting irretrievably stuck, or worse: helplessly sliding down the bank, road and all, into the dammed-up water rising all the while.

We had just overcome a moment's fright when there suddenly appeared a dark crack across the road as the ground sagged away where the water found a passage underground. It was too late to try to brake the heavily loaded vehicle, for we would have slid into the growing gap . . . So I called up to the boys to hold on tight, and accelerated instead, jumping the void. The ground had been softened throughout, so the front fender and axle simply bulldozed a ramp up and, as luck had it, got us back onto the central tracks.

Minutes later, while carefully progressing along the top of another high landfill, I could hardly believe my ears when there came from behind the sound of a horn being blown insistently! Although this might not strike the habitual city driver as so extraordinary, we were in the middle of nowhere, on a road still unsettled, where you encountered another vehicle only very sporadically; the relations between drivers were, of necessity, reciprocally helpful. Besides, it was not only obviously impossible for me to move over to either side, but also totally unnecessary for anyone to have to overtake then and there instead of waiting another minute or two until we reached a cut, where it was safer.

When we reached a cut I swung to the right.

One look at the driver's flushed face as he cut in across our path with his Kombi microbus and braked was sufficient to remove any doubt that he was bent on aggression. By then I had jumped out even before the jeep came to a complete halt and knelt in the mud with my

12-bore coach gun aimed at his head. His only passenger scrambled out on the opposite side and rushed around the back of the car while my peons scattered for shelter—all malaria momentarily forgotten in their hurry to get out of the line of fire. The passenger emerged from behind the vehicle with one hand under his coat. Swinging the shotgun around I told him to get it out of there, which he did in a hurry, fortunately with his fingers spread wide open.

Meanwhile the driver, cursing all the while, went ahead and pulled a revolver from his glove compartment right in front of the muzzle of my gun, bragging that he, too, had a weapon! A more jumpy guy in my place might have shot either or both with every right and all my employees as witnesses.

Eventually the passenger got back inside and urged the driver to continue on, which he did, still cursing. As my people came out from their shelters, muddy and scratched, nobody could fathom what the guy's argument had been about. But there was a consensus that his red face betrayed he'd been drinking. Opening the cabin door I picked up a cartridge lying on the floor, which had slipped out of one of the chambers when I opened the breech in my hurry to cock the hammerless gun . . . only I knew that all the while I'd had just one cartridge.

Neither could my boss understand the incident when I described it to him that evening in Marabá. "The only fellow I know here who fits your description and drives a Kombi is as gentle as a woman!" he opined.

About a year later I was traveling out to one of our work sites in a Kombi as a passenger with my rucksack and coach gun, my jeep having broken down. As we passed this particular place I told the driver about the experience I'd had here. He was very respectful and quiet. Then a thought struck me, and I discreetly observed the man more carefully from the corner of my eye: Though his face—now sober—was so different that I had not recognized him, it was, as my boss had guessed, the same man!

HEALTH AND SAFETY—SOME CONCLUDING THOUGHTS

Although the number of accidents involving animals, insects, or fish in the jungle may seem negligible when compared to car accidents and crime, you must stop to reflect that the number of people walking in the jungle is likewise minuscule next to the millions of city dwellers. Also, accidents get only occasional media coverage; much of what happens here remains unknown.

And just as someone coming from the hinterland to the seashore or the metropolis grows much more accident-prone, so are you—the city dweller—when in the jungle. And for the same reason: Danger recognition hasn't had time to settle into your guidance system and grow automatic. In other words, you are not yet sufficiently aware of the colors and shapes and movements that you must automatically be on guard against.

So your chances of accidents are really much higher than statistics might suggest. But by diligently studying the jungle's "traffic laws" in this guidebook and preparing yourself accordingly you will be able to reduce them to the very minimum.

As you see, walking in the jungle is potentially as dangerous as driving a car, requiring the same constant attention, observance of safety rules, and care with equipment and maintenance. For, just like on the highway, when involved in an accident you may be lucky and get off with only a few scratches or cuts—or you may be crippled, or gone.

Note that in my family alone no fewer than three people have been bitten by venomous snakes—my grandmother, my uncle, and myself. And I was saved from being bitten at least twice more by wearing appropriate clothes.

If, on the one hand, in the jungle you are more fully and directly rewarded for your own precautions—let's call it "defensive walking"— since you are not a hostage of thousands of other drivers on the road, on the other hand you are not as experienced in the jungle, where the signs and warnings of dangers aren't always as visible or easily perceptible as traffic signs.

And the distance from medical help, plus the potential hardships and delays involved in getting the victim to a city hospital, may immensely aggravate an otherwise minor injury.

However, by preparing yourself adequately and observing these instructions, you will find in walking in the jungle an exhilarating, stress-free experience full of interesting events constantly renewed. A therapy for mind and body, in an endless laboratory for study, an adventure to be reexperienced year after year, each time more intimately, as you get to know and love the jungle, and to belong.

> I'd be an Indian here, and live content
> To fish, hunt, and paddle my canoe,
> And see my children grow, like young wild fawns,
> In health of body and peace of mind,
> Rich without wealth, and happy without gold.
>
> —Naturalist Alfred R. Wallace,
> *Travels on the Amazon and Rio Negro*

PART THREE

EQUIPMENT

11

GEAR OF ALL SORTS

Let's suppose you wish to take an exploratory trip across the tropical South American hinterland by car, boat, or both, with short excursions of from an hour to two or three days on foot, on horseback, or by canoe branching off wherever you are lured by something that interests you. (That's the way I travel; later I'll discuss these excursions specifically.) What should you bring?

Well, rather than trying to tell you what to wear, carry, and do in the jungle, in this section I will just tell you what I wear, carry, and do, and why. Then you can decide for yourself whether the equipment you already own will serve, can be adapted, or requires either additions or substitutions.

Should you have practical suggestions to offer from your experiences, please write or e-mail me, so that we may together improve future editions of this guide.

Colors

Whenever you have the option to choose the color of your clothes, hats, hammock, sheet, blanket, rucksack, companion bag, and so forth, give preference to solid light shades on which you can immediately spot anything that doesn't belong there. Avoid military camouflage, which seems to serve only to hide biting, burning, and stinging insects.

THE INDISPENSABLES

First, you'll want a light, foldable aluminum chair. This is a most convenient item to carry in the car or boat for comfort.

The indispensable compass—bussola or brujula—is best carried on a nylon cord or nonmetallic chain around your neck, long enough to hold it away from your body with the hand that does not contain your watch; otherwise it will give you an untrue reading. It should be sturdy, to support collisions with branches and so forth, and have a locking pin.

When purchasing, test two or three compasses at the store entrance where you can see the sun and away from metals, for uniform accuracy. Buy two, keeping one in your companion bag as a reserve.

In my shirt pocket I permanently carry four items, wherever I am: a **wallet** containing the necessary documents and bank cards (but no money!—cash should not be shown when presenting car and driver's documents to policemen), address, blood type, calling cards to give new friends and write messages on, and, last but not least, a couple of condoms. It can be awfully frustating to go out into the wild with your spouse or companion, bathe nude in a clear pool below a waterfall, dry yourselves in the warmth of the sun . . . only to remember that your protectors remained safely back in the glove compartment.

Besides the wallet there is an **address booklet,** which also contains important information such as my car identification, the numbers of my documents in case of loss, the names or formulations of medicines, and the like. A foreigner who does not speak Portuguese or Spanish may want to write in key words or phrases for everyday use, a basic conversion table for the metric system, a currency-exchange rate table, and so on. Both the booklet and the wallet are laminated, for every now and then I drop one or the other into the water, mud, or dirt.

I also carry a **comb** and **two ballpoint pens,** one red, one black. All these items are stuck tightly into one pocket so as not to fall out. If you can close your shirt pocket, so much the better.

A wristwatch—it needs no special features other than giving the time and date—is important in cloudy weather, when you need to turn in with enough time to prepare your camp in daylight; and during the night, when natural light can fool you.

Once I was camping in the Serra dos Agudos Grandes in southeastern state of São Paulo with my school friend Milton Correa and some caboclos. I was sixteen, and this was one of my first entries into real jungle. The day before we had encountered puma tracks. It had been raining heavily and the mountain creek by our hut was flooded and roaring. We had had to erect a trunk platform covered with palm leaves to keep above the water oozing from the ground, but even so it was hard to get any sleep that night given mosquitoes, smoke, and leaks in the thin thatch roof (which had already threatened to collapse).

Then it began to get lighter. Anxious to explore these exciting wilds in the first light of dawn, I picked up my rifle and set out along the brook. But it had been only a momentary thinning of the cloud cover, filtering down some weak moonlight for a few minutes. I was several hundred meters (yards) into the jungle when all-enveloping darkness set in again, and soon rain came prattling down anew. Now I had to feel my way back, with the gurgling stream as a guide, rather uneasy as to what might stand or lie across my path . . .

CLOTHING

Beginning from the top of the head and heading down, I take three hats in the car: a medium-brimmed straw hat for the open spaces—savannas, rivers, and beaches—with a ribbon to tie under the chin when there's wind or branches; a light ventilated cap for everyday use; and a leather cap for dense thickets and rainy weather. If I had to choose just one, I'd opt for the light cap.

In my particular case I also need a hearing aid, plus extra batteries and a battery tester. And glasses, with an older pair in my companion bag (see chapter 13) as a reserve.

I take five shirts, all light cotton, with at least one pocket each. Two have long sleeves to wear on the trail or river, two have short sleeves to wear while driving, and one is a T-shirt as a reserve in case I get wet. This T-shirt I keep in my companion bag, padding my photo lenses, together with a light woolen jacket, a scarf, and a plastic raincoat. The other shirts go with the remainder of my clothes in a rucksack (see chapter 13).

More necessities include four pairs of underpants, cotton, no elastic, bermuda type. One bathing suit in the companion bag.

I bring four pairs of pants as well. Two are long jeans or a pair of soft chaps and shorts to wear underneath, for trail and river; one is bermuda style for driving; and one is long, light, and soft for evening wear around camp. Pants, underpants, and bermudas must fit snugly around the beltline, and be free of rivets and knots that might press or rub your skin. But otherwise they should all be as loose and ventilated as possible, avoiding anything tight around the thighs, for two good reasons besides coolness:

First, tight pants will either tear at the knees or hinder your freedom of movement when climbing; and second, they are sexually destimulating for men. The male scrotum is located outside the body for the purpose of cooling, like a radiator. Hot, tight clothes hinder this process, acting like those Japanese communal baths, taken with friends and relatives, which are overheated precisely to deaden the sex stimulus. In the pristine atmosphere of the wilds this stimulus is usually powerful.

Also bring a strong, relatively new, solid-leather belt with a heavy-duty saddle buckle, as wide as the loops on your pants will take.

The narrower the belt, the more uncomfortable it becomes. Attached to the belt I carry, when on the trail, a pair of good garden pruning shears in a leather holster, a machete or hunting knife, and, where necessary, a canteen.

Let me introduce you here to a most practical belt that some imaginative cowboy figured out, which is now standard garb for work and even travel in the cattle-breeding states of Mato Grosso and Rio Grande do Sul. The guaiaca is a double, 7.5-centimeter to 9-centimeter (3- to 3.5-inch) wide belt of soft leather with one or two double-pronged swivels that close over a pad for absolute comfort. Back when the revolver was an indispensable part of a man's working tools, the guaiaca contained a short holster, with one large pocket behind for items such as bandages, tweezers, gauze, and emergency medicines, and two small ones in front, for the watch and compass, which fold out when unclipped so that you can read the dial without removing the instrument. The two spaces between the three pockets were occupied by a double line of cartridge holders. In the lower row you inserted your cartridges in the normal, upright position, from the top; in the upper row you fed them in upside-down, from below, by slightly folding the belt. The idea was that the bullets in one row kept those in the other from slipping out and being lost in the twist and tear of work with brute cattle and wild animals, where the belt serves, furthermore, as a protection against hernia. As mentioned, the guaiaca is a double belt: When you unbutton the snap fasteners and unfold it, you have, on the inside and fully protected from weather, wear, and thieves, a couple of long pockets for documents and money.

Today carrying a gun in public is no longer permitted, so now you can find guaiacas with extra attachments in place of the holster and cartridge holders—except two, for the toothbrush—such as a scabbard for your pocketknife, cell phone, and perhaps an extra pouch for keys and things that may become uncomfortable in your clothes when you're walking a lot. So it continues to be a utilitarian belt that you wear over your clothes and can turn whichever way you want in order to reach this or that pocket, all items in it being easily accessible.

In my particular case I also wear braces because of an inguinal hernia. I carry two: one for all-day wear, the other just for showering or swimming. When the former needs washing I invert the order.

All my pants and bermudas must have six pockets, and the contents of each are always the same: the small, right-hand "finger" pocket is for the car keys, the left one for coins. The right rear pocket is for cash—bills only, loose, no wallet. The left rear pocket contains my checkbook, toilet paper, and some Band-Aids, all inside plastic bags so as not to wear away with sweat, rain, or friction. You may wish to equip your pockets with covers or zippers for extra protection.

In the left front pocket I carry an unused, reserve handkerchief for cleaning lenses; I transfer this to the right-hand pocket each time I wash the one there. When I have a cold and running nose I keep two handkerchiefs in each front pocket, although I prefer a T-shirt to blow my nose; it's softer and bigger.

Footwear

No amount of care is ever too much when it comes to choosing and conserving your footwear; for if your feet are not comfortable, your walk in the jungle is going to be impaired.

I carry three pairs of very comfortable leather shoes and boots for the trail, regularly oiled for softness, water resistance, and conservation, free of ornaments such as rings, swivels, or chains that are likely to get caught in the vegetation and cause an accident. There's an extra pair of shoestrings in my companion bag. Leggings, if you can find them, are another option.

When buying shoes for walking, they must conform to the profile of your feet, feeling snug all around without pressing in anywhere. The soles must be sturdy and well stitched. Very soft soles will make you feel every root and pebble, and as a result your feet will soon be hurting.

You'll want four pairs of socks: one with the shoes, one in the companion bag, and the other two in the rucksack.

You may prefer sneakers, which so many people are wearing nowadays. I find them too hot, but that's a personal matter.

In your companion bag there should be a tube of Super Bonder Loctite instant all-around glue. Shoes and equipment must, like the pockets, be examined every day along all joints. When anything begins to come apart on the trail, such as a shoe sole, clean it, dry it well, and glue it, placing a weight on top for a safe ten minutes. Then stitch as well, if possible.

Add a pair of Rider press-shut sandals for bathing, driving, and walking where it's clean.

SLEEPING ARRANGEMENTS: THE HAMMOCK AND MOSQUITO NET

If there is one absolutely indispensable set of items in the Tropics, be it in the jungle or in the towns and villages where hotels are usually low quality, it is the proper hammock and mosquito net.

I'm not talking about that combination "military" piece of junk consisting of a canvas mat with screens on the sides and a plastic cover. The mosquitoes bite you through the bottom, as well as each time you

lean against any of the screens—which soon rip apart anyway. That's no good.

You'll instead want to buy the two items separately. The mosquito net for a hammock is an independent item, its netting of a very fine mesh (otherwise our "torpedo" *Anopheles* climb right in), with a sleeve at each end through which the hammock fists pass, and a couple of thin, 1-meter (3-foot) rods that you cut locally, to stretch it.

When you buy one, it comes open at the bottom. This may be acceptable in clean indoor places, but not out in the field or jungle. Thus you must have it sewn together underneath and a 1-meter (40-inch) zipper installed in the middle, so that you—and nothing else—can get in and out.

This is how the hammock and mosquito net should look when set up. The net touches the hammock only at each end.

The hammock you also purchase locally, and for a tall individual a sleeping hammock should be no less than 3.5 meters (12 feet) long so that you can lie in comfort, at an angle of about 20 degrees to its axis, with a small pillow under your neck to get the head right. The material must feel strong, especially at the cords and fists, and be free of ornamental fringes. I hate these fringes that people seem to think hammocks and blankets have to have. The wind flips them over, and you wake up thinking there's a spider walking on you. Or then it's the other way around: You think it's the wind blowing the fringes on you, when it's really a spider—which you find out when you touch it! So the best thing to do with fringes, when you can't find the item without them, is to take the nearest pair of scissors and clip them off.

The only place where the mosquito net touches the hammock—which swings freely inside it—is up at the wrists. So you are entirely isolated from insects and small animals, while enjoying total visibility for your security (unlike a tent, outside which anyone or anything can sneak up unseen).

Above the hammock you tie a rod or rope parallel to it, over which you stretch a 4-by-3-meter (13-by-10-foot) plastic tarpaulin for protection against rain, falling fruit, debris, and bird or bat droppings.

Tying the Hammock

A hammock should be tied to trees whenever possible on high ground and in the darker recesses of the forest, away from exposed beaches, trails, and animal paths, both for protection and for sufficient darkness to be able to sleep well. Good sleep is important because disease enters the body when it finds the door open—and insufficient sleep is one condition that will open the door.

As you tie up the hammock, there's no need to wield a machete right and left to clear away the underbrush, only the odd interfering branch or bush. Since your mosquito net is totally closed, the less it touches the ground, the longer it will remain clean and dry and free from destruction by termites. So it doesn't matter whether you have a cliff, river, swamp, tree branch, rock, or what have you beneath you, as long as there is a firm step from which to enter or leave the hammock.

Shoes should remain outside the mosquito net in order not to dirty or force it—but don't put your socks inside the shoes; hang them up separately. In the morning shake and beat your shoes well before putting them on. I have placed my boots on top of a foldable chair inside the screen-fringed tarpaulin and still found a dozen large ants in one of them!

Hammocks and Lightning

Here is another significant advantage of the hammock: You aren't grounded, which means you're safe from a direct lightning stroke. But precautions must be taken to avoid being indirectly hit. You don't want to stay close to the tallest trees or rock outcrops upon a mountain ridge or other high ground, nor alongside wire fences.

On a ranch I managed near Valparaíso in the west of São Paulo in 1966 we came upon an isolated tree in a pasture after a storm, under which lay, like the petals of a flower, eleven fat steers, all dead. And a friend who owns a small farm near Charqueada some 225 kilometers (140 miles) northwest of São Paulo found sixteen of his yearling calves lying dead along a fence. When storms come in low across the upper Serra da Bodoquena, fences become electrically charged even without lightning.

And speaking of storms, there is, besides lightning, the wind and the softening of the ground to recommend staying clear of the tallest, or inclined, trees.

Bamboo or Taquaruçu

Wherever you find bamboo, it is by all means your safest choice for tying your hammock. Bamboo is a gramínea—a grass—and therefore extremely flexible and weather resistant. No bamboo stem can fall on top of you, for the simple reason that bamboo stems don't fall: They jackknife and fold down slowly.

Back in July 1977 Maria and I arrived late at night at our chosen campsite beside the Aquidauana River in the Piraputanga canyon some 130 kilometers (80 miles) west of Campo Grande, Mato Grosso do Sul. Behind us the sky was ablaze with lightning. Nearby stood an old shed with a corrugated zinc roof. Upon the cliff above the river grew a line of bamboo, and we tied our hammocks and shelter there.

Minutes later that storm came roaring and firing down the canyon like a massed, charging tank division. The zinc roof was torn off the old shed, and we could hear trees snapping along the cliff walls. We swung to and fro as our bamboos flexed; that was all.

The main precaution to take under bamboo is for fire: A gust of wind can blow a handful of dry leaves across the firebreak, into the flames, light them, and blow them on out the other side and start a brushfire. Also take care regarding snakes, for rodents live in bamboo.

The Fall of a Giant

As the rainy season advances in the Amazon forest and the ground softens to increasing depth we are at times given the opportunity to witness the demise of one of its giants. Join me in this experience.

It was past two o'clock in the morning and the electrician and I were on our way to replenish the generator's oil sump as our team was working straight through the night hammering in the screws with which I had only just managed to arrive from Marabá, to fasten the assembled 105-meter (345-foot) Tuerê River bridge in the face of a rapidly rising flood.

Although the generator wasn't far from the illuminated bridge in a straight line, it took a couple hundred meters (about 650 feet) to get around to it because of invading floodwater, and the electrician was afraid of going alone in the dark. When we got to the far side we perceived a sound, like a muffled punch, that seemed to come out of the ground.

My immediate fear was that one of the bridge's bases, which had suffered the impact of a ferryboat—ripped loose in a previous flood and thrown against it—might have sustained undetected damage in the rock ledge it rested on . . . Still, the men on the bridge didn't seem to have noticed anything.

While we poured the oil there came another thump. Then, as we began to make our way back, we actually felt the ground shudder as another tearing sound came up from beneath, this time accompanied by some alteration up in the high crowns of the forest a little downriver, where some birds let out startled cries while our hunter's dogs began to bark from the road.

We were just concluding that the ferryboat—now moored downriver—was in the process of being ripped loose once again, when there occurred another punch in the ground as one more anchoring root let go, followed by a growing howl like that of an unlubricated gate being opened, then there began a crashing and roaring like a furious wind coming across the forest, heavier trees breaking, and finally the shuddering crash as the tree hit the ground, followed by the tumbling of lighter trees brought down by the big one and its network of attached lianas.

That tree opened a swath in the forest 50 meters (more than 160 feet) long and nearly as wide with the other vegetation it pulled down.

Height

The height to tie the hammock should be such that from a standing position you can sit back into the middle of it. Or, looking at it from another angle, when you swing your legs out over the side and sit up, your feet should touch a solid surface in order to stabilize the swinging hammock in case you have to aim a gun or camera, or just want to observe wildlife, or pinpoint some noise. Thus try for about 1 meter (just over 3 feet) high in the middle, no more. As a matter of fact, a meter is a good measure for most things in the jungle, as you may have noticed: the walking stick, mosquito net separators, zipper.

The Danger in Tying a Hammock Too High

Along the Apa River there have always been some jaguars and pumas. In the mid-1960s a man, who may have been an American, came to this region to fish, taking with him into the jungle some local individual as a guide.

Fear of the big felines caused the man to tie his hammock at an absurd height. Unaccustomed to sleeping in hammocks, the visitor—who was apparently overweight—fell out and crashed to the ground on his back in the middle of the night, seriously injuring his backbone. Unable to move and in great pain, he could not drive his car. The guide had to walk to the nearest cattle ranch and arrange for the man to be hauled out on the flatbed of an oxcart as far as another farm, where there was a pickup truck to take him into town along rutted trails.

All this took days and nights due to the distances and the need to go slowly with the man. The small local hospital could do no more than alleviate the patient's pain with sedatives until the arrival of the twice-weekly plane . . .

A hammock should be tied to green wood, with knots that become tighter the more you pull, while easy to undo once pressure ceases. And then test it to make sure the hammock, cords, fists, ropes, and trees are all sturdy enough.

Give yourself extra time the first couple of days until you get the hang of the procedure, after someone with experience has shown you how to tie it and what to bear in mind. Setting up and adjusting the hammock takes a little longer than the tent, but to me it's worth it. See The Danger Regarding a Tent, below.

A Light Hammock

For extremely warm weather and nature-watching you can find in sporting goods shops a hammock made of fishing net. This is very practical, cool, and transparent; it weighs next to nothing and allows you 360-degree visibility.

The Hammock Camp

Your flashlight, pistol, knife, and objects from your pockets should be kept in an easy-to-reach pouch while you sleep, strapped to the hammock cords behind your head, or on the ground inside the mosquito net, within reach. You can have a saddle ring sewn to each end of the hammock mat, along the central line, for this purpose, because you never know which way you'll lie. Flashlight and gun should be placed so that you can reach them without noise—thus the bag must be open.

Fish and meat are to be kept suspended from a branch some distance from the hammock to avoid disturbance by alligators and other carnivores.

When breaking camp you simply untie and remove the two separating rods from the mosquito net, then roll up the hammock together with the net, tie the bundle with the ropes or leave these wrapped around loose, insert the roll into a plastic bag, and pack it on the bottom of your rucksack, followed by the sleeping bag and the folded tarpaulin on top.

SLEEPING ARRANGEMENTS: THE TENT

Like a rucksack, a tent is a well-known item to all campers. Today there are very practical and light "igloo" tents with telescopic nylon or carbon fiber rods that can be assembled in five minutes and occupy little space.

Let's therefore concentrate on details you must keep in mind when choosing a tent for the Tropics.

Screens, or tela, must be of a fine mesh, with holes no larger than 1 millimeter.

Zippers have to be closed completely, leaving no open hole at the junction through which all sorts of insects, including leeches, and even snakes might slip in. There should be a flap with a magnetic press-on closure inside, over the zippers; or you can stuff the hole with a handkerchief or sock.

The floor must be made of a heavier material and waterproof, and arranged so that when the tent is erected, the edges of the floor are turned up all around in order not to let in rainwater. The floor has to be wiped clean and then examined against sunlight for holes every time you've camped where there are thorns, sharp stumps, or the like, and then repaired with the boat-repair kit. Otherwise water will infiltrate and soak your clothes and sleeping bag.

Always take twice the lengths of ropes, cords, and string you expect to need, because the best branches to tie on are sometimes distant. All should be nylon; while sisal ropes are easier to handle and tie, they stretch when dry and shrink with rain to the point where they might overstretch the tarpaulin, pulling out the eyelets. When breaking camp always save every length, for you will need them all again.

The Danger Regarding a Tent

Even when you're traveling in a larger group and apparently secure, you must, when choosing your campsite, be conscious of the possibility of flash floods, cattle, alligators, and thieves.

Alone, I would not risk sleeping in a tent anywhere other than in the deepest recesses of thickets with only one approach open—and that one I could control. Otherwise, in case of an attack by robbers or vandals, you are a sitting duck, with insufficient all-around view to enable you to assess who or what is out there, how many there are, and where they are. From the outside, on the other hand, your shape is perfectly visible when there's a light on.

Because a tent must be set up on flat, clean ground, people know where to look for it. A hammock on the other hand, can be tied up just about anywhere that suits you as long as you have a couple of trunks, branches, or pitons to attach it to: on a cliff, in a tree, a cave, a boat, and so forth. No need to clean the brush around: The denser the vegetation, the more difficult it is for anyone or anything to approach unnoticed.

SLEEPING ARRANGEMENTS: NOISES IN THE NIGHT

Let's suppose you are asleep in your hammock or tent in the jungle when you wake up believing you've heard some noise. You probably did, and your subconscious prodded you from your slumber so that you might defend yourself if necessary.

What to do? Tropical South America is not India of a hundred years ago, where perilous animals slunk around camps to pounce upon the unwary, as Jim Corbett described in his fascinating *Man-Eaters of Kumaon*. But all sounds should be identified, both for the sake of your reassurance and for your enlightenment, since each mystery you solve is one more point added to your lore, and a satisfaction.

At first you are likely to wake up quite frequently since your sixth sense doesn't know jungle sounds. Later, as they become familiar, you will sleep right through the lesser ones.

The variety of small nocturnal animals going about their errands in search of food, partners, and marking their territories can only be assessed when—while camping in the sandy savanna—you pull a branch along the trails in the evening to erase the day's tracks and then go see the next morning what marks you find. Many of the smallest ones (especially of arthropods) I don't know myself, although each time I see something moving on the trail I look for its tracks.

So now you are awake, suspecting it is due to some noise you heard, and wondering what to do. My first act is to noiselessly reach for my two indispensable companions: flashlight and pistol. Then, having made sure the hammock is not bathed in moonlight—in which case any movement I make will be perceptible through the shifting shadows on the ground—I sit up in slow motion and listen, trying to meanwhile fig-ure out what could have produced the sound, if it's not repeated. Has some wind sprung up and perhaps flapped the tarpaulin, caused the central pole supporting it to fall, or dropped a branch on it? Might the handle of a portable radio or the undercarriage of a foldable table have settled back into its resting position, or an empty plastic soft-drink bot-tle been too tightly screwed, causing it to burp with the drop in tem-perature? Could it have been myself, beginning to snore? Was any pot of food left uncovered or dishes unwashed, where a wood rat or opos-sum—gambá—might be nibbling? In July and August in the dry mid-west some leguminous trees such as *Cenostigma* crack their pods like air-gun shots to throw their seeds as far as possible from the mother tree, right into the night. Cattle may at times move until late out in the open, Indian Brahma bulls belching very much like jaguars. When there is a bright, full moon several birds call throughout the night. Of those you are unlikely to know, the rhea hums a *huuum hum!* like someone agree-ing to a suggestion. A shorter, more repetitive *huh-huh, huh-huh!* is the guan's (mutum) call. Of the larger animals, the tapir whistles in one note and prefers to move in weaker moonlight or none at all.

What you should *never* do is switch on the flashlight before the source of the noise has been identified—or, even more foolishly, fire a random shot into the dark! Darkness and anonymity are your protec-tion. If you fire a shot, you give away your position, as well as the fact that you have a gun and are nervous; not to speak of the possibility of injuring some fisherman or animal completely unaware of your pres-ence and offering you no danger. Use your night binoculars instead, and give yourself plenty of time to identify what's going on.

I have heard some very strange sounds in the jungle. When I was sixteen I accompanied my grandfather to the virgin forests of the Paranapanema River's headwaters east of Capão Bonito in the south of São Paulo state, where he spent a couple of months painting pictures of nature while I cooked and hunted. On those jungle trails I used to hear odd gurgling, slurping noises, which the local caboclos told me were made by the giant earthworm—minhocuçu (*Glossoscolex wiegreeni*)—as it moved inside its subterranean galleries.

One very cold evening in the Swampland after dark a sound began to issue from a stand of tall trees on an island near our camp—some-thing like a lot of motorcycles parading at a constant, low speed. This grew in intensity as the night progressed and lasted until daybreak. The moment the sun emerged the noise suddenly grew to a roar like a pis-ton airplane taking off, and then the sky was black with a flight of sev-eral hundred bare-faced ibises (*Phimosus infuscatus*). The poor birds had been beating their wings throughout the freezing night to keep warm.

One night back in 1957 when I was in the army I had camped alone deep inside a beautiful limestone cave in the Swampland some 4 kilometers (2.5 miles) from Fort Coimbra, south of Corumbá. Around midnight I woke up, thinking I had heard a noise. I listened, feeling the occasional breeze from the wings of curious bats coming in close to examine me. Then I heard it again: a long, drawn-out, muffled roar. I sat up in my sleeping bag and placed the rifle across my lap, flashlight and machete lying alongside. On entering the cave by a relatively small hole under the roots of a strangler fig in the saddle of a forested hill late in the afternoon I had spotted the freshly torn remains of an armadillo, indicating that one of the larger carnivores lived there. But I was some 150 meters (500 feet) into the pitch-dark interior, where it was unlikely that a jaguar or puma would venture. Still, I sat beside a crystal-clear subterranean lake. Alligators are known to migrate overland when their lagoons dry up in the late winter and early spring. Could one such beast, in crossing between the hills, have smelled the water of this lake down here and descended, thenceforth surviving on the occasional blind catfish (*Typhlobagrus kornei*) living in these waters? But this was not the call of an alligator, whose three or four short belches are sharp and openmouthed. What I was hearing—and it was getting louder and more frequent, thus seemingly approaching—sounded more like a long growl issuing from a closed or semiclosed mouth.

Though my rifle was entirely dependable, I realized that only as a very last resort should I fire it, for the concussion of the powerful 7-millimeter Mauser might dislodge some of the spectacular stalactites hanging like Damocles' swords, slowly dripping, from the vaulted ceiling high above my head . . . Then I perceived a different, equally mysterious sound, something like what lithe feet dabbling in shallow water might produce. I couldn't place this, as it seemed to be approaching from all around, especially the pond. So I stood up, feeling at once the impact of cold water on my face. Illuminating the scene with my flashlight, I saw that the stalactites had greatly accelerated their dripping. The mystery was solved: A storm was raging outside, and the growling I'd heard was the roll of thunder, its sharper edges rounded and subdued by echoing along the labyrinthine passages down into the depths of the cave.

A GUN

On the inside of my handkerchief, so as not to show its outline, and because I'm left-handed, I carry a small, 12-centimeter (4.9-inch) 6.35-millimeter (.25-caliber) semiautomatic Beretta pistol, in a thin leather holster inside a plastic bag to keep sweat and dust out when I'm walking in the jungle. This gun has been accompanying me for more than twenty-six years. It has an eight-shot capacity, which, with the addition of an extra clip in a leather pouch and plastic bag in the other front pocket adds up to fifteen quickly available cartridges. The Beretta has the assets of an exposed hammer that I leave on half-cock for safety, and a flip-up barrel, which permits instant checking of the cartridge in the chamber or replacement by hand in case of a malfunction—though I have never had a failure with this gun, which is all-important.

If I were given the choice, I would conduct a comparison test with larger-caliber guns of the same size—no more than 5 inches in overall length—available in the United States: semiautomatics of 7.65 millimeters (.32) and 9 millimeters (.380) with five-shot magazines to make room for the more voluminous cartridges and reinforced frame; and derringers with superposed barrels that can likewise be carried well concealed in a pocket, in .32 or .38 special at the most. Fewer shots but more powerful. I would only opt for one of these, though, if its safety and reliability matched the Beretta's. The ammunition mentioned is available in Brazil, but a license is required for the gun, with which the cartridges are also purchased.

Although safer and more dependable than a semiautomatic in the hands of a nonhabitual shooter, a revolver is too bulky to conceal within a pocket. Also, in our tropical climate there is no way you can carry it in a shoulder holster: Not only will the straps and contours show through a sweat-soaked shirt, but people in Latin America have the habit of clapping each other on the back or embracing amiably, when they might feel the straps or holster.

When I was a cavalry sergeant serving in Ponta Porã, now Mato Grosso do Sul, one day I had to go across the border to the Paraguayan garrison with my boss. My Paraguayan colleague embraced me warmly, placing his hand right on my shoulder holster . . .

Why a Gun?

And why concealed? Am I suggesting that the average tourist coming to the Tropics on a guided tour, in a group, should carry a concealed weapon?

Under no circumstances. Not even a machete. I've already described, in Dangerous Companions (see chapter 10), what problems this can cause.

But the present manual is more specifically directed, in this respect, at the autonomous hiker, camper, naturalist, or explorer, who is determined to go it on his own, alone or with one or two companions. Like myself. Then it's reassuring to feel a solid little gun in your pocket, just in case.

Many years ago I saw a western in which a wounded stranger dropped into the yard of some religious settler's family, who doctored him as best they could. But the feverish, unconscious gunman would not rest, thrashing about in bed, his hand forever searching, and with that his wound wouldn't heal. The farmer had an idea: He took the man's big Colt out of the cupboard where they had placed it, unloaded it, and pressed its wooden grip into the man's searching hand. As soon as his fingers closed around it, he calmed down.

That's the way I feel, too. For others a knife or a club may do, or a Bible or Koran. For a baby it is a pacifier that suggests the security of the mother's breast. No wonder they called one of those Colts a Pacifier!

Although I have never needed to use this pistol, I feel tranquilized by its presence. And should I suffer a debilitating accident in the wild, or get lost, the gun will gain importance as a means of signaling, survival, and defense. See part 4, Survival.

I carry my gun concealed, because there are things you should never display at random: money, valuable objects, conjugal intimacy, a gun. Its anonymity gives me an advantage if I have to resort to it for self-defense. Also, people's feelings may be affected by the ostensible presence of a firearm: Some could feel offended, seeing it as a symbol of mistrust; others are afraid of it, as something liable to go off by accident; or they may suspect its owner of being outside the law; whereas the criminally minded covet the gun, besides reckoning with it in case of a planned holdup, which is exactly the main reason I carry it.

There is no more suicidal gesture than reaching for the glove compartment or anywhere else in the face of a holdup. With the gun tucked away unobtrusively in my pocket I keep open the option to decide whether, and when, to use it.

Maintenance

This weapon must be kept holstered, clean, dry, and, when you're sweating, inside a plastic bag. Keep your pockets free of dust, sand, and crumbs that might find their way into its mechanism, clip, or barrel. For smoothness, apply only a minimum of oil to the moving parts such as the hammer, trigger, sliding rails, safety, and tilting axle if there is one. No oil must touch the ammunition, barrel bore, bolt face, or tip of the firing pin.

Unload and operate the pistol every time there is any dirt, water, or rust on it. A tightly fitting holster and a pouch for the clip make all the difference in keeping dirt out. Clean all corners with a stiff, dry paintbrush, but be careful not to leave bristles caught anywhere. Unload the clips and check their springs and guides for smooth, constant pressure on the cartridges. Should they get caught anywhere, disassemble the clip inside a towel—or else your spring may fly away into the scrub or water—polish the parts with steel wool, and wipe first with a dry cloth, then one lightly moistened with oil.

Upon putting everything back together, operate the gun to check its feeding mechanism. This should be done with firm, full-length strokes, holding the weapon level, as when you're firing. Test the reserve clip, too. After wading through water—especially brackish or salty coastal water—everything must be disassembled, dried, and, except for the ammunition, lightly oiled.

Sand is both your friend and your enemy. Sandy ground is the best, driest, and cleanest to camp on. But if you happen to drop your pistol, clip, pocketknife, or pruning shears, every last grain must be patiently removed until you neither see, feel, nor hear any in the moving parts; otherwise your tool may fail and will surely spoil rapidly.

The gun is to be kept fully loaded, including a cartridge in the chamber, with the hammer on half-cock or "safety." In an emergency it is the first shot that counts, so the firearm must be ready.

When a Gun Feels Good

In 1967 I was cattle section manager at Fazenda Bodoquena in the Swampland. As I rode in from the field one morning the agriculture foreman asked me to oversee a group of some fifty Kadiwéu Indians harvesting corn at the foot of the mountains, because he had another errand to do.

The Indians were going about their work as I came upon the scene, but I noticed they were leaving all cornstalks standing, which made it difficult to know what area had already been harvested. So I asked them to tread down the stalks, leaving only one standing at each pile of ears, which they did.

Then, out of nowhere, a man quietly approached and challenged my right to give orders in *his* area . . . Nobody had told me there already was someone in charge. And if there was, it made my presence unnecessary. I told him that.

"So, who's in charge, then," he demanded, "you or me?"

An alarm bell began to ring persistently somewhere inside me, like a rattlesnake's tail, as my sixth sense warned that my predecessor had been murdered here!

Get some distance between this guy and yourself, I thought.

"Now that you mention it," I said quietly, trying to sound pleasant, "I don't know. But I tell you what: Go over to the offices and find out with your boss. Tell him what's happened. There must be some confusion. If you're in charge, I'm leaving. This isn't my section and I have other work to do."

Instead of leaving, the man stepped nearer, mumbling something about being in charge here, not at the office. It was time to change my tone. "Go on, man!" I ordered, "let's have this thing cleared up!" With that I walked away, as if to check some work detail.

Slowly the man left. He appeared to be in no hurry, but seemed undecided about what else to do.

Sometime later, just before the end of the morning shift, I was jerked to attention by a glimpse, from the corner of my eye, of the man coming toward me from behind. When I deliberately turned to one side, this individual sidestepped in order to remain behind my back, approaching all the while. I felt myself growing tense. One more test, just to make sure: I turned the other way, and sure enough, the man again went out of his way to remain concealed.

Now there was no longer any doubt: He was sneaking up on me. What to do? The man had no visible weapon—though surely he had a knife under his shirt, like everyone else in rural South America—so I couldn't just turn around and shoot him. He hadn't done anything to me. I wiped my left hand on my jacket, to remove the sweat. *Be calm, but firm!* I reminded myself. *You know what he's up to, so you have the advantage. And he must be nervous. Just don't let him get within arm's length.*

I steadied my hands against my hips to keep them from shaking. When something happens all of a sudden, you react instinctively, instantly; and by the time your nervous system comes on, the party's over and it no longer does you any harm. But when you have to watch murder develop, slow motion, by degrees, irreversibly, without a break that might allow you to enter action and get it over with, as aptly exploited in thriller novels and films, then your nervous reaction tends to break in ahead of events and helps mess things up.

My heart beat loudly. I tried to tell myself not to overreact, but the man's intention, by deliberately staying behind my back, was irrefutable. Nobody else seemed to notice what was happening. I felt strangely alone, like in a dream, as if it were all unreal.

The man was about 3 meters (10 feet) behind me when I swung around, facing him. "So what did they tell you?" I asked sharply. The man's eyes were on the ground and he kept on coming, mumbling something unintelligible. I got disconcerted, consulted my watch. Just four minutes to go before the bell rang for lunch.

"Wait here a moment!" I said, and walked off as if I'd spotted something requiring my presence at the far end of the field. There I remained until the bell struck. Then, as I spotted the agriculture foreman walking toward his house, I called to him and cut straight across the field, waving the other man over to have the matter out.

"I just wanted to get near because I don't like to talk in front of peons," the guy said lamely. Two or three days later he stabbed someone else.

In the right-hand front pocket of my pants I carry the extra clip for my pistol, loaded and protected from dust, debris, and sweat inside a little press-shut bag or sheath and plastic bag. I also have a handkerchief or two and a Swiss pocketknife that has been with me longer than the pistol. All pockets must be of strong material and well sewn. The pockets are the most important part of your pants because of the essential items they hold, and therefore they must be checked every day for holes or wear. Add matches or lighter or both in a plastic bag, together with a small candle, well sealed.

OTHER WEAPONS AND TOOLS

A Swiss Pocketknife

There is a large variety of Swiss army pocketknives to choose from, some having insufficient attachments for our purpose, others quite simply too many. Mine, which my mother selected very well some thirty years ago, has the following: red side plates for easy location if you forget or drop it in the jungle or water, cutting blade, saw, file, pair of scissors, can opener, cap opener, corkscrew, awl, toothpick, tweezers, and two screwdrivers.

All are important. Only the tweezers on my knife should be sturdier. The awl should be perforated, so that you can pass thread, string, or leather through and stitch equipment with it besides extracting thorns. Given the option I would add one more cutting blade, because it's what wears most, through honing and use; and a miniature Phillips screwdriver for lens and camera in place of the useless toothpick, which you can shape yourself from any match or twig if you need one. Some knives have pliers, which are also useful, especially for fishing.

Machete or Facão

If you haven't got the more civilized pruning shears and foldable saw, or you are walking in places like the thorny, cactus-rich caatinga of our northeastern semidesert, you will need a machete, for with this tool alone you can provide everything you need: shelter, food, firewood. You can hack, cut, polish, stab, clear, dig, and make other tools and accessories.

Therefore a machete must be comfortable and practical. Otherwise it will hurt your hand and wrist—even if you're wearing a glove—and thus become useless. Its grip must conform to your hand and be free of rough or sharp edges. Because this is a violent tool that you have to wield with an effort, blisters and sore wrists are potential problems if you're not accustomed to using one. So is cutting yourself and others.

Our cowboys prefer the lighter butcher's knife. Those top-heavy European hunting knives with thick, stiff blades and beautiful deer-antler grips are absolutely useless for anything more than sporadic and brief employment. I've had a Solingen for over thirty-four years. The blade must be thin enough so that you can sharpen it on a sandstone, and light and flexible so as not to force the wrist. It should not be of excessively hard steel, like a saw blade. When misused, it dents almost as easily as softer steel, but requires much, much more whetting to remove. The knife should have a strong scabbard that it will not perforate nor slip out of, together with the steel for sharpening it. (See Sharpening Knives below.)

A good, comfortable grip or hilt should have three things. First is a small, downward-curving shield or rib in front, to protect and prevent your hand from slipping off the hilt and onto the blade in case you need to thrust, push, or support yourself upon the knife—which can happen very easily when your hand is sweaty. Second, the grip should end in a sufficiently downward-curving "beak" to support your small finger and keep your hand from sliding off the hilt backward when you have to draw, pull, or extract the knife. Third, on the top front—the beginning—of the blade, there should be an anatomical support for your thumb, usually serrated or checkered, for when you need to press down to cut.

The British Martindale jacaré (it has an alligator under the name), made in Birmingham, is an old favorite in the Tropics, followed by the American Collins. Although workable blades are up to 43 centimeters (17 inches) long, for a newcomer not yet accustomed to fencing with such a knife amid tangles of lianas I recommend a more prudent 30- to 35-centimeter (12- to 14-inch) blade. It balances better. If you must use such an anti-ecological weapon, that is.

Because there are downsides to the machete. After decades of making a fool of myself and blistering my hand unnecessarily, I have finally stopped to think and, seeing the light of common sense at last, curtailed the tool's use drastically as inappropriate for the wilds in our ecology-conscious times. Unless, as mentioned, there is no choice.

Besides injuring your hand and tiring yourself out in the stuffy jungle heat, causing you to sweat and attract biting insects, a machete is noisy, giving away your presence to every living being within 100 meters (yards). Its blade requires a wide arc to swing, where it may get caught on vines or branches and end up deflecting against your own body or a nearby companion. And it produces a strong smell of cut vegetation, irritating bees and wasps, which then zero in on you.

I can only think the machete must be some remnant from the days of slavery, when a wide swath had to be cut clean in order for His Excellency's litter to be carried through . . . If you're a caboclo who can only afford a single tool, okay. But for anyone prepared to spend an extra $30 to $50, there are better, less laborious options: good old-fashioned garden shears (any experienced gardener will tell you which are the best makes) and a foldable green wood saw.

For walking in the jungle, that is. In the car, in the boat, or at camp the machete is a useful tool to have on hand, which is why it is included in the rucksack. Of course some feel better with it in the belt.

The Danger with a Machete

Dr. Tola, from Rio de Janeiro, was a keen jaguar hunter back in the late 1960s, when he, his charming wife, and three guests from Florida landed at an outpost of Fazenda Bodoquena.

This outpost lay at the edge of a practically impenetrable jungle known as the Big Swamp, or Brejão. From the security of this spot the big felines made forays on cattle in the adjoining, open Pantanal. As a matter of fact, the very first day the group rode out they shot a young specimen.

The next morning they happened upon a fresh kill by a pond at the edge of the Brejão. The dogs were released and the strong scent led them into a thicket of low acurí (*Scheelea phalerata*) palms, followed by the cowboy guide, the tracker, and the hunters.

In an instant there occurred a turnaround as a counterattack took place: Two jaguars came charging after the hounds under the acurís and very nearly overran the team, who executed a fast strategic retreat out into the open with their dogs among their legs.

There the group was reorganized and a new advance mounted, with the guide and the tracker reentering the swamp in front, hacking open a trail with their knives. These were experienced men, brought up in the Swampland, to whom the knife was an everyday tool, permanently carried in the belt. But tension ran so high that presently, the tracker accidentally hacked the guide's arm, causing abundant hemorrhage and putting an end to the hunt.

Pruning Shears

This is a silent, smooth, effortlessly operated tool that does not tire or hurt your hand (though a thin leather glove—luva de couro—is necessary because of thorns, caterpillars, and so on). You use it to cut only what is minimally necessary—selectively, without disturbing other plants or wildlife.

Pruning shears have to be of good quality, to cut well and repeatedly while rarely requiring adjustments. Mine are Swedish Sandvik, very satisfactory, that I carry in a holster in my belt, like a pistol. I also have a Brazilian Tramontina that cuts well.

On the trail your pruning shears need a drop of oil in the moving parts every two or three days; watch out for grit, removing it if you find any. Sand the excess, dried sap from the blades with wet, soaped steel wool.

When purchasing, look for the following points:

• It must conform to your hand and feel comfortable, for you will be operating it for hours, sometimes the whole day long.

• The cutting blade and the support must be absolutely flush, like good scissors. Ask for a pencil in the shop and cut it up to try the tool.

• The adjusting screw has to have a locking device so that it will maintain the adjustment.

• The return spring that opens the blades and handles must be sturdy and of good quality. Do not settle for lower quality, or it will spoil your trip.

Foldable Saw or Serra Dobrável

When thicker wood must be cut, as in the construction of a shelter, or firewood, the foldable saw is another fine tool that requires minimal effort and is almost noiseless. Mine is likewise a Swedish Sandvik, 23 centimeters (9 inches) long when closed. I also own a Brazilian Tramontina of similar dimension that isn't bad, though its axle and locking system are weaker.

Sharpening Knives

Your knives, from the machete or heavy hunting knife down to the Swiss pocketknife, must be perfectly sharpened before you enter the jungle. Moreover, you must know how to sharpen them as well, for a blunt knife is useless.

To check whether a blade is sharp, you turn it up so that the sun or an electric light shines directly upon the cutting edge. If it has been properly sharpened it will not reflect any light. If it does reflect light it needs further whetting on the medium oilstone or sandstone you carry in your car, after which you give it the finishing edge on the small, fine stone in your companion bag, or the steel.

A pocket- or hunting knife blade must be ground by pressing it flat on its predesigned angle, so that as the blade wears with years of use, the angle always remains the same. Simple blades of pocket- and kitchen knives are thin on the cutting edge and thick on the back, so that you simply lay them flat on their side to grind them. But hunting knives, which often have a thicker, more elaborate blade, show the angle to be followed. Always do both sides, alternately.

Keep the stone well lubricated while grinding. I prefer sandstones, lubricated with water, because they don't dirty the luggage. An oilstone must be wiped with a cloth every now and then during the process, to remove the oil full of residue, and wrapped in a couple of plastic bags when putting away so that it doesn't seep out. The oil-soaked cloth you can save for lighting the campfire.

Cowboys, however, don't carry a whetting stone. There's usually a big sandstone on the farm patio, principally for removing dents. Cowboys carry a steel in the same sheath with their knife. You can buy the complete set in any cutlery of the cattle-breeding states. I use it and recommend it, for the steel—which is as simple a tool as its name: a candle-shaped piece of steel like a round file, with a handle—is much faster and more practical for giving your blade a quick and very sharp edge than a stone, and your cutting edge will remain sharp ten times longer between stone grindings, so long as there's no dent.

A steel does not remove dents. That will have to be done on a stone or with a file. When you haven't got a steel you can friction the blade of one knife against that of another with the same result.

MISCELLANEOUS GEAR

Flashlight or Lanterna

Carry a small reserve in your companion bag for emergencies, and a large one in your rucksack for general use. I recommend the four-battery model (two each way) with a handle and a large lantern, yellow or coral, sold in Brazil. It conserves the batteries perfectly, so there is no need to unload it when not in use, and you have easy access to the installation for minor contact adjustments in case it fails. These consist of three points: the central spring, which may need pressing in a little; the lamp spring, which perhaps needs pressing out; and the screw-on cover, which should not be tightened beyond the point of contact. If these fail, try moving the switch housing a bit.

Walking Stick

This simple item is by far your most useful companion on the trail; used to push aside spiderwebs or vegetation in the way, harvest fruit, retrieve objects from the water, prod things, test the ground, flip snakes off the path and even kill some when absolutely necessary. It must be remembered, however—and this seems so difficult for some people in this part of the world to grasp—that out in the wild these animals and insects and plants are in their home; we are intruders with no business harming them unnecessarily.

The walking stick should be at least 1 meter (3.3 feet) long, half that length again if you feel more secure; of a thickness between that of a thumb and that of a middle finger; flexible while green and slightly arched in case you need to hit an exceptionally aggressive snake or insect. You cut it just below the fork where another limb branches off, so that your grip forms a curve, beak, or hook just large enough to enable you to pull things up close to you—fruit too high to reach by hand, an object dropped in the water, a stone on the bottom of a stream—without becoming uncomfortable. When you must walk a trail at night without a flashlight, you push it along the ground ahead of you as a "sensor," which is another reason why it should be slightly curved.

Bamboo is only suitable while green. Dry, it becomes too light and brittle. A solid rod of almost any tough wood will do if it feels good and is straight enough. It is the most easily replaceable piece of equipment. A thick, stiff, and heavy piece is inappropriate. Because most of the time you will be carrying the walking stick upright in front of you, to fend off spiderwebs and twigs, it must not be something that begins to weigh you down over time, or hurt your wrist. Remember, you'll be wielding it all the time you're walking, like a good fishing rod.

The tip of the walking stick should not be sharp, but rather flattened so that you can ease it under snakes and things you want to move. Or, if you wish, it can be sufficiently forked (about 2.5 centimeters or 1 inch of free space) to immobilize a snake behind the head for identification.

By locking your walking stick in your armpit with the curved end forward and downward—like a child with a pretend rifle—you can use it as a stock to stabilize your pistol for a careful shot.

Binoculars

Nature-watching, as well as your own protection, calls for a handy pair of these useful glasses. You can, of course, pay a lot of money for the best equipment, but this should be insured.

Our nature-loving friends Dean and Susan Greenberg, keen bird-watchers, had just bought themselves two new Nikon glasses when their house in Campinas, state of São Paulo, was burglarized and the Nikons stolen.

When I was in the army in Ponta Porã, I lost my Leica C3 camera and a Winchester 1894 carbine in a similar way. Then I bought a Leica

M3 complete with a set of lenses for my Latin America journey by motorcycle. Near the Popocatepetl volcano in the region of Cholula, Mexico, I hitched a ride on a truck full of people. After I had alighted and the vehicle was gone I realized I had left my bag on the truck bed along with my camera, lenses, film (with photos taken throughout Central America and Mexico), passport, and more. And that was it. I didn't know where the truck was from, nor did the people on board—mostly Indians—have any idea where to find me.

Thus I recommend secondhand or not-so-expensive equipment, following the traditional American line of thought. When I came back to Brazil in the mid-1960s after working for the American arms and ammunition industry in Connecticut and California, I brought along a pair of Bushnell 7x35 wide-angle night binoculars, which served me well and cost less than $40 at the time. Now I own another, smaller set of the same make, made in the Philippines, which sells for about $100. It's inferior to the old Californian glasses. At night it's definitely no good. Anything more powerful makes me dizzy, though that's a matter of individual suitability and choice. The rule is that for fast, freehand focusing you want lower-power glasses, in the 6X to 7X class, because the larger, 10X-plus glasses require a stable support and more time to find and focus your object.

Night vision is a quality worth going after in binoculars, as well as a wide angle for quick scan; this gives you a definite advantage in the case of someone approaching in the dark. If you have a gun, for example, the first rule is never to fire at an unidentified shape, much less in the direction of some noise. We all know enough cases of tragedies that have occurred because someone opened fire against a shadow.

When it's so dark that you cannot see what's making a noise through your night binoculars, you can be sure that if it's a person he can't see you, either, and may not even know you're there. And if it's an animal, leave it alone, for it's just going about its business of foraging for food.

Should it be people, they will need at least enough light to find their way. So you will see them through your glasses and have time to deduce what their intention is and how to defend yourself if necessary. That's why you should not camp right on or beside a path. It may be a passage for people living farther inside the forest who have just arrived and are completely unaware that there's anyone camping.

Incidentally, if you happen to arrive after dark anywhere inhabited in this country, don't do so stealthily. Talk aloud, and before approaching clap hands and call "O de casa!" to advise you are there. A stealthy approach is in principle suspect; though it must be remembered that people stepping softly may be doing so because they, too, don't know what's ahead.

The Raincoat, Capa de Chuva, or Capa Pluvial

Like many of the items in your equipment, your raincoat also has more than one purpose. It should have either buttons and buttonholes or eyelets installed in parallel fashion, so that cords can be attached with which to stretch the coat open over a horizontal branch or rope as a makeshift tarpaulin in case you need to spend the night out in bad weather. A roll of cord can be kept in the raincoat pocket if it has one. Mine doesn't.

Umbrella, Guarda-Chuva, or Paráguas

In the rainy season or cloud forest an umbrella is a must, enabling you to sit out a heavy shower in relative comfort when it's too warm to wear a plastic raincoat. It should be large sized and nontelescopic so that it will also shelter your bags and, when closed, serve as a walking stick. Examine carefully and test when buying. Oil both springs and all the hinges.

PROTECTING YOUR EQUIPMENT

If you plan to write during your excursion, your paper must be fastened to a clipboard in order not to be blown away in a sudden gust of wind such as often precede rainstorms. This clipboard should have a snugly fitting, strong plastic "pullover" to protect the papers from rain. Your umbrella should likewise have such a cover of the toughest plastic to shield it from thorns when using it as a walking stick in the intervals between rain showers; otherwise the webbing will soon be torn. Some umbrellas come with such a sheath when you buy them. Ants don't usually destroy equipment, though cutter ants (see chapter 5) may scissor through sweat-soaked clothes left lying about; but termites are another story! As a matter of fact, people who claim plastics are nonbiodegradable don't know our tropical termites, some of which work their way right through concrete. In camp they will attack things—wood, leather, clothes, plastics, anything—left on the ground when it's moist. One rainy period while

The plastic raincoat doubles as a makeshift shelter by having eyeholes inserted all around to stretch it.

This is what an umbrella—which can double as a walking stick in uncertain weather—will soon look like in the jungle unless it is fitted with a sturdy plastic or canvas sheath.

revising these notes in 2002 in central South America north of Cuiabá, Brazil, I left the lifebelts for a rowing adventure with my youngest grandchildren on the ground under the tarpaulin for some twenty-four hours while organizing my camp. When I picked them up the termites had eaten through the nylon of one of them. They've also chewed to pieces the tip of my mosquito net that touched the ground.

WHEN YOU LOSE SOMETHING

The jungle is characteristically full of liana tangles, thorns, and thickets—especially where there is more intensive competition for the light, such as along the fringes, rivers, and clearings—so it's important not to have things dangling about you from slings or straps, chains or hooks. Otherwise you may find yourself hooked or hung up at every few steps, if not literally hanged. Therefore it is not advisable to have essential items, such as your Swiss pocketknife, attached to a chain or cord, for this will get caught on things and the knife be ripped from your pocket with annoying frequency.

And you will, every now and then, have little accidents in which you lose an essential piece, the necessary recovery of which will demand all your creativity and initiative. See what happened to me on a recent excursion with my family:

We had been exploring an ancient, overgrown canal alongside the Rio Claro at the foot of Chapada dos Guimarães in Mato Grosso, hewn out of the relatively soft, flaked rock by prospectors in order to detour the water at a falls farther upriver so that they could sift through the gravel and sand on the river bottom after diamonds. It was a very dry, rather warm winter, and ticks were abundant, with brown lumps of thousands at a time transferring from leaves to our clothes.

On returning to the river I stopped to scrape off the worst concentrations with my pocketknife prior to wading across the strong, waist-deep current. This was sheer laziness on my part, because I had the much more practical hunting knife in my companion bag, with a better grip and larger blade.

Well: The pocketknife slipped from my grasp, tumbled down the steep bank, and vanished in the white wavelets of the rapids.

All of us—my wife, my eldest daughter, Beatriz, and her children—spent the next hour searching for the small knife, without success. Later some friends of my grandchildren's arrived and also contributed their efforts, to no avail. Everybody was sorry, as I'd had this knife for over thirty years.

A couple of nights later, back in Cuiabá, I woke up around 4 A.M. and figured out what needed doing. After breakfast we bought a couple of small cans of paint, one bright red and the other aluminium, along with a brush and a screwdriver to open them. Next we collected a total of nine stones closest to the size, shape, and density of the pocketknife. These we washed and painted, four red and five aluminium, since we didn't know which would appear best nor how many we might lose.

The next day we returned to the site of the loss, attached the rope from the companion bag to a trunk in the water for us to hold on to in the current, tied an aluminium-colored pebble to a length of about 3 meters (10 feet) of very thin, 8-pound-test nylon fishing line for minimum water resistance, and let it roll three times down the bank into the rapids where the pocketknife had disappeared, each time marking the place where it came to rest on the coarse, multicolored gravel bottom.

Then I proceeded to feel about this area with my bare foot, removing branches and things until I was able to reach every crevice. And presently, there it was.

In deeper water, or at the edge of a high cliff, we probably would have needed all the painted pebbles in order to determine the most probable location.

And the next January something else happened in the same general region: I had been walking in the pathless jungle one whole morning, exploring an area at the foot of the northern Chapada dos Guimarães buttes. In the early afternoon I drove home to Beatriz's country house, where I was staying. When I got out of the jeep at her gate, I raised my hand to switch on my hearing aid . . . and found, to my shock, that it was gone.

The loss of the tiny device meant not only its monetary value of nearly $2,000—hard to come by in a Third World country—but also the time and incovenience involved in ordering and fitting a new one back in São Paulo. The very next evening there was going to open in Cuiabá the yearly Congress of the Association of Municipalities, attended by some 150 mayors, besides congressmen and other authorities. And Beatriz had set up a booth at the convention center to offer the municipalities the services of her language school, such as English and teacher training. Together with the prospects describing these services she had decided to donate to each municipal library one of my books on the Swampland and the Amazon. So I had to be present, not only to autograph the books but also to talk to these people and, most important, hear and understand what they wished to say and ask.

So there was only one thing to do, and that was to drive back to where I'd spent the morning walking and redo my entire itinerary. I had the rest of that afternoon and most of the next day—but thunderclouds were gathering around the buttes, promising rain later that afternoon, which would erase my tracks in the sand and wet the humidity-sensitive hearing device.

During the drive back I made a mental note of the most likely places where I might have lost the hearing aid. There was a long stretch of thorny caraguatá (*Bromelia balansae*), in crossing which I had stopped and bent down several times to slap biting horseflies, mutuca, and unhook the clawlike thorns from my legs. It could have been knocked down somewhere there. I had also stopped for a rest and to eat a couple of oranges in the shade of a pequi tree (*Caryocar brasiliense*), where I had removed my cap, and possibly pushed off the device. Down by the river I had crossed an extensive growth of wild bamboo—taboca (*Guadua* spp.)—where I'd had to duck and crouch several times. It might have gotten hung up or knocked off there. Plus there was the odd branch and liana brushing past every now and then.

Having parked the jeep in the same place where I'd left it in the morning, I first had a couple more oranges. The task ahead demanded a calm, methodical procedure, looking well—on all fours where necessary—in order not to have to go over the same ground more than once. I took the umbrella along, in case I had to wait out a shower or two, and a flashlight, should it become too dark to see under the trees with the incoming storm.

Wherever a branch or vine swished past my face I stopped to inspect it, in case the device had been caught on it, and then the ground below, lest it had been knocked down. Thus I crossed the thorny caraguatá, searched under the shady pequi, climbed among armadillo holes on cliffsides, waded across tall ferns and bogs of razor grass—capim navalha (*Rhynchospora corymbosa*)—came upon the tracks of a small deer and a large tapir, straightened my back to watch a flight of squawking macaws.

When I reached the end of the stretch of taboca bamboo and thunder rumbled ominously, I stopped to get my bearings, for it seemed that this was not the way I'd crossed in the morning. Looking about here and there I came upon a marmeleiro-do-campo (*Alibertia sessilis*)—a small tree whose round fruit looks and tastes rather like chocolate—which indicated the direction I'd taken the first time. And the hearing aid lay on the ground a few steps into the taboca.

12

FOOD AND DRINK

My daughter Beatriz's father-in-law, Jaime Siqueira, is a land surveyor, retired now, who in his lifetime opened up and measured off much of the Brazilian Mato Grosso in central South America, a region he knows, without exaggeration, like the palm of his hand. There isn't an Indian tribe or a jungle profession that he doesn't know all about: gold and diamond prospecting, medicinal ipecacuanha root, Brazil nut and rubber collecting, difficult pequi (*Caryocar brasiliense*) planting . . . you name it, and he will spend patient hours explaining every detail, right down to the quality and frequency of diamonds found at each site, with history thrown in along the way.

Jaime's surveying stretches lasted on the average three to four months in the jungle each time. His teams consisted of five or six professionals to mark and clear the new trails, plus again as many carriers—"ants" or formigas—to lug their supplies from one campsite to the next every day.

There is no grass in the jungle to feed a mule, nor can the animals negotiate the straight line through swamps, along steep mountainsides, across crags, and over the sharp stumps of freshly cut taboca bamboo or caraguatá bromelia thickets, often far from water. So from the base depot where the airplane, truck, canoe, or mule pack train unloaded the supplies, everything had to be carried forward on the men's backs: 30 kilos (66 pounds) of supplies per individual, plus his personal gear.

The cook was the first to rise, at 2 A.M., to prepare lunch for 5 A.M. Yes, five in the morning. Then he washed and packed his kitchen on his back and set out for the next campsite, way ahead of the brush-clearing team, followed by the formigas carrying the supplies.

He would normally reach his destination, preferably near water, early in the afternoon; then he'd set up the kitchen, cook dinner, and go to sleep.

153

When the men arrived at dusk they ate in silence so as not to disturb the cook, for he'd be getting up again at 2 A.M. so that they could eat and leave at daybreak.

They carried shotguns and plenty of ammunition to supplement their stock with game, fish, and palm cabbage, or palmito. Where there was no water they resorted to the water-containing liana during the day on the trail while the "ants" had to transport it on their backs in double plastic bags inside sacks for kitchen needs.

Edible supplies consisted mainly of jerky, manioc flour, beans, rice and macaroni, coffee, sugar, salt, and oil. Salt had to be well packed in several waterproof sacks so as not to leak onto the carrier's sweaty back with rain. Still, sugar was their biggest problem, because of bees: Attracted by the sap of freshly cut vegetation, they would invade camp and sting people when touched.

THE FOOD BAG

This is that nylon market bag that in my jeep has its place under the driver's seat (see chapter 14), where it is free from pressure and well ventilated. While in the car, it contains the perishables—fruit and vegetables.

When walking in the jungle the food bag is carried in one hand while in the other you carry a walking stick. Because the bag is washable and easily replaceable, it can be instantly set down anyplace without damage when you need your hand. When buying this bag (sacola de feira), check the seams to make sure it has been properly stitched.

The contents in the food bag have to be rearranged according to the needs for each excursion you undertake away from your car, boat, or camp, based on how long you expect to stay (see below), plus something extra, just in case. Never bet you'll be back when foreseen.

For all these professional walkers' hardiness, however, two great explorers are my models for life in the jungle—John Muir and Candido Rondon. Muir, a Scotsman-turned-American-conservationist, is remembered and revered through place-names like Muir Glacier in Alaska, Muir Woods in California, Yosemite National Park, and others; and so is Marshall Candido Rondon, who erected thousands of kilometers of telegraph lines across the Brazilian wilderness and became the staunchest protector of Brazil's Indians, in whose memory were named the state of Rondonia in northwestern Brazil, the city of Rondonópolis in Mato Grosso, Marechal Cândido Rondon in Paraná, and more.

Both lived frugally. Muir's famous camping provisions were, in his words, "A sack of bread, some tea, and jump over the back fence!" For Rondon's team it was often but a sack of manioc flour and mate (*Ilex paraguayensis*) tea; meat was shot and dried when luck provided it.

Therefore I shall list the basics—for us, that is; to all of the men above these would have been luxuries—to which you are free to add whatever you're prepared to carry. I am physically lean and require little, though I recognize that some people need more food. But food and comfort were never a consideration to interfere with the countless missions that Muir, Rondon, and the Amazon surveyors set themselves.

Food for a Single Day

I would stock the food bag with the following, per person: four small oranges, two apples, ten rolls of bread (bread weighs little and constitutes a good reserve), a can of sardines, a foam plate of cheese and one of salami (about 200 grams, or 0.5 pound, each), or a roasted or fried chicken—frango assado ou à passarinho; three lemons and sugar for lemonade, salt as a reserve, tea, a packet of biscuits, and a small pot with a half-moon handle to hang over a fire.

I expect to consume no more than half of the above in one day, at the most, the rest being a reserve for the case of a delay. I may add a couple of cans of beer (cerveja) or Coke. Chocolate melts with the heat in the Tropics, and so does margarine; thus they must be packed in leakproof containers inside plastic bags closed with elastic, pegs, or tape.

For a Lengthier Trek

For a lengthier trek across the jungle, assuming you will be carrying your food and gear on your back, the heavier items such as gas cooker and bottle, liquids, glasses, fresh potatoes, etc. must be replaced with light or concentrated foods of high yield, like powdered milk and chocolate, oats and other cereals, rice, beans, macaroni, wheat and manioc flour, bread, jerky, salami, eggs, cut or prepacked cheese, lemons and rapadura—a hard, brown, homemade cane sugar that is healthy, nutritive and can be used both as sweetener and as tasty dessert together with a piece of cheese.

Knorr and Maggi are long-established producers of instant soups, to which you can add food items threatening to spoil, such as bread going mildewy, a salvaged piece of tomato, leftovers from an earlier meal.

Breakfast you can prepare cold if you don't want to light a fire. A 500 grams (1 pound) can each of Quaker oats, powdered milk and chocolate will give you a week's breakfast.

Rice, macaroni and potatoes take 20 minutes' cooking on an open wood fire. Since jerky takes longer, it should be chopped together with a tomato and an onion and fried in margarine or oil plus a little water for about half an hour, stirring frequently, for a tasty sauce. The jerky—500 grams (1 pound) will last you for a week—already contains salt so there is no need to add any.

Beans—a kilo will do for a week—must be put to soak on the eve. Cut out the A 3 times their volume in water. In the morning replace the water, add chopped jerky or salami, onion, garlic or palm heart and allow to cook for 1 to 1¼ hour, which depends on how old the beans are. When serving, add roasted manioc flour to the hot bean brew on your plate and mix.

BEWARE OF MANIOC! With this tuber, also called *cassava*, you need native assistance. Never harvest or cook your own when you happen upon an abandoned plantation because, being an outsider, you are unlikely to distinguish the edible, cooking varieties from the toxic one that has to be leached and roasted for flour.

Your cooking and eating utensils on the trail should consist of: two pots of the kind you hang over a fire, that fit into each other for space. Clean only inside, no sense in wasting steel wool scrubbing off the soot between fires. Carry them inside a plastic bag or two so as not to dirty the other things. Plus a couple of ordinary knives, forks and spoons, aluminum plates and plastic cups (one can easily lose one while washing in the evening); a lemon press and a small sieve to strain ants out of lemonade and honey.

Your food bag is of interest to a lot of wildlife—from ants, bees, and wasps through mice, rats, and opossums all the way up to alligators—so it must always be hung apart from your other gear.

WHERE TO OBTAIN YOUR FOOD

The safest places to buy food to take with you on the trail are the supermarket, the baker's (padaria or panificadora), the butcher's (açougue), and the greengrocer's (frutaria). These shops cater to regular, local customers, so they have a large daily turnover and the food is normally fresh and clean—though ultimately you must go by your eyes and nose.

I don't usually take an icebox, so when I buy fresh meat it is to be prepared and consumed that same day.

At the Bakery

I buy my main camping staple: bread. I also purchase cheese and salami in more or less 200-gram (0.5 pound) portions usually precut on foam plates wrapped in transparent plastic film, which are practical for one-day meals. I take the common rolls of bread everybody buys, and when they get stale I toast them over a flame; or packed, presliced bread.

When there is no supermarket nearby, or the small price difference isn't worth going after, you can also buy other basics at the bakery, though they will be a bit more expensive: salt, sugar, honey, oats, cornflakes, beer, soft drinks, tea, coffee, milk, and so forth, thus completing the ingredients for breakfast or a snack in the field.

The bakery is also the best place to have a light meal in town while you're there, the most popular being pingado e pão com manteiga—coffee with milk plus bread and butter. Or try a medium misto quente—oven-heated bread with cheese and ham, two of which make a satisfying meal with coffee or a soft drink. Beer is sold but not served at bakeries. You can also get the universal hamburgers and cheeseburgers (which have the same names in Portuguese and Spanish), if the place looks decently clean, as bakeries generally—though not always—do.

If you must eat at establishments of questionable hygiene, ask to see the ground meat (carne moída) beforehand. First-class ground meat should be uniformly red, whereas dark means old, and grayish with a lot of white tallow is second-class.

Another popular food item that is quite safe and tasty, especially when fresh, is cheese bread—pão de queijo or pan de queso—a rounded roll smaller than a hamburger, containing no filling of any kind. The cheese is in the dough.

Among soft drinks, one that foreigners are fond of in the region is guaraná, made by Antarctica, which contains a small proportion of the caffeine-rich berry of the Amazonian vine *Paullinia cupana*. They also make good água tônica if you prefer something a little more bitter, and soda. And there's the omnipresent Coke—Coca.

You can buy beer at bakeries or at supermarkets, where it is cheaper. There are half a dozen good national makes, preference being a matter of taste.

Ham—presunto or jamón—and mortadella must be consumed the first day out of refrigeration. When buying, check the expiration date stamped on the prepacked container and look at the color: Even the lightest shade of gray means *reject!* Many bakeries slice ham on the spot, which is best.

At the Supermarket

Most supermarkets in the Amazon region don't have snack bars, nor do drugstores. But they usually have a butcher's, a baker's, and a section where they sell salted, dried, and smoked meats, salami, sausages, cheeses, and cold cuts.

I am rather lazy, and I admit that at the end of a day's walk, drive, ride, or canoe trip I don't want to get involved with a lot of cooking, if any at all. I usually settle either for a cold supper or else something that can be quickly prepared in a pan, like oatmeal, or eggs to have with bread, and a raw vegetable like a cucumber.

So here's what I usually buy at a supermarket to take in the car or boat. You may improve upon my list with a few more items, but if you're going to carry these on your back you must keep the weight factor in mind. Thus, besides what I've already mentioned at the baker's:

- **Meats.** Sardines, eggs, jerky, fresh beef for the first day only. Kippers and dried cod are expensive. Perhaps corned beef.

- **Cereals.** Oats, rice, wheat and corn flour.

- **Vegetables.** Potatoes, onions, cucumbers, carrots, greenish tomatoes, green or red peppers, sweet potatoes, cabbage.

- **Fruits.** Plenty of small oranges, some apples, a few bananas at a time, a pineapple and a papaya if well packed in newspaper, a peeled coconut, various dried fruit, peanuts, other nuts, and raisins. Go easy on peanuts because of the carcinogenic aflatoxin common in humid tropical climates.

- **Candies.** To give children and for consumption, but only well packed in individual wrappings and boxes, because of the heat.

- **Others.** Margarine—to be transferred to a leakproof container—serves as cooking oil as well. A can of precooked, ready-to-heat beans with meat (feijoada), one of chocolate powder.

Do your shopping preferably at the best supermarkets in the larger cities, and take your time looking at everything before purchasing what's most practical. Salt, sugar, honey, and other sweets should be bought in plastic containers that can be sealed after each use because of ants, bees, and so on. Polenghi cheese comes prepacked in individual tablets, while cappuccino coffee is premixed with milk and sugar.

Where There Is No Supermarket
You can buy fruit, vegetables, eggs, and basics at greengrocers (frutarias) or the open street market (feira livre). Seasonal fruit can be purchased from kids or stands selling them along the road (see below).

All fresh fruit and vegetables should be washed in water, well sprinkled with vinegar or chlorine and left for about five minutes, then rinsed in clean water.

FRUITS AND JUICES
Fruits and juices sold at the roadside consist mainly of sugarcane juice (caldo de cana), green coconuts, and fruit in season, such as mangoes or pineapples. Of these, the only one safely free of contamination is the coconut, because it's cut open on the spot in front of you and you drink

directly through a straw, after which you can scrape out the pulp with your spoon.

The most popular is the sugarcane juice, but that goes through a press and has ice added to it. How cleanly this press is maintained and what water the ice was made of is anyone's guess. Of course, if the place looks clean enough you can always order your juice sem gelo—without ice.

Fruit sold by the roadside must be well washed. Especially mangoes—in December and January—which grow on rather large trees and are therefore often knocked down with rods on ground roamed by pigs, dogs, and fowl. As for wild fruits, it is unlikely that the kids harvesting them wash their hands.

In the Amazon there are a number of delicious juices of native fruit: cupuaçu (*Theobroma grandiflorum*), graviola, soursop, or bacurí (*Platonia insignis*); and, the most popular, cabbage palm or açaí (*Euterpe oleracea*). People put out a little red banner above their door to announce that they have açaí "wine" for sale. Fortunately this drink, which is prepared by tumbling the ripe fruit and is quite a meal by itself, has spread in popularity beyond the borders of the Amazon fast enough to save the cabbage palm from disappearance through cutting for the palm-heart industries. In cities like Belém you can also find tasty ice creams of these fruits.

Another fascinating experience is going out with a native and harvesting some of the fruit yourself. When my sister came from England with her children for a short stay on an island south of Rio de Janeiro, my nephew, who was about eleven, got the greatest kick out of a little "expedition" the two of us made into the woods, where he had the experience of cutting down a banana tree and harvesting its ripe bunch of fruit.

A few observations are in order here. Each banana stem produces only one bunch of fruit, after which it dies, so it is cut to facilitate harvesting the bunch. Keep alert for snakes and spiders around bananas.

Guava—goiaba—should be cut open and the core, where the small hard seeds are concentrated, be eaten or removed by means of the sturdy medium-sized spoon you carry in your companion bag, prior to eating the pulp of the fruit. This not only prevents your breaking a tooth on the stone-hard seeds, as has happened to me—although I ought to have known better—but also reveals the presence of a worm if there is one, which is also indicated by a small hole in the skin. Fruit worms are particularly fond of guava, and it's a popular local saying that "it's better to find a whole worm in a guava, than to find just half!"

If you plan to fish, save the worms with bits of guava in a small bottle or plastic bag, for bait.

Some of the fruits in the Amazon are not harvested; you wait until they drop on their own. This is true of the Brazil nut, or castanha do

Pará, for the simple reason that it hangs so high—from 30 to 80 meters (100 to 260 feet)—above the ground when the tree grows on a steep hillside, and out at the tips of branches often more than 20 meters (65 feet) from the trunk of this giant, that it is impossible to harvest. And it's true of the cupuaçu, because it will spoil rather than ripen off the tree.

Beware of Brazil nut trees during the months of December and January, when the fruits are falling. A pod, containing some twenty nuts, weighs about 1 kilo (more than 2 pounds) when fresh and crashes down like a cannonball, breaking anything it hits.

RESTAURANTS

Here some special precautions must be taken, as a standing rule, for it is at restaurants that most people catch intestinal infections. Mayonnaise is to be avoided outright, and so are all uncooked vegetables, since you don't know how well they've been washed. Nothing cold, even if cooked, due to flies and handling. Eat fish only at city restaurants in whose parking lots you find a majority of local license plates, meaning the establishment has the patronage and confidence of the populace.

At the roadside you look for the trucks: Where they are all parked, that's the place to eat. Here you will find the food basic, plentiful, good tasting, healthy, and cheap. A restaurant catering to truck drivers cannot risk serving doubtful food, for the truckers' grapevine would quickly destroy it.

On entering, choose a table at the far end of the restaurant so that on your way there you can look at what people are eating. It's usually standard: beans, rice, fried potatoes, salad, and barbecued meat, which the waiter brings every few minutes, cutting the piece you choose.

The people eating here are, incidentally, your best friends on the road when you know how to treat them—although it may not always seem that way—for they are well informed about roads, conditions, assistance, and so on. The secret in dealing with truck drivers is to facilitate their passage when they come thundering up behind you, especially downhill and at the beginning of an ascent—where there is, as a rule, a third lane for slower vehicles—when they are taking advantage of gravity. As they slow down farther uphill you are perfectly welcome to overtake when conditions are safe.

Eating, however, should never be the main concern on your excursion, but rather a necessary complement. The exercise and fresh air out in the wild tend to develop a healthy appetite, so that almost any food will taste good with minimal additions or preparation.

In December 1973 the blacksmith of our bridge-building team on the trans-Amazon highway invited me to explore the upper Cajazeiras River, approximately 100 kilometers (60 miles) upstream from the road, to look at some land there, where he had already staked out a plot with squatter's rights for himself.

We set out in a canoe with an outboard motor. Along were the blacksmith Domingos and his wife Maria, another companion, and myself. In the boat we carried a sack of manioc flour (farinha)—the local staple—a few oranges, and a crate with two or three live chickens.

The river was flooded and turbulent, and it had taken us a whole day without respite to inch our way up a kilometer-long rapids amid rocks, whirlpools, falls, countercurrents, submerged trunks, and frightful waves. Dona Maria operated the penta—the heavy-duty Archimedes outboard with a long tail that is standard in the Amazon (see chapter 15)—while her husband and the other man waded and clambered along the bank hauling on a long rope that they looped around trunks and stones, and I stood on the prow with a forked pole to push and steer the boat clear of obstacles.

By midafternoon there remained one last delicate passage to overcome in order to reach a deep, quiet pool at the head of the rapids. It was a narrow gap, just about wide enough for the boat to pass between the steep wall of a boulder on our right and the sharp drop of a waterfall on our left.

Just then a propeller pin sheared; the boat stalled, then nosed out into the flood and dived down the white falls . . . *"Drop the rope! Drop the rope!"* came the warning calls amid the turmoil. I unhinged and cast off the lifeline as we tobogganed down into voids and up wave crests, speeded past emerging rocks and overhanging branches, water pouring inside from backwash despite the fore and aft castles these boats have for protection against this very kind of accident.

Some 150 meters (nearly 500 feet) down the roaring cascade our canoe stabilized long enough for me to risk grabbing a sturdy branch and holding on, thus braking the boat, while the crate with chickens rolled back and forth with the waves inside.

Having secured the boat, our first step was to bail out the water, then replace the pin and get the motor functioning in order to restart our ascent from where we were.

We finally made it just as darkness was descending. Beside the pool there was a ledge to which we moored, then dug through our wet belongings to see whether there remained anything edible. There was half a bottle of pinga—sugarcane rum—and the bag of manioc flour, half of it soaked in water with chicken shit.

With the blade of a knife the dirty part was removed, the remainder divided into four equal little hives on the rock surface . . . And I tell you, did that simple bit of food taste good, with a swig of pinga!

Which serves to show that when you are hungry, food needs no sophistication.

DRINKING WATER

Never drink directly from the source. Always use a cup, your cupped hands, or a clean leaf, and examine before drinking. Any doubtful water should be sterilized. It takes only one drop of Hidrosteril or a tablet of Aquatab—both sold in pharmacies—and a three- to five-minute wait or as recommended in the instructions.

Under Piranhas (see chapter 8) you will have read the case of Mr. Thomas Horton, an Englishman who lost the tip of his nose when he lay down to drink directly from a flood channel in the Swampland.

When I came to Campinas from the Amazon in 1974 there was a story going around of a small child who had drunk water from the pipe or bamboo of a fountain at one of the hydromineral resorts in this region. He immediately felt severe stomach pain. Doctors had no idea what the cause might be, and the child died. An autopsy revealed a small snake, which had bitten his stomach walls. The snake apparently slipped in through his mouth while he drank from the tube.

In his book *First Footsteps in East Africa*, British traveler Richard Burton warned of the danger of drinking directly from pools in the North African desert, where he told of some French foreign legionaires who died as a result of swallowing leeches when drinking directly. Although I have not heard of any case in Brazil, I see no reason why leeches in the Amazon shouldn't do likewise when given the opportunity. And then there's the candiru (see chapter 8).

Thirst can do things you wouldn't believe. We had been riding the whole morning across the swamps of Fazenda Bodoquena checking fences. It was early September and we hadn't come upon a single drop of water. Around noon we did find a shallow pool in the shade of a stand of piri reeds. The trails leading to the dirty water were full of tracks and droppings of all the animals in the surroundings, and at the far end a dead cow lay in the water. We allowed our horses to choose the best spot from which to drink, and there we, too, dropped our drinking horns, from which we sucked up the precious liquid through our mate-drinking filters, with no ill consequences.

13

Packing

THE COMPANION BAG

I've spoken so much of the companion bag that it's now time for me to introduce her.

The object of the companion bag is, as the name I've given it suggests, to accompany us at all times out in the wild, like a woman's handbag in the city. It contains not only the essential items we may need during a regular day out in the field or forest—other than food and drinks, for which there is a specific bag—but also basic survival equipment in case we have to stay out longer, be it because we got lost, suffered a delaying accident, were cut off by a flood or fire, failed to make a planned crossing within the expected time, or simply couldn't resist going on to explore that enticing cliff, canyon, cave, peak, swamp, or woods up ahead. Or perhaps there is still more investigating to hold us up, or the agreed-upon rendezvous with others has been fouled up. Naturalists are notoriously disposed to following the trail to their object regardless of time, food, and comfort, and that's how it should be.

Therefore, while containing the essentials, the companion bag must be as light as possible though sturdily made. The weight factor is all-important in long walks. Mine is an excellent Brazilian-made Abu Garcia. It has one central or main compartment with a lateral "curtain" division that is practical for accommodating such things as this guide, list of contents, camera manual, notebook, set of mini screwdrivers, small flashlight, and the like. It's also detachable, washable, and can be transformed into an extra carrying bag.

Add three outside pockets of good size, all closed with zippers. The central compartment is reinforced by two straps besides the zippers and a handle for carrying the bag like a suitcase when desirable, instead of slung from the shoulder. If you can find one with straps that enable you to carry it on your back as well, like a rucksack, so much the better; you never know in what position you may need, or wish, to carry the companion bag, depending on circumstances. But it is important that any straps not in use should be tucked in somewhere, or detachable, for otherwise they will get caught on every branch and creeper.

Some will no doubt find it handier to take everything in the rucksack, and while in camp dump the bulkier sleeping items. What matters is that the companion bag's contents be with you at all times. Let's examine what we've got in this bag, guiding ourselves by a most practical and indispensable item, the camping list.

Camping List

I am quite forgetful, so I must compensate for this deficiency by organizing things in a "findable" way. The camping list saves us the frustration of digging around in our luggage and thereby getting things wet, dirty or scattered on the ground while trying to find a missing item—especially those of us who are not everyday campers with the position of every item memorized.

When you have one or more companions along, the list becomes of even greater importance, so that everybody is able to find things needed without having to ask or dig around, and afterward—equally important—put them back in their right place. Not to mention the simplicity of drawing up a shopping list, packing, and finally checking whether everything is there.

Try to avoid depressing arguments, especially between spouses, about where something ought to be, who got it, and why it's not there. The camping list takes care of that. It is constantly being updated in the light of most recent experiences.

My list is just per place. Even more useful, however—especially when there are newcomers in the group—would be a double list, per place and per item in alphabetical order, after which you'd have its location.

Number the items, especially those purchased at supermarkets and packed in plastic bags. Give each kind of food (for instance) the same number each time, tagged to the bag so that you don't need to open it to find out what's inside.

Order is indispensable in camp. Build yourself a raised platform of rods on which to place your gas stove and food items in chronological order per number. Remember that meats must be hung high because of rats, ants, and so on.

Another advantage of the camping list is that you don't need to keep your gear packed and gathering mildew. You pack it on the spot, with the list in hand, ticking things off.

The camping list, as well as this book, your checkbook, toilet paper, notepad, and anything else that might spoil in contact with humidity or friction, must be carried wrapped in strong, transparent plastic folders or bags.

Main Compartment

Camera (wrapped in a T-shirt), lenses, films, batteries, manual, light meter (if separate), camping list, *Walking the Jungle*, notepad and pens, light jacket, scarf, bathing suit, socks, gloves, minimal fishing kit (see below), rope, extra shoestrings, mini screwdriver set, needlenose pliers, light hunting knife with sharpening steel (if not on belt), extra ammunition, and, on top of it all, a raincoat. This should have a hood and reach below your knees, with buttons (not zippers) so that it can be stretched over a pole as a makeshift tent. If you can't find a raincoat with buttons, have a shoe repairman install a line of eyelets on each side, for tying.

The scarf is an indispensable item that provides incredible warmth and coziness for the space it occupies in your luggage or tied around your waist.

The rope—10 meters (33 feet) long—should be strong enough to support a couple of people climbing up or down a cliff or tree, or swinging across a stream or gap. Sisal ropes give you a better hold and knot, whereas nylon ones are more resistant. These you need to briefly burn at both ends so that they don't fray. When there is a space problem, the rope can be tied around your waist.

To climb a tree you cut a sturdy length of wood about 60 centimeters (2 feet) and tie it to one end of the rope, by the middle, like a crossbolt. Then you tie a fishing line to one of the tips of this crossbolt, and a lead sinker or small stone to the other end of the fishing line. This weight you throw up across a tight fork in the tree, then pull the crossbolt and rope up through it and adjust until it's firmly locked across the gap. Check that there is no danger of the crossbolt slipping before you begin to climb. Leave the fishing line attached, to disengage the crossbolt when you are ready to leave.

Outer Pockets

Emergency kit (see below), small towel, soap, sponge, toilet kit (see below), toilet paper, mirror, small flashlight and batteries, battery tester, extra compass, magnifying glass, spare eyeglasses, rubber gloves, spoon, several plastic bags (for garbage, wet clothes, and collecting things), a little salt, lighter, candles and matches, foldable saw, file, Super Bonder glue, small magnet or ímã for recovering metallic objects from the water, small can of oil, and box of large paper clips for closing plastic food bags and securing drying clothes to lines.

- **Fishing kit.** This can consist of: two light 100-yard lines (linha or hilo), one a 12-pound test, the other a 6-pound test, plus a sturdier, 30- to 50-pound-test piece about 30 meters (100 feet) long for paternoster line. Very small (mosquito) to medium hooks (anzóis or anzuelos), leaders, sinkers, and two or three red- or coral-and-white Daredevil lures. When necessary you can even fish with dental floss and fashion hooks from pins and leaders with your pliers.

- **Toilet kit.** This contains toothbrush, toothpaste and floss, comb, soap, razor, and scissors. Mine is a little cotton bag with a zipper like the ones schoolchildren carry their pencils in; I keep this in my pocket when I eat out.

- **Emergency kit.** Of variable size depending on need, it should contain antisnakebite and anti-arachnid (polivalente) serum, syringe, and needles. Dry sulfa powder (Anaseptil-em-pó) for bleeding or wet wounds; aspirin; Band-Aids; Fenergan (prometazina) ointment for burns and insect bites; Foldan (tiabendazol) ointment for *Larva migrans* and other skin parasites; vitamin A and D (Hipoglós) ointment for rashes; cotton, gauze, and bandages; needles and thread, including a couple of saddler's needles and nylon thread for repairing things; nail clippers, tweezers, and safety pins; bulbs for the flashlight; battery tester; extra matches. Add iodine tincture in a double-sealed jar—with a plastic stopper plus the cap—for most skin problems, Hidrosteril or Aquatab for water purification, and Lavolho and a dropper for eye cleaning.

- **Adhesive tape.** Do not economize on this item of multiple uses. Take a roll about 10 centimeters (4 inches) wide by 4 to 5 meters (yards) long, of good quality. Besides protecting wounds, blisters, cracked footsoles, and more, it also serves for makeshift field repairs of ripped clothes, tents, and mosquito netting. Apply it to both sides of the torn part, face to face; otherwise it will stick to things and make a mess.

Your heaviest equipment in the companion bag consists of camera and lenses, which you may prefer to carry separately—vegetation permitting—if the bag gets too heavy.

THE RUCKSACK

Your rucksack, or mochila, contains the bulkier items you'll need for spending the night out in comfort, plus supplements to the list already in the companion bag, for a longer stay. Since a rucksack or backpack is an item most people are well familiar with nowadays, I shall only mention the points that are important for our specific purpose of jungle walking.

No Protruding Odds and Ends

Unlike the relatively clean temperate forests, tropical jungles are characterized by a rich assortment of lianas, or cipós, from the thickness of shoestrings all the way up to that of tree trunks, often competing fiercely for space and light. These form bewildering tangles, mainly along the fringes of forests and riversides, some equipped with thorns, others serving as suspension bridges for colonies of defensive-minded ants.

So it stands to reason that a rucksack for the jungle must not have anything protruding such as top ends of frames, tents tied across, or foam mattresses and sleeping bags piled high above the head. Otherwise you'll find yourself hung up at every step before you even get inside the jungle!

In such places your rucksack should be transportable on your chest as well as on your back whenever necessary, so that you can duck under the vines or use the rucksack as a shield when crossing aggressive vegetation. Therefore it must not be taller than from your hip to your chin when fully loaded. Otherwise you won't see ahead of you, or else you will lack sufficient space at the groin to duck under obstacles.

If the backpack of your choice has a frame, to keep your back ventilated, this must be as unobstrusive as possible, without "horns" or "feet" sticking out anywhere. I have a beautiful rucksack here beside me that I once practically discarded because of its incovenient frame, but I have since subjected it to the hacksaw and file to reduce the frame to a usable size.

Bringing your backpack down to a more compact volume isn't as difficult as it may initially seem, because in first place here in the Tropics it doesn't get as cold as in temperate zones. Still, frost is not entirely unknown in winter (May to August), even in such low altitudes as the Swampland on occasion, which averages only about 100 meters (330 feet) above sea level. And hammocks can get very cold indeed. While in summer a poncho will do, in winter a pantaneiro cowboy may have to line his hammock with the saddle blanket plus two sheepskins, then roll himself up in his poncho.

In the Amazon basin it gets no more than pleasantly cool when it rains. People there call the rainy season (October through April) "winter" for that reason. But actual cold weather is only encountered in the higher altitudes that fringe the basin.

Thus your sleeping bag, while warm, should have more insulation to keep out the cold rising from the forest floor and less padding—which you don't need in a hammock—to reduce volume. You can always place your raincoat between the hammock and the sleeping bag if insulation is not sufficient. Wherever cold is foreseen—especially accompanied by wind, as in high mountains—a leather jacket is a must. In a hammock you don't need a foam mattress. Should you prefer a tent, then an inflatable mattress occupies less space, though it requires more care: The ground under the tent must be clean, free of thorns and sharp stumps. And you need to take along the boat-repair kit in order to be able to seal punctures.

While a hammock is best set up inside the darker forest, the preferable ground for a tent is always a sandy beach. Bear in mind, however, that in a tent you are much more exposed, both securitywise and in case of a flash flood.

The floor of the rucksack—which gets lowered onto rocks, branches, and stumps, and scratched by sand, thorns, and protruding things—should be reinforced with an outer lining of leather or canvas, glued and stitched on, and waterproofed. You should be able to wipe this clean with a moist cloth and oil (in the case of leather) when dry.

Rucksack Pockets or Bolsos

A practical rucksack should have several (at least three) good-sized outside pockets. Don't let a lot of small pockets into which nothing much fits tempt you into putting the contents of the companion bag in the rucksack, unless this is absolutely indispensable because of other equipment you may be taking. The companion bag is supposed to be with you at all times in order for you to have your basic needs within reach; if it's all in a heavier and bulkier backpack, your tendency will be to leave it behind whenever you think you can, because you're just going here, or there, and don't want to be bothered hauling the voluminous thing about all the time . . . And that's when things happen.

If you happen to be, say, half an hour's walk from your camp—where you left all your things in the rucksack—and are bitten by a rattlesnake or *Micrurus* coral, you stand a good chance of not making it back as your eyesight and voice fail. Even if you do make it back, it's unlikely that you'll be in condition to medicate yourself. Our caboclo says of some snakes that their poison allows just enough time for them to get out from under you before you drop dead! But whatever the accident, you will have thrown away critical time and resources by not having the medicines on you.

All compartments of a rucksack and companion bag should be closed by good-quality zippers protected by a hood, not just straps with swivels, for a simple reason: Zippers won't allow insects to climb inside during the night or the trek and then bite you when you put your hand in. To keep zippers running smoothly, you can rub a candle or apply silicone, oil, or fat on the tracks.

You will notice that some indispensable items appear twice or even three times, in different places: flashlights, matches, Band-Aids, toilet paper, knives. That's because out in the wild we can never discount the possibility of an accident involving loss of equipment: a fire, a mishap on the river, forgetfulness, a partner who turns back and takes vital equipment with him, and much more. As my boss at Fazenda Bodoquena in the Swampland used to say, "We've got to have at least two of every essential item in order to have one!"

Rucksack Contents

> • **Inside.** Machete (if not in your belt); hammock with mosquito net; tarpaulin and pertinent ropes and cords; the clothes mentioned in chapter 11—pants, shirts, underpants, socks, handkerchiefs, flip-flops; and sleeping bag.
>
> Instead of the hammock and tarpaulin you may, as mentioned, prefer a small tent with telescopic fiberglass rods and an inflatable mattress. But do read the warning on page 131 before deciding. Pillow, large four-battery flashlight, coals where lighting a fire is difficult, a leather jacket where it gets cold at night.
>
> • **Pockets.** Top: regular medium-sized towel, sponge, soap, toilet paper, pegs, and, in my particular case, a mouth harmonica. A musical instrument is a passport to all homes. Rear: extra ropes, cords, candles, matches, plastic bags. Lateral: fishing gear, flashlight batteries, honing stone and oil, transparent plastic bottle of fuel for lighting a fire in rain and cloud forest. The honing oil will do in an emergency.

You'll also find information on packing your food bag in chapter 12, and on packing your car in chapter 14.

14

TRAVEL BY CAR

CHOOSING YOUR VEHICLE

The vehicle I drove on my 4,000-kilometer (2,500-mile) trip to the north of Bahia in December 1998 was a fiberglass jeep with a Volkswagen 1600 motor that I've had for twenty-five years. With a good preliminary revision it functioned like clockwork. There's no need for anything newer, if you can't afford it. It's a matter of maintenance rather than age.

This small car has a hand-operated winch and a reserve-fuel container but little else—not even four-wheel drive, which I didn't need anyway. What is important is that the vehicle must be high enough above the ground and short enough to simply drive off the road shoulder and up or down banks, gravel-extraction trails, and erosion gullies with minimum need of buidup with rocks, wood, or dirt to camp in peace off the beaten track. This requires new tires with good grip.

Your vehicle need not be a jeep, though a word of warning is in order here: Front-wheel-drive automobiles perform poorly up steep, muddy slopes. The Volkswagen Kombi microbus is suitably high and does well in mud, but it's bad in uneven ground: The moment one of the rear wheels loses its grip, you're stuck and spinning helplessly. It's all right when you have company: One or more people stand on the rear bumper and thus give the spinning wheel traction. It's not a car for a loner—nor do you need so much space, anyway.

The car should also be in common use in the country, so that you don't get tied down because of unavailable replacements.

Four-wheel drive is helpful though not indispensable. It's more important to give yourself extra time to wait out improper weather until the road is dry enough to drive without forcing the car.

Another important detail, in the case of a jeep, is that it must have a solid cabin that can be locked. Loose canvas flip-ups let in rain, dust, insects, and thieves.

If you happen to be coming from abroad just for this trip, you will probably want to rent a car, choosing the best from what's available and completing the equipment needed. Several of today's cars are appropriately short for uneven terrain, and you can roll your seat back to sleep. So the main item you'll have to prepare is the indispensable screen-fringed tarpaulin (see below). Also buy a hand winch with a 25- to 30-meter (80- to 100-foot) cable (below), a length of iron tube to facilitate removing the wheel, and a pair of wheel chains.

For the Swampland

There is no such thing as an ideal car to enter the Pantanal or Chaco in any weather, other than the oxcart. Finely granulated limestone clay is like soap when wet. You need to come in the right, dry season—June or July to October—take along a local guide, and be patient in case it rains, as it sometimes does out of season.

A FEW EMERGENCY PROCEDURES

Since the automobile is the daily transport of most people who read this book, I will restrict this section to a few backwoods experiences that may be of value in an emergency out in the middle of nowhere. If you expect to do extensive traveling by car or motorboat along the fringes of civilization, I advise bringing along a good emergency repair manual.

Broken Axle-Spindle or Ponta de Eixo

This can easily happen when you get stuck in deep mud or sand and attempt to force the car out through sudden acceleration. A moment's thoughtless impatience that can jeopardize your entire trip. It happened to me while crossing a silted creek on a farm near Nova Granada in the north of São Paulo state.

It can also happen by accident, as it did to my former father-in-law, Santana, in the region of Itiquira, southeast of Rondonopolis, Mato Grosso. They were out there far from every recourse, but Santana was a man of Indian blood, a master at improvising. So they made a crutch—or travois—for the car from a piece of tree trunk, which they tied to the front end of the spring and under the axle so that it descended to the ground at a rearward-tilting angle, since the wheel had to be removed. Then they shifted the car into four-wheel drive—of which, in this case, they only had front-wheel traction—and that was how they made it, slowly, to the nearest assistance.

Back and Hernia Precautions

Back problems and inguinal hernia are potentially debilitating problems you must beware of at all times out on the trail, where a lot of unaccustomed-to physical effort may come your way. Whether you are jacking up the car, dragging or pushing a fallen tree out of the way, digging or shoveling mud or sand out from under the car, hauling a boat past a rapids, or picking up a gas container, the procedure to follow is the same: Keep your body straight and balanced, feet firmly on the ground, and weight and effort distributed uniformly between your two arms. Kneel down instead of bending down, and avoid sideward-twisting exertions, beginning with slinging on and off the heavy rucksack. This should always be placed or lowered onto an elevated stump, trunk, rock, or bank.

Bad Brakes, Freios, or Frenos

I was conducting a group of Swiss travelers across the Swampland when the power brake master cylinder, or hidrovácuo, of my microbus began to fail, locking the return from "brake" to "free" once the wheels got hot, forcing us at intervals to stop in the shade and wait for the wheels to cool. Since taking the car into town for repairs would have robbed the group of two days' touring, we decided to risk carrying on with the excursion without brakes since the Pantanal is all flat; thus the master cylinder was disengaged. Where there was any danger I'd shift to lower gear or, to stop entirely, switch off the engine. It went all right until we drove to Corumbá where the visitors were scheduled to catch their plane. That meant not only facing traffic and holes on the highway, but also boarding the ferry and entering the city—which lies on a hillside—all without brakes. So we left with plenty of time to drive slowly and, by using utmost care—and not inconsiderable apprehension—managed to finish the tour without accident.

The dealer in Corumbá didn't have the spare parts to repair the cylinder, so I had to buy an entire new unit—another problem you're faced with at these end-of-the-road places. But the master cylinder doesn't fail all at once. If I'd had it checked before the trip, the problem would most likely have been detected.

On rough backwoods trails it isn't uncommon to develop a leak in the fluid-distributor pipe from knocking against rocks or roots. Close the leak with soap and adhesive tape, then refill the fluid container located under your hood. This means taking along a bottle of brake fluid, or fluido de freio.

Problems with the Ignition or Ignicão

On my way from the Swampland to the opening trans-Amazon highway in the early 1970s I stopped at a place called Estreito for lunch.
Here the Tocantins River narrows down to a width of about 150 meters
(500 feet) between cliffs, and nearly as deep. The scene from the bridge
was beautiful: Local women dressed just in panties sat on the rocks
washing clothes while tiny brown, naked children gaily hurled themselves from an outcrop into the clear emerald water.

So after lunch I went down for a swim. Not wanting to disturb the
women I slipped behind a cliff wall to change clothes. With a shock I
saw my car keys drop down the sheer wall and vanish in the bottomless depth . . . Now what? Peering over the edge of the wall, I spotted
something reflecting the sunlight from deep down in the water: The
smallest elbow of a ledge protruded from the cliff, and upon this tiny
platform lay the keys! Now all I had to do was hire one of those kids to
dive down and retrieve them for me. Otherwise I would have had to
take out either the rear window or the windshield in order to get the
spare keys from the glove compartment. The lesson is that spare keys
should be on your person, but where you cannot lose them, such as
strapped to your belt.

In the early 1990s my friend Edgar Piereck and I were taking a
small group of American fishermen to the region of Corumbá in the
Swampland. We had stopped at a hotel on the way for the night, where
the guy in charge of the parking lot insisted on maneuvering the
microbus himself. I noticed that the key appeared slightly bent, but the
brute had managed to do a more thorough job than that: The next
evening we were lined up for the ferry crossing of the Paraguay River,
with cars ahead and behind us in the dark, when upon switching on the
motor the entire starter lock came out in my hand! There was no way
of fitting it back in. Fortunately Ed saved the day by inserting a screwdriver into the starter housing and thus managing, after finding the right
position, to start the motor. So we drove all the way to Corumbá with
him holding the screwdriver in place. If that hadn't worked we would
have had to tear out the wiring and make a direct connection.

Problems with the Roller Bearings or Rolamentos

During my trip north described above, I began to hear a clacking sound
from one of the wheels when I was approaching Gurupí, now state of
Tocantins. The mechanic told me it was the roller bearing. This was on
a Saturday afternoon, the part was not available locally, so I'd have to
take a bus back who knows how far to find it—perhaps all the way to
Goiânia—and the next day would be Sunday. "No problem," the man

assured me, "go ahead to Belém, and when you get there, you replace it. You'll make it all right!"

That was well-intended but poorly based advice. After a while the clacking noise ceased. But just as I came round a bend in Marituba—a small town before Belém—my left rear wheel came off spectacularly, speeding across the highway past a bus stop to bump to a stop against a mango tree . . . fortunately without hitting either cars or people.

Unprepared Companions

When traveling it is not uncommon to find yourself hitching a ride in someone else's car. Given the opportunity you should check whether this vehicle is minimally equipped, because some people live on nothing but faith that God will provide—ao Deus dará . . . Better to foresee such a contingency, which is otherwise likely to reveal itself only after you're hopelessly stuck.

Mud or Barro

If you're stuck in mud and there happens not to be a pair of chains on board—a winch is almost certainly absent—you can always improvise by tying segments of the hauling rope, or corda, around the wheels in a spiral. This rope should be amply long, preferably about 25 meters (80 feet), so that you can afford to sacrifice a couple of lengths and still use it for towing.

If no rope is available, either, you'll have to build a support for the jack, then raise the car on one side, pad its wheels with rocks or wood or branches, move over to the other side, and do the same. Once the wheels are well supported and above the mud, you can proceed to line the rest of the bog, because you'll have to drive out slowly or else your car will in no time be right back in another hole, and the entire process must start all over again.

In case the jack doesn't function, or there isn't one, you'll have to cut a sturdy pole, and you will need help: two people. With the aid of one you'll be able to fit the pole under the axle and thus raise the wheel by pushing up or down slowly and evenly, while a third person pads the wheel. Be careful about back and hernia problems—see above.

Or you may find yourself in the company of some wise guy, like myself thirty-plus years ago. In June 1969 a gentleman from Tecumseh, Michigan, named Jens Touburg was coming to the Swampland for a jaguar hunt with me. Jens was flown directly to the ranch from Corumbá. The rancher had urged me to go the same way, but I knew better: I had good mud tires, two jacks, and so on, and so forth. So I left about three days earlier, by rail to the nearest station—Carandasal—and from there continued on in my pickup with the gear, dogs, and a tracker.

But meanwhile it had rained heavily, quite out of season, and while crossing a vast carandá palm forest we soon found ourselves mired in bog after bottomless bog, jacking up the car, padding, clouds of mosquitoes trying hard to carry us away, falling into the next bog, starting all over again . . . the fine limestone clay holding on like glue.

By nightfall of the second day we were still in the woods, dirty, exhausted, bad tempered, with no prospect of improvement. And Mr. Touburg was already due!

To make the best out of a bad job I sent my assistant ahead to borrow a horse somewhere, ride out to the farm with a message to the visiting hunter, and send back the oxcart.

The oxen also failed to pull the car, nearly overturning the heavy cart loaded with equipment transferred from the pickup, which we then had to leave behind, where it stayed for one full month.

Sand, Areia, or Arena

In other parts of the Pantanal the problem is fine, deep sand that, when dry, can be as thwarting as mud.

With sand the procedure is different. Chains would only aggravate the situation by digging the car in deeper. What helps here is deflating the tires to about half their normal pressure—say, about 15 to 18 pounds, or libras—in order to increase and round out their surface while making them softer. The harder and narrower the tires, the deeper they cut. Padding with vegetation also helps.

When returning to higher-velocity roads you must remember to reinflate the tires or then continue at low speed as far as the next borracheiro.

Wheel Chains, Correntes de Roda, or Cadenas de Rueda

It's best to fit chains onto the traction wheels *before* entering doubtful ground, because then the job is cleaner, more uniform, and more comfortable. The procedure is to spread out the chains lengthwise on the ground, aligned with the wheels. Then drive on top, to the midpoint, hand-brake the car, and wrap the chains around the tires, being careful to centralize them as well as possible. Then lock them in place by means of a hook on each side, which you pass through the last chain link you are able to reach, then fold it back and lock it into an existing ring.

Should you happen to get stuck before chaining your wheels, as often happens, the easiest way out is usually backward, along the tracks you've just made. Go slowly—no wheel spinning, or else you'll sink in to the axles.

Winch or Guincho

If the vehicle won't move either way, this is where your hand winch, or talha-guincho manual, comes in. With it you can pull the car to the best place, and right onto the chains.

When the going gets bad despite chains and driving outside the ruts, your best option is to camp until the weather improves. Your schedule for the trip must allow time for such setbacks. But if for some reason you have to go on—like an oncoming flood, danger of a landslide—then the necessary procedure is to take out your machete and pad the worst mudholes with branches and thatch, being careful to lay the cut ends away from the car so as not to get them caught in the chains or rupture your brake-fluid pipes. Proceed only as far as necessary in order not to spoil the car.

Before going to the extreme of forcing your vehicle beyond the radius it was designed to operate in, see if there isn't a farm within walking distance, where you might hire the service of a tractor, a couple of oxen, or three or four cowboys with their ponies to pull the car. The cost, if any, ought to be incomparably smaller than a breakdown in the middle of nowhere.

When there is no outside help available—a situation I often faced during the rainy seasons on the opening trans-Amazon highway—then each doubtful-looking stretch ahead requires that you stop, go out on foot and study its whole length, trace your proposed itinerary across the bog, and prepare a branch padding, or estiva, where necessary. Then take off in second gear as fast as she will go, shifting down to first if your speed drops or when you foresee the need, before the car comes to a halt.

Short, high, and light vehicles such as the American military jeep are best for mud.

Alcohol Cars

In Brazil there are alcohol-fueled cars. All service stations have both gasoline and alcohol pumps, which are clearly marked.

CAR CONTENTS

So now let's look at what to bring, what each item is for, how the luggage is distributed inside the car. Then we'll be ready to hit the trail!

Sleeping Platform

You'll want a plywood sleeping platform for a car whose seat does not roll back; it's for one person only, 1.2 centimeters (0.5 inch) thick, and has a couple of wooden crossbars screwed to the underside to keep the rack supporting it from slipping out of place. It fits snugly into the passenger space—seat removed—and is supported in the back on the rear seat. The rack, cavalete, holding the platform in the middle is a simple structure like a chair without a backrest.

For the VW microbus—our family camping car for many years—we have an identical arrangement using a slightly thicker, 2-centimeter (0.75-inch) platform that fits tightly into the space between the first and third seats. It is likewise supported on the backseat and in the middle by a wooden rack. The equipment and supplies are arranged on the floor around the rack, which can be shifted in any direction to accommodate less flexible items, before putting on the platform that in camp serves as table.

In the jeep there isn't that much space under the platform, but enough to accommodate the needs of one person.

Screen-Fringed Tarpaulin

This is a most practical piece of equipment for the car, boat, and camp. It isn't available commercially as far as I know, but can be manufactured in one morning. You buy the tarpaulin, or encerado, according to the size of the car: for small vehicles, 4 by 4 meters (yards); for pickups and station wagons, 6 by 4 meters. The extra width is so that you can stretch it to one side as a porch. These come ready-made with reinforced edges and eyeholes, most of them a coral color, and cost between $25 and $50. Next you buy the screen, of a fine, faultless nylon mesh, as wide as you can get (about 1.2 meters), preferably of a green color, because white shows dirt. Buy double length; for instance, if your tarpaulin measures 4 by 4 meters, instead of 16 meters buy 32, for you will need double width, sewn together at the seam, so that you have a total screen height of around 2.4 meters. If it were just to spend the night in the car you could do with 1.2 meters. But when you're camping out, you will want to tie the tarpaulin to tree trunks and branches high enough to walk around your vehicle in comfort without having to crouch, and to avoid the heat and moisture that tend to accumulate under a low-slung tarpaulin. One side should be tied sufficiently lower than the other for the rain to run off freely.

These you take to an upholsterer (estofador) or saddler (seleiro or guarnicionero) to sew with durable nylon thread and double-stitch all around the tarpaulin, joining the ends. You will need a length of cloth seam upon which to sew this single vertical joint, since the screen itself won't have any seam there. Or you can fold back each end about 2.4 centimeters (1 inch), place one upon the other, and have the saddler run his machine up and down a couple of time for sturdiness. Then he can

The screen-fringed tarpaulin—a most practical travel companion for overnight stops with sufficient lateral space for camping.

also sew on a set of rings round the bottom of the screen, at intervals of about 1 to 1.5 meters, so that the screen can be secured to hooks or stumps on the ground in case of wind. These rings should be attached to the screen by means of leather straps glued and stitched on for adequate resistance. Before tying down the screen, the tarpaulin must be likewise secured like a tent; otherwise its flapping in the wind will end up tearing the screen at the seams. If there is no wind, there's no need to tie anything. When the weather is warm you can leave your car door open.

This instant system rids you of the need to find a place to set up a tent or sling a hammock, which in rainy weather can be most inconvenient, and you are more promptly ready to leave if necessary. And when you aren't out in the wild, or prefer a service station for security or convenience, you can have your meal at the local restaurant or snack bar, use the bathroom, then park your car right next to the big trucks, throw over the tarpaulin, and go to sleep in peace.

But like everything else we are not accustomed to, spreading the screen-fringed tarpaulin over the car, when you are alone, takes a little practice. With two people it's easy—you just spread it out on the ground on the side of the car that is cleanest, then close the doors and windbreaks and pull the screen over the top, being careful not to get it hooked anywhere. Alone it's best to place the folded tarpaulin on top of the car before untying it, then unfold it from there. If you spread it on the ground and then try pulling it over the car, it will slip down one side while you pull up the other, besides getting caught on things or burned on the hot exhaust.

When camping you can tie it more to one side or the other for extra space. But make sure there is enough tilt for heavy rain to run off without forming "bellies."

Newspaper or Journal

Normally I carry four or five whole newspapers in the luggage compartment. With some of them, moistened with water, I wipe the windows, mirrors, lights, and license plates. With the paper dry or slightly dampened I give the windshields and rearview mirrors their final polish. Besides, I use them for wrapping tools to keep these from rattling and banging around, cleaning my hands of oil and dirt before washing them, and so on. They can also be held against the windshields by the wipers while parking during the day to keep the sun out, or used at night to darken the car for sleep.

When camping I double the number of newspapers because they also serve to pad such potentially leaky fruits and vegetables as pineapple, papaya, tomatoes, potatoes, and onions, plus eggs. They are the best thing for lighting fires, especially when dirty with oil or grease, and if it gets cold newspapers provide some of the best insulation for hammocks, beds, and even inside your clothes. Ask any of the poor people living in the streets.

A Flyswatter or Mata-Moscas

Whereas on a foot trail you can cut yourself a suitable branch or palm leaf for swatting or removing insects, in the car a plastic fly swatter is a necessity, especially in the warmer equatorial regions, where the common housefly is most prevalent.

Arrangement

Here's my internal organization for the one-person Gurgel Jeep: In place of a passenger seat, I use a plywood sleeping platform on a wooden rack. On top of this platform are my rucksack, companion bag, mattress, blanket, sheet, pillow, and tablecloth (for dining on the hood). Underneath are shoes or boots, flip-flops, and nonperishable foods such as sardines, dry fruit, nuts, and soft drinks. A sharpening stone. Candies for gifts. Jack, ax, oars, walking stick, hand pump.

• **On the rear seat.** Tarpaulin with insect screen, binoculars, flashlight, light hammock, camera, hat, leather cap and jacket covering things, bread up on top.

• **Behind the rear seat.** Books, umbrella. On rainy days, trail permitting, you can carry the umbrella instead of your walking stick; it does the same job, besides providing shelter when there is a shower. In the Tropics a raincoat is often too warm.

• **Behind the driver's seat.** Inflatable boat in its own rucksack (see chapter 15), containing foot pump, repair kit, cords, brush, and towel.

• **Under the driver's seat.** A machete and a ventilated nylon market bag containing fruit and vegetables (see chapter 12)—lemons, oranges aplenty, apples, a few bananas, hard pears, melons. No fruits that leak—papaya, pineapple, figs—unless they're well padded by several layers of newspaper. Cucumbers, carrots, greenish tomatoes, peppers, onions, sweet and common potatoes. No other items here, because this bag must remain well aired. It should also be emptied every day and each item checked, replacing any moistened newspaper. Read the newspaper's headlines while replacing; this gives you an idea of what is going on in the country.

• **In the left front corner,** by the door. Five-liter (quart) square, hard plastic bottle with drinking water, renewable from bottles purchased along the way at service-station snack bars and mini markets.

• **On the panel.** Maps, fly swatter.

• **On the passenger's grip handle.** A small towel and a cloth for washing windows. After washing, wiping with newspaper gives best visibility.

• **In the glove compartment.** Basic car-tool set plus fine sandpaper, file, metal saw blade, tire gauge, vise wrench, silicone glue, smaller spare parts such as points, condenser, and fuses. Also, extra hygiene items like toilet paper, soap, sponge, matches, candles, and tire-repair kit if you wish.

• **In the extra fuel tank,** screwed on outside. Either fuel or water for washing, renewable at any pond or stream and disinfected with chlorine.

• **In the luggage compartment.** Spare tire, extra tube, larger spare parts such as fan belt, accelerator, and clutch cables, spare oil and braking fluid, manual winch and jack handle, wooden blocks, wheel spanner with iron bar, spade, towing rope, newspaper, plastic bags, signaling triangle, a child's beach shovel and a brush for cleaning, cooking stove and gas bottle (be sure to take extra rubber washers for the contact of the stove valve with the gas bottle and tape them to the valve so that you can find them when needed; wipe with saliva or water to check whether there's gas leaking and seal with soap scraped from a bar), chlorine, washbasin, pot and pan, cleaning set (steel wool, soap, sponge, hose to transfer water), margarine, a set of wheel chains.

• **In front, outside.** Winch and cable if fixed.

Before sleeping, whatever is in the way inside the car goes onto the roof. After supper the tarpaulin (see above) is thrown over the lot and, if there is any turbulence, tied to nearby branches and anchored to the ground, protecting everything from rain and insects.

Preventive Hygiene for the Car

Keep the car clean, brushing the floor, replacing the newspapers underneath fruit and vegetables the moment any leakage is spotted, washing with soap those parts of the car you touch with sweaty hands (steering wheel, gearshift handle, doorknobs or latches, or seat covers) or with dirty footwear (accelerator pedal, brakes, clutch, and floor). And keep yourself clean, by washing and bathing daily.

The sweet, odorous juice oozing from a ripe pineapple is especially attractive to bees and wasps. The same goes for sweetsop, mangoes, and jackfruit. When they're after food, bees and wasps won't sting you unless you accidentally touch them. But if you start swatting about indiscriminately you're going to attract even more insects through the smell of their squashed companions, and that's asking for trouble.

Except for swarming season in the spring, when they have wings, ants will not enter the car unless, through oversight, you pack things away from the ground or a rock without brushing off hitchhikers. But housecleaning should be performed every time a cockroach is found.

WHERE TO CAMP ALONG THE ROAD

Service Stations or Postos de Serviços

While driving on highways, your most practical stops to spend the night are the service stations—preferably the large ones, where you see lots of trucks. Besides fuels, with attendants on duty throughout the night, these stations have a restaurant, a snack bar, and a complete bathroom where you can even have a shower—some charge a small fee, others don't. Some also have a hotel, mechanic, and tire repairman. In the ample lot there's plenty of space to choose where to park your car (preferably within view of the attendants and truck drivers), throw your screen-fringed tarpaulin over the top, and sleep in peace, even with your door open when it's warm. This is how I spent most nights during my trips to Cuiabá, Mato Grosso, and back to Campinas, São Paulo, at the beginning of 2001 and 2002.

On secondary roads service stations remain an option, though you will find sanitary facilities and standards lower, to the point where it's often preferable to camp out in the savanna or scrub.

Whenever possible, drive up to the nearest farmhouse and, if there's a family, ask for permission to spend the night inside the property. This is always safer than sleeping off the road.

The Roadside, Beira da Estrada, or Orilla del Camino

Brazilian federal roads have a standard elbow room of 40 meters (130 feet) from the axis or middle of the road to the fence along each side. Deducting the asphalt and shoulder, this leaves about 30 meters (98 feet) of vegetation.

When it's savanna or woods dense enough to conceal the car I often park there for the night, preferably if it's at a higher or lower level than the road, or by a curve. But not at any rest area—area de descanso—or trail. Off the road, period! That's why the car should be high and short. Grass must be avoided when it's dry due to fire hazard, snakes, and insects. The ground should be clean. And don't park in the vicinity of any suburban or otherwise populated area. It's much more city thieves than rural criminals that you have to guard against.

15

TRAVEL BY BOAT, HORSE, AND BIKE

TRAVEL BY BOAT

If you have in mind a long trip down some river, letting the current carry you along at leisure while you watch wildlife, write, fish, explore, and camp along the banks, living when possible off the land, by all means do it, for it promises to be one of those great, unforgettable experiences of life.

A few considerations are important during the planning stage. The first of these is the time of the year: Such an undertaking must be scheduled for the dry season—winter and spring, May to October—when the water is low and clean, rains are few, and there are sandy beaches and dry banks to go ashore and camp.

The next important point is that your boat and equipment must be light enough for you to portage them over difficult rocks and cliffs around waterfalls, which requires the utmost patience and care to avoid accidents and damage to your gear. Some of the series of waterfalls and rapids in rivers of the Amazon can be many kilometers long; you may find yourself clambering around on rocks for days or weeks on end without much respite, depending on the river you choose. And if there is one place where rashness can destroy your trip or your life, it's by the waterfalls with all their traps.

When you expect to take one or two companions on your trip, you must first of all be sure you know these people well enough to trust them under stressful conditions. Next you go together to the store and try the weight of the aluminium or inflatable boat of your preference by carrying it back and forth, in twos, above your heads. Dragging won't do because of narrow, winding passages among cliffs. If you aren't taking a motor, then the Canadian canoe-type craft is the best to row.

Canoes with a flat poop for motors can be rowed if there is no other choice, by turning them around and rowing backward with the flat end raised above the waterline. In the case of an inflatable boat, you must remember that it has to be maneuverable in an emergency, such as moving out of the path of larger boats, in fast-flowing bottlenecks leading to waterfalls, or being sucked under overhanging ledges, fallen trees, or into whirlpools.

More important than oars in fast jungle waters are a couple of forks—rods about 4 meters (13 feet) long with a fork at one end that you prepare by the river, preferably of bamboo—with which to push away or stave off obstacles in your path. One you use, standing up when necessary; the other you keep as a reserve or for your companion if you have one.

If you're going it alone, an inflatable boat by itself is inappropriate for the reasons above, and so is a canoe, for in an emergency there will be no one to help you out. The Canadian canoe, which has a rounded or oval bottom, tends to tilt sharply when it runs aground upon a rock or trunk, with danger of overturning, or at least dumping part of your luggage into the water, as was the case with my photo equipment when my family and I were trying out our new canoe.

The solution that I have devised to my satisfaction is a "happy in-between": My Canadian canoe weighs only about 27 kilos (60 pounds) and is fiberglass, so a simple kit enables me to make repairs on the spot when necessary. To the side of the canoe I tie the inflatable boat. This arrangement prevents the canoe from tilting, and keeps everything manageable under the oar or fork, while the weight for portage is reduced. I also carry a grappling hook on a long line to cast out onto the bank or into overhanging trees to brake the boats in a hurry if necessary, plus an anchor at the opposite end of the same line. When I wish to go someplace quickly I can always untie the inflatable dinghy and go in the canoe alone. Likewise, if there is bad weather I can distribute the luggage between the two boats as necessary, or go ashore, put all the equipment in the canoe, and tilt the inflatable boat on top, to protect things from the rain. Even myself.

It goes without saying that upon approaching any narrows or change in the speed of the river you must immediately go ashore, tie up your boat, and investigate overland before venturing in, because it may be a canyon with smooth walls where you cannot get out, and a waterfall ahead! Your reserve oar should be tied to the boat, and all important equipment tied up in sturdy, floatable plastic bags. Rough rapids can quickly upset things. Wear your life jacket preventively in all doubtful stretches.

Bear in mind, though, that this is no whitewater rafting gear intended to face man-high waves, boulder-strewn currents, and countercurrents with sucking whirlpools. This is equipment for mild, manageable waters.

Unless it's a small drop that you can safely handle alone, you will need help. So one thing to verify during your preliminary exploration is whether there is anyone living or fishing nearby. These are the people to talk to, for they know the trails and rapids and can give you good advice. Still, play it safe by checking out the information.

Settle the price for this and any other job in advance, to avoid surprises. If you think the fee charged was extremely modest, you can always add a small tip after the job has been completed. Some people don't want to charge for their help, but you can give something for the children or the wife.

Carry different quantities of money in separate pockets, inside plastic bags, so that you never need to show much to anyone.

If you're a beginner I recommend the Swampland for your first trip, for here you have practically no drop and thus no waterfalls to cope with. You have time to familiarize yourself with your equipment without the apprehension of a surprise at the next bend.

The Inflatable Boat

An inflatable boat with its rucksack is a practical piece of equipment for exploring rivers, ponds, and swamps; camping on islands; and more. I wouldn't advise using one on lakes, because this little boat doesn't row well. It consists of a main oval tube, plus four other minor and separately inflated chambers: one on each underside of the main tube, to protect it from sharp rocks or stumps in the water plus one on the central floor and the seat at each end.

It has a nylon line attached to the outside to hold on to and tie it up with, a foot-bellows pump with the appropriate terminals for each nipple, and a repair kit containing plastified or rubberized material and glue.

The boat, designed for two adults and a child, is so light that a good clothesline is sufficient to tie it up, and a brick-sized rock will do as an anchor.

This kind of boat is good for fishing and bird-watching in ponds sheltered from the wind by reeds, swamps, and just drifting down rivers with the current as far as you please. But it will not allow you to row it back upriver, because it's impossible to maintain any steady direction; and anyway, that would be the most laborious and least recommended way to do it.

A much easier procedure is to take the boat out of the river when you've gone far enough, then deflate it on a clean stretch of pasture or beach while you have your snack or bath and wash your clothes, for it takes about an hour to deflate completely when left to itself. Of course you can shorten this interval when desirable by deflating the remaining air pockets with the bellows. Then you just throw it onto your back and march straight across the fields or along the nearest trail back to where you left the car.

But this is an uncomfortable way to carry the boat with its equipment, oar, companion bag, and so on. That's why I built a sturdy rucksack for mine. In the large main compartment goes the deflated, folded boat. There's a central rear pocket for the bellows and tube, with a small outside compartment for the nipple terminals, plus one long, narrow pocket on each side for the cords and a brush and towel to wipe the boat clean and dry before folding it. These were my wife's good idea. And there's a swivel to fasten a short oar on each side of the cover.

Thus the boat and everything needed for it is together in this rucksack. Likewise, every item for a one-day outing (or even two or three days if necessary) is in the companion bag, except food. And the supplementary equipment for camping out longer is ready in the rucksack.

It's important to have each set of equipment together and ready for an emergency. The boat is also a good alternative when you don't feel secure on land: You simply put your sleeping gear and valuables inside, row out to a conveniently camouflaged spot, drop the anchor or tie up to some reed or branch, and go to sleep on the water. You can stretch a piece of tarpaulin over the boat in case of rain or cold wind, hooked to the eyelets and raised in the middle by an oar or stick. It also offers a means of flight if there is a threat on the road, an accident, or the car breaks down in the middle of nowhere and you are too far from any assistance to walk, or unable to do so because of an injury. This also works if the car is caught in a flood and you must transfer your luggage to higher ground. Just pack your most essential equipment and belongings in the boat and let the current carry you along to the next riverside inhabitant or village—though attention must be paid to possible rapids and falls, which are often found in narrowing valleys or gorges, and you tend to hear them from below, not above . . .

You may not need to go to the trouble of making a backpack for your inflatable boat: Depending on the model and how it can be folded, you may be lucky and find a large conventional rucksack into which it fits.

Anyway, if you plan to take the dinghy in your backpack on a foot expedition into the jungle, then you need one more companion to carry the camping gear and food—unless you carry all your needs in the food and companion bags and sleep in the inflated boat, dispensing with the other rucksack. Then you would carry a small, light oar in place of the walking stick. But it's a fairly heavy load, mind you, and in case of rain you'd have to turn the boat upside down on a clean spot of sand and sleep underneath.

The Motorboat

The first thing that calls your attention when studying a good map of the Amazon basin are the impressive strings of arrowheads in practically all the rivers indicating waterfalls and rapids. You need only look at the tributaries of the Rio Branco in Roraima to get the idea. In reality there are more than the map shows, because there are simply so many rivers that some of the smaller ones aren't even marked.

So much so that when you arrive in the Amazon your curiosity is likely to lead you first of all down to the riverside to see how local man has adapted his equipment to cope with this condition. And you won't be disappointed.

- **The boat.** An Amazon canoe has, like seagoing ships, a slightly elevated, covered forecastle with a gunwale across the back, for two purposes: first, shielding the open hull from water as the boat dips into wave troughs in traversing the rapids and falls; and second, serving as a platform for a standing crew member with a pole or fork to stave off obstacles when crossing the inundated forests, or igapós, and prop or push in the rapids.

- **The outboard motor or motor de popa.** Preferred in the Amazon is the heavy-duty Archimedes Penta type with a long shaft leading out at an angle, where the propeller operates in shallower water behind the keel, relatively sheltered from rocks and stumps, as opposed to the Evinrude type with a vertical shaft, where the screw functions below the keel.

- **The oar or remo.** The Amazon oar is such a slender, streamlined piece that it makes most other oars look like clumsy logs. Made of tough wood such as the attractive, black, weather-resistant acapu (*Vouacapoua americana*), it has a large, round or rounded blade and a short, 1-meter (3-foot) shaft ending in an elaborate flat or rounded grip such as that of some walking sticks to fill the palm of the hand. It's operated in a sitting or kneeling position near the waterline, with one hand closed around the shaft and the other pressing down upon it.

In the Swampland it was the Paiaguás Indians—prime boatmen and feared pirates who inflicted much damage upon expeditions on the gold route between Cuiabá and São Paulo in colonial days—who developed a specialized, double-purpose oar. Unlike the Amazon model, the Paiaguás oar had an exceptionally long, sturdy shaft and a narrow, sharp blade, for it was at the same time the battle lance.

Otherwise the serene rivers of the Pantanal or Chaco, unruffled by turbulence other than the weather, have not encouraged much creativity. Here the important detail is a flat bottom and shallow draft, so as to be able to negotiate the shallows during the dry season, and beach the craft in a hurry or drive it into the floating mats of hyacinths—camalotes (*Eichhornia azurea*)—when a storm whips up the river unexpectedly, within minutes converting its usually placid surface into ocean-level turmoil with waves that look meter high.

Since—unlike the Amazon—Pantanal riverbanks rarely have beaches or rocky ledges for easy landing, your wisest procedure at the first signs of a storm in the making is to seek the bank or cove that appears most protected, and either beach or moor your boat in the shelter of the vegetation. In late autumn, winter, and early spring these storms come accompanied by rain and a violent drop in temperature.

I was caught in such an emergency at Fort Coimbra back in 1958. I was fishing from a rather heavy wooden boat downstream from the fort one afternoon when a storm raced in upriver out of the south. This was my first entry into the Swampland, and I had no idea such waves could build up so fast as they came in at a 45-degree angle from my left.

The bank on my right was high, steep, and fairly straight; the current ran fast alongside because the fort is exactly located at a bottleneck in the river. Now the additional turbulence of the incoming waves lapping up and knocking down chunks of silt made it impossible to moor here, let alone beach the boat.

With water spilling in and the evening not far off, I realized from my experience in the sea around Santos that there was only one thing to do: I swung the prow into the wind and rowed for the opposite bank, which was here about 600 meters (650 yards) away. It was hard work and slow progress against the wind, to the point that I came to wonder whether I'd make it at all before dark.

But about two-thirds of the way across I could see that the agitation ahead was soon going to get milder once I managed to make it into the area shielded by the wall of jungle upon the bank. From then on things got progressively better and I was able to rest enough to make my way upstream in the relatively calm waters close to the bank until I was opposite the lights of the fort and ready to cross back with the wind.

RIDING A HORSE OR BICYCLE

In the Swampland the horse is the best and therefore the most-used means of individual transportation. For loads it is the oxcart—with wheels 2 meters (6.5 feet) in diameter and pulled by six to twelve oxen—or the tractor.

But there a cowboy-guide is absolutely indispensable, even for us old-timers, because you don't know the flat, repetitive country, its dangers, the trails, gates, swamp and lagoon crossings—which change according to the height of the flood—the local procedures the horse is accustomed to, or the equipment used.

Should you fall behind or stray away from a group and feel unsure of the direction, give the horse the reins (relax your hold on them), and let the horse go where it wants to. It will take you either to the party or back home.

When it's dry, the Swampland is also ideally suited for the bicycle: flat, crisscrossed by cattle trails, with no stones. Where there is deep sand or borocotó—stone-hard limestone clay—you can always push or carry the bike. It is silent, permitting you to approach wildlife, and cool, providing a welcome breeze in the usually high heat while enabling you to cover large distances with minimal effort.

When wet, the Pantanal or Chaco permits the use of a bicycle only in sandy areas, such as Nhecolândia, east of Corumbá.

On savanna-covered plateaus, using a bicycle requires more attention, since cattle trails are frequently eroded or crossed by rocky outcrops in the hilly terrain. In the northeast caatinga and the cities and villages in the Amazon the bicycle is the people's vehicle; but in the jungle its use will depend on the existence of trails, since in the latter region the canoe is the number one option for any longer stretch, and in many places the *only* option.

Of course your tube-repair kit, a good pump, and basic tools are indispensable wherever you go, because there are always thorns that may cause a puncture. Necessary, too, is a canteen or bottle of water.

Your bicycle should have a luggage rack, upon which you may buckle your companion bag, and if possible one of those baskets attached to the front of the handlebar, for food. If not, you can tie your nylon food bag to the crossbar.

If your object is, like mine, exploring and nature-watching, then your best bet is the most common bicycle, without gears, or with no more than three if you wish, and soft, well-rubberized tires, provided with light—in case you stay out late—and mud guards to shield your clothes and equipment from splattering. Since my purpose is not speed,

I don't wear a helmet. But a straw hat with a medium brim and a lace to tie under the chin because of the breeze is important. Just a cap is not recommended because your ears and neck will become sunburned. For the same reason your shirt should be long sleeved.

PART FOUR

SURVIVAL

16

BUILDING A FIRE

I divide the South American jungles into three categories with regard to building a campfire:

• **The Swampland, savanna, and caatinga** semidesert. There is always dry wood available, but careful precautions must be taken before lighting a fire to prevent its breaking away, bearing in mind the possibility of a sudden gust of wind.

• **The Amazon basin forests,** where a campfire is not inordinately difficult to start providing you allow yourself an hour's time before dusk to gather and prepare wood.

• **The mountainous cloud forest,** of perennial humidity, where building a fire can be a near impossibility. I have shivered through cold nights in the Serra do Mar mountains around Santos after my efforts to build a fire failed despite taking along kerosene to start it with.

So let's concentrate on this most difficult and frustrating area, for once you succeed here, there will be no place in the Tropics where you won't be able to light a fire!

Advance Preparation

Before starting out on your excursion into the cloud forest, buy and take with you in a plastic bag a small package of charcoal—which isn't heavy—and a small, preferably transparent plastic container of kerosene, alcohol, lighter fluid, or other fuel. Figure out how much coal you will need to use to start a fire each evening, or divide your coals into plastic bags for the number of days you expect to stay, plus two as a reserve. You will be able to replenish this reserve with leftovers from campfires as you move along.

Firewood

When stopping to make camp, allow yourself about two hours of daylight in which to locate useful firewood—the most difficult item. The best place to look is among the boulders of open mountain streambeds, where the wood is more exposed to the scarce sunlight than under the dense canopy.

All the wood you come across will most likely be more or less moist, and clouds drifting in and building up throughout the afternoon won't make it any drier. On the contrary: Rain is likely to start after sundown and last through most of the night until the clouds have gotten light enough to rise and drift on over the summits. So sapwood is out of the question, for it will usually be soaked. Therefore you have to search for hardwood, which is comparatively impermeable. You will easily identify its denser, usually darker grain by hacking a dent with your hunting knife or machete.

Unless you are lucky enough to get a brief dry spell—which is not to be counted on—you will almost certainly have to peel off the outer layers of bark and sapwood to get to the drier inner core.

Lighting the Fire

Once you have assured yourself of a sufficient wood supply for the night and—to be on the safe side—the next day, the first thing to do before constructing a fire is to put up your tarpaulin shelter high enough not to be spoiled by the heat, for no fire here will resist the mist—if not the frequent rain—of the night.

Just a shelter is not enough. Arrange one portion of your coals on top of dry newspaper or plastic in a hollow protected by rocks, bark, or stumps of wood to hold the precious warmth and keep out the drifting, moist air.

Divide your liquid fuel by the number of nights foreseen plus two and mark the divisions with a pen on the plastic bottle. Use only the minimum necessary. Close and put your bottle away in its place in the rucksack before lighting a match to ignite the coals. Blow as necessary to get the flames going while you pile wood around to dry, in the following order: first shavings, then thin splinters or parted pieces, finally thicker wood and stumps.

The matches sold in the Amazon region must be struck against the shoulder of the box in order to light, so the box has to be kept perfectly dry inside a plastic bag. Fiat-Lux makes a large-sized, palitos longos, match that is suitable. When you need a longer-lasting flame to light your campfire, you can glue or tie the match to a dry twig or a piece of cardboard long enough not to burn your fingers, and lubricate both.

Maintaining the Fire

Once the fire is going strong you can afford to lay the surplus wood, as it dries, back a safe distance from the flames but within reach of their warmth, adding from this stock as necessary. Pay attention, though: While wood is steaming, it is not yet dry and must therefore remain close to the heat. Although it can be used on a strong fire, it will hardly be suitable to restart one if you wake up in the middle of the night and find only a few glimmering coals among the ashes. Always provide a safe store of firewood, for you may find yourself tied down for the next day or two by rain—or worse, an accident or illness.

Before moving on, save all leftover bits and ends of dry, partially burned wood and coal in a plastic bag for starting the next campfire. That makes it a lot easier. In the morning there are usually a number of such ends around the dormant fire. You will need only a few to rekindle it as you blow away the ashes and expose the live coals underneath. Carrying a reserve of firewood or coal for kindling is as important as food in the cloud forest.

Before going to sleep, reinforce your campfire and make sure it is sufficiently sheltered in case it starts raining, for if you allow it to go out, that will be it for the night. And without the warmth of a cozy fire it can get most uncomfortably cold in your hammock with only a light sleeping bag and the humidity coming up from underneath.

If the fire goes out and it gets cold—and there's no rain—the best solution is to insert your plastic raincoat between the hammock and the sleeping bag to protect your back, preferably lining the top of the raincoat with your towel and extra clothes to absorb condensation. Otherwise your sleeping bag will get moist. All moist items must be dried by the fire in the morning before they are packed away in the rucksack, or they will develop mold and smell.

No Dry Fuel

If you have neither tinder, coals, nor liquid fuel to light a fire, creativity and patience will be the order of the day. There is likely to be some paper, cardboard, or plastic in your equipment, such as film boxes, toilet paper, nylon cord, plastic bags, or the like. Onto this you cut fine shavings of the driest wood you can find—from under overhangs, ledges, or inside hollow trunks—then add gradually coarser and thicker pieces.

You may come across the odd palm leaf that is dry enough to burn, perhaps one hanging under the tree's crown that's dead but hasn't yet dropped. Add a little margarine, cooking oil, or a slice of bacon—whatever you've got that's oily—to your kindling for it to burn longer. Only the minimum necessary. A tiny square of bacon or a few drops of sardine oil on top of a piece of the cardboard tube inside your toilet paper may give you all the fire you need to get started. Then proceed as above. The secret is to keep your toilet paper wrapped in a plastic bag in your pocket for dryness, and lay your hand upon dry-enough wood by patiently chipping off the outer layers with your knife.

Or try the driest piece on hand. Can you guess what I mean? Your walking stick! If you've had it for some days, it's most probably the driest piece of wood in the vicinity. And it will take you less than ten minutes to cut and shape yourself another one.

Extinguishing the Fire

Before leaving camp—whether it's for a few minutes or for good—you must always, as a standing rule, make sure there is no way in which the fire, flaring up with a gust of wind or the collapse of a piece of wood that's burned through, can reach anything else that burns and thus get out of hand or damage camp equipment. This means that not only must the firebreak be about a meter (3 feet) wide all around, but the inclination of the terrain must also be taken into account, so that no live coals or burning pieces go rolling down the hillside and set the brush on fire.

When you are definitely breaking camp, take what bits you may need for your next fire, then pour water on the remaining coals until there is no longer any smoke, or use sand, or soil. Should you want to keep the coals alive for the day, place a heavy stump on top, but lock it in place with stones so that it cannot overturn when gravity changes as parts of it are burned away.

17

LOST

Our bridge-building work site by the Tuerê River, 280 kilometers (175 miles) from Marabá and 220 kilometers (138 miles) from Altamira along the path of the opening trans-Amazon highway across south Pará state, lay in a wild, mountainous region as yet untouched, back in 1973, by the settler's chain saw.

One sunny Saturday in December—it was my first day up after a week in the hammock with malaria—I felt an urge to get away from the noise and smell of people for a few hours. So after nibbling at some tasteless bits of peccary, rice, and beans I got into the jeep and drove about 3 kilometers (2 miles) out of the river valley up into the mountains, which were fingers stretching north from the ore-rich Serra dos Carajás. I took only my heavy knife and shotgun with me, completely neglecting my usually indispensable accessories: a game bag containing compass, matches, flashlight, first-aid kit, and cape. My intention was to enter only the very edge of the forest and listen to the sounds of nature away from man for a while.

I came upon a wild cashew tree, in the high crown of which toucans and oropendola hopped about, occasionally dropping a juicy red fruit that I ate. Once in a while I could hear the thud of a heavy Brazil nut pod dropping to the ground. When you're under one such giant you have to pay attention to the telltale swish of a branch tip freed from the heavy pod—and run for cover!

A distant row of monkeys and macaws enticed me on, over a ridge and down a slope into the deep forest. I came upon a fountain in a hollow, where colorful little frogs tingled in the dripping maidenhair. It grew into a stream and had gotten deep enough to contain fish by the time I reached the approximate site of the racket, which had meanwhile ceased. Had the monkeys and macaws been fighting each other over nuts, or was there a third element involved, perhaps a jaguar?

Presently I perceived a dull rumbling, interspersed with sharp clicks of fangs, and soon found myself in the middle of a herd of some thirty white-lipped peccaries—queixadas (*Tayassu pecari*). I climbed upon a large prop root, from where I was able to observe the pigs rooting the marshy ground among clumps of cabbage palms in relative security. This is a much-feared animal (see chapter 7), though it only becomes dangerous when you are accompanied by dogs, which it hates. Eventually they retired up a hillside, and their rumbling gradually faded.

It was time to turn back. The sky had meanwhile become overcast and I no longer had any indication of the sun's position. Still, all I needed to do was walk back up along the creek to its beginning, and then proceed in the same direction up to the mountain ridge and down the other side, where I should find the road. But somewhere I lost my tracks in the poor light under the three-layered canopy and followed the wrong tributary upstream; though that only meant I would have to ascend a different ravine and was likely to come out upon the road perhaps 0.5 kilometer (0.3 mile) or so to one side or the other of the place I had started out from.

On reaching the beginning of the gully I had been following, I proceeded to scale the slope until I got over a crest and started descending. Now it shouldn't be far to the road, which lay absolutely silent, for it was cut off by flooded rivers on both sides. It was taking longer than I had expected, though. A new stream had meanwhile emerged, grown bigger . . . Presently it was the size of the other one at the point where I had stopped to watch the wild hogs—and darkness was approaching!

Stop, man! I told myself. *Rest a moment and think clearly, for something has gone very wrong!* I washed the sweat off my face and sat down. This couldn't possibly be the side of the hills where the road ran, for I now remembered the highway did not bridge any brook in this area. If that was so, then I was heading *north*—*away* from my destination! I checked my reasoning and concluded that I had not crossed the main ridge after all, but rather a secondary one branching off to the north, after which I'd unconsciously turned back in the same direction I had been coming from. This decided, I jumped to my feet and ran back upstream in order to cover what ground was possible before the twilight vanished altogether.

It had become totally dark when I was stopped by the sudden crashing and churning of a large animal breaking away ahead of me, probably a tapir. Well, with visibility now entirely gone, there was no longer any sense in hurrying. Gradually a growing number of frogs and toads, momentarily silenced by the animal's stampede, resumed their hammering and croaking. There was a bog in front of me, into which I would have dived headlong if I had not been stopped in time by the frightened animal. No question of pausing here, though, for mosquitoes were already attacking in whining clouds.

I noted that the largest concentration of batrachian musicians was straight ahead of me. I covered my eyes—which were totally useless now anyway—with my arm in order to protect them from invisible thorns and twigs and, by feeling the edge of the soft mud with my right foot, proceeded to grope my way along the swamp until I had the loudest crowd of frogs on my right again. This meant I was now directly opposite the spot where I had stopped when the animal broke away. So here I turned 90 degrees to my left and, with my back to the orchestra and my free arm outstretched ahead, began to walk, step by careful step, away from the swamp, thus continuing in the same direction in which I had been running. I was pleased to feel the ground rising, seeming to confirm that I was heading the right way.

Walking was not impossible in the pitch-black night, despite the thorns, spiderwebs, lianas, ants and other crawlers, and frequent stumbling until I got the hang of it. As long as I could still hear the amphibians behind me, I'd be okay. The moon would be rising late, and if the cloud cover wasn't too dense by then, I might get an idea of my position.

Wishful thinking! There was a flash of lightning over on my right: rain soon! But meanwhile the lightning would serve as a beacon, too.

The moment came when the last sounds of my helpful frogs faded and the ground began to level off. So far, so good! I moved on—and promptly fell, as the terrain dropped away! One more attempt convinced me that it is absolutely impossible to walk downhill in the dark. What to do? I sat down against a tree to rest and think anew. An animal called. If I stayed where I was, I'd be in for a miserable, wet, cold night with mosquitoes and ants and—worse—a probable relapse of malaria . . . Besides, it meant giving up, failing. The men interrupting work in the morning—we worked Sundays, too—to go out and search for me . . . No: Tonight I was given the most fascinating challenge in my life. Fate dared me to find my way out of the Amazon jungle in absolute darkness, and I had the whole night ahead of me with nothing else to do but try!

Maintaining the occasional lightning on my right, I edged forward by holding on to whatever my hands could reach. In case the lightning should cease or move away I'd be left with any one of ninety-nine wrong directions to stray in, so I could not afford to waste this beacon.

While progressing at a snail's pace I was reminded of the many infamous accounts of lost people who had perished miserably in the jungle. Only recently a surveyor's assistant—of all professions—had vanished in the region.

But the jungle was known ground to me. And its dangers, mainly the vicious bushmaster and other snakes, were risks worth braving under the circumstances.

A fallen tree I had begun to cross collapsed into some unfathomable hollow, and I was left dangling in a web of lianas around my neck and under my nose and armpit. An army of ants, which had apparently been using the creepers as a bridge, swarmed all over me. On feeling about, I discovered that I hung inside a growth of prickly mumbaca (*Astrocaryum gynacanthum*) palms . . . It was hardly the kind of downhill travel I usually pictured!

As time passed I began to hear thunder, gradually getting louder. My hands and knees had by now collected a lot of thorns and cuts. Presently I perceived the distant sound of a motor! I froze where I stood, all ears: It was our truck, the only possible vehicle moving on the stretch. And it seemed to be getting nearer! I realized that I had to mark the direction where I should hear it loudest in relation to the lightning, for that ought to be where the road passed closest to me. Gears shifting in the hilly country, it was coming nearer all the time. The driver must have gone to visit some girl by the Aratú River in the next valley some 20 kilometers (12 miles) east.

Then I felt a surge of joy as I saw the beam of the vehicle's headlights passing no more than 200 meters (650 feet) ahead of me! It was now only a matter of proceeding easy and carefully until I broke out on the road.

Three-quarters of an hour later I'd had a bath in the river and sat in my hammock with crackers and hot coffee, extracting thorns and cleaning out cuts. Around me the camp slept. Rain began to prattle on the thatch roof, and I felt magnificent.

A HYPOTHETICAL SITUATION

Let's suppose that, as evening approaches, you realize you won't be able to make it to your expected destination. Besides, rain is approaching, and you're already wet from some accident in which you lost all your food plus your rucksack with the sleeping gear . . . All you were able to save was your companion bag, and you don't know which way to go.

WHAT TO DO FIRST: A SHELTER

First of all you must build yourself a shelter, or abrigo, because there is rain coming. No use gathering firewood or starting a fire until you have a roof to protect it and yourself. The exception would be a case where it's already getting dark and you need the last daylight to gather wood, and the light from the fire to build your camp. Then you can protect your fire from the rain with palm leaves, wood bark, or flat stones.

Building a shelter for one or two people is a very quick and simple thing, since you've got a plastic raincoat in your companion bag. Bend down a more or less straight sapling about 4 meters (13 feet) long and tie it horizontally to another tree, high enough above preferably level ground so that you can sit comfortably underneath—say, about 1.25 meters (nearly 4 feet). Stretch out your raincoat over this beam and tie it fast to the surrounding vegetation with cords attached to the eyelets or buttons and holes, at a sufficiently dropping angle that heavy rain can run off freely without forming pockets of accumulated water on the surface. You may have to cut, sharpen, and knock into the ground a few extra stakes so as to obtain a firm, uniformly stretched cover.

Where to Erect

Build your shelter near water if possible, though palm trees are also important. You definitely don't want to be down at the bottom of any gorge, gully, or narrow valley subject to flooding. Look out for high-water marks on the vegetation and rocks. Nor do you wish to be on the lower side of an inclined tree that might fall in a storm. But don't waste time—unless you've got plenty—searching for an ideal campsite, because your source of warmth, light, and comfort is going to be the fire. Try to be a short distance from some driftwood or a fallen tree, if possible, for fuel—but not too close, since there may be snakes living under the wood.

WHAT'S NEXT: FIRE

After your shelter is in place and has been secured, the very next thing to do is to bring in firewood, or lenha, cut with your foldable saw, and store it under the shelter. Hard, stiff, crisply cracking woods are preferable to half-rotten sapwoods, especially if it's already raining, because the latter get soaked, besides being inhabited by a lot of insects undesirable to share your shelter with.

To build the fire, see chapter 16. Save termites, maggots, and wood worms in a plastic bag for fishing. As soon as the fire holds its own, it's time to build a proper roof for it. The pole over which you stretched your raincoat has more than a meter (yard) protruding, unused. Against this extension you lean freshly cut palm leaves. If these are the long, horsetail kind, you indent them with your knife or saw, then jackknife them against your knee into a V-shape that, placed over the pole, provides a firmer structure. Should you have only rather fragile fan-shaped leaves of small palms available, it may be necessary to first place some sturdier rafters underneath, for support; otherwise the weight of the rain may bash them down and extinguish your fire, after which it can be very laborious to start another one.

There should remain an open, clear space of about 25 centimeters (10 inches) between this shelter for the fire and your raincoat, for the smoke to rise, and to avoid the danger of the palm leaves catching fire and burning the raincoat.

Mosquitoes

Your mosquito net has gone with your rucksack. Should there be a significant mosquito problem, you will have to increase the smoke by throwing green or wet foliage onto the fire. That ought to keep them tolerably at bay. But if possible, collect a tree termite hive and ignite it; its smoke is especially mosquito repelling.

Bedding

Since your hammock has also been lost, you will have to collect the remainder of the leaves necessary from nearby palm trees (provided they have no thorns!) to line the floor of your shelter so that you can sleep with a minimum of comfort. Should they be wet, then lay them with the wet side down. They make quite a soft padding if you're patient. But you may need to construct a preliminary platform with the palm trunks laid side by side before padding with leaves, because of infiltration of rainwater.

FOOD

Now that you are the lucky resident of a dry shelter, with a cozy fire and a bearable bed to lie down on, it's time for some food!

Palm Cabbage or Palmito

Palm trees are wonderful plants. You can chew the fruit or, when necessary, cut down the tree to reach the area up where the trunk joins the leaves: There's a kind of "cartridge" there, inside which the leaves develop. This you cut off just above the trunk, and again where the leaves spread out. That gives you a more or less cylindrical piece of varying size, depending on the species and age of the palm, which you now cut longitudinally and peel away the leaves on the outside. Save these, for you may want them to cook things in.

Stick this cylinder into your fire and allow it to cook for about an hour or until the core is tender, which you check by periodically prodding from one end or the other with your knife. When ready, allow it to cool, then peel off the outer layers. Each of these becomes progressively whiter and more tender. Once you have reached the point where you can chew it you have come to the palm heart or cabbage, which is edible. Some are bitter, others sweet, but all make a good, nutritious vegetable available throughout tropical jungles. Add a little salt from the reserve in your companion bag.

A few species of short, thick palms like the acurí in the Swampland require a lot of patient cutting to get to the edible part, but their heart is delicious and can be eaten raw. Those with thorns on the trunks and leaves, like the bocaiúva (*Acrocomia aculeata*) and tucumã (*Astrocaryum* spp.), are inappropriate for building a hut and bed but produce edible fruit. The easiest to harvest and handle are the açaí in the Amazon and the juçara (*Euterpe edulis*) farther south, from both of which commercial palm heart is extracted. Guariroba (*Syagrus oleracea*) is also edible but bitter.

Bow and Arrow

I'm not an archer, but one of the easiest weapons to manufacture is a bow and arrow, or arco e flecha. Although the Indians use special wood such as the stem of the tucum palm, from whose leaves they also braid the bowstring, for your short-term purposes any flexible green wood cane of uniform thickness such as your walking stick will do, though it may require some whittling down of the thicker half to balance the bow's resistance and elasticity. At one end you carve a notch to slip on the bowstring, which you smooth out with the file on your Swiss pocketknife.

Almost any piece of strong-enough cord will do for a bowstring, including your heavier paternoster fishing line. You tie it firmly to one end of the bow and make a permanent loop at the other so that when not in use you can slip it out of the notch and let it slide down the bow shaft to preserve the bow's flexibility. When you want to use it you bend the shaft and slip the loop onto the notch. That's how the Indians do it. Polish with beeswax or paraffin.

Taquari—which is Guarani for "small bamboo"—occurs in one species or another all over tropical South America and is ideal for arrow shafts, although there are usually various other straight, thin canes that can be used. Sharpen the lower tip and cut a notch into the upper one with your pocketknife—by the joint, in the case of bamboo, for resistance—to fit the bowstring.

And you're all set to shoot fish at short range. Accuracy at longer range, such as for hunting, requires tying feathers to the arrows for flight stability and target practice.

Your bow can also have a double string—called a bodoque—separated at the ends by 3.5-centimeter (1.5-inch) wooden pegs, with a leather or canvas net in the middle, like a slingshot, for shooting small stones. When you're ready to practice, you must tilt your string enough for the stone to bypass the bow shaft and your hand. Wear gloves until you've gotten the hang of it, or you'll stone your fingers!

Fishing

By the time you have cooked and eaten your palm heart it may be close to 10 P.M. Time to go see what kind of fish inhabit the water down at the bottom. For even the smallest creek in the jungle contains fish, sometimes surprisingly large, as was the case of a jeju (*Hoplerythrinus unitaeniatus*) swimming upstream in just about its own depth while I was watching the herd of wild boar that day I got lost. During the day you normally see only a few lambarís (shiners) of various species and guarus (minnows), but hidden in deeper pools under roots and drift-wood or burrowed in mud or holes in the bank there are usually some bigger fish like mandí, jundiá, and traíra (see chapter 8), unless you happen to be above some high waterfall that larger fish are unable to overcome.

How to Fish

You have at your disposal all of four means to fish, from which to choose the most suitable: line and hook, machete, pistol, and spear. The latter you need to prepare, if its utility seems warranted: Cut a straight, stiff sapling about 3 meters (10 feet) long with a small fork at one end that you can whittle into a sharp, double prong with your pocketknife. This will also be useful to free your hook when it gets caught, and to capture animals like snakes. A throwing net, or tarrafa, is useful to have in the boat or car, incidentally, for night fishing, but too heavy to carry on the trail, due to its all-around necklace of lead sinkers.

Should the water be so muddy from the rain that you can't see a thing below the surface, you have only one option tonight, and that is to try with line and hook for catfish. This requires a hook no larger than 2 centimeters (0.75 inch). You don't need a leader because these fish have no teeth, but you do need a sinker as they feed close to the bot-tom. There are several varieties of catfish that grow to about 24 cen-timeters (10 inches) if you happen to be near a small creek. In unpol-luted jungle rivers these are clean, good-tasting fish (some of the South American catfish are among the most appreciated freshwater fish) that are quick and easy to prepare because they have neither scales nor small bones. But handle with care, for some have sharp and very painful fins. Do not disembowel directly in the river because there may be piranhas or alligators. Save the entrails and heads for further fishing, but hang them in a plastic bag where ants and animals cannot get them. You will now be able to use the palm-leaf sheaths you removed from the palm heart to roast your fish in the coals.

If it's raining and there is no sheltered cove from which to fish, you can stretch a paternoster line, or espinhel, either across the stream or from one branch to another along the same side. This is a cord or heavy line to which you attach a number of short lengths of fishing line, each with its baited hook on a leader, with or without a sinker depending on how much of a current there is.

The length of each line and size of hook depend on how deep the water is and what it has to offer. In larger rivers where there are more powerful fish, the paternoster should be tied to flexible branches in order not to snap. When there is enough time and you are close to a siz-able river, such a line may be put out before you even begin setting up your camp; but remember that in the daytime it will be more subject to smaller fish stealing your bait, so it's better to wait until nightfall.

When assembling a paternoster it's important to be aware that the distance from one line to the next must be larger than the combined length of both, so that they won't get tangled. Run all nylon lines between your fingers and remove any part that feels rough.

Where there are piranhas you should not use a paternoster or leave a hand line unattended, because they are likely to not only eat up any fish that's hooked but cut your line as well. And you cannot afford to be losing fishing gear, because you only have a minimum in your compan-ion bag. Piranhas don't normally occur in shallow waters of small creeks—say, 30 centimeters (1 foot) or less in depth. But wherever they may be present your hook must always be on a steel leader. Piranhas are edible, though unlike catfish they have one hell of a lot of bones, as do traíra, jeju, and peixe-cachorro—predatory fish you are likely to encounter in the smallest streams, ponds, and swamps. These you need to cut crosswise with a sharp knife, at 0.5-centimeter (0.2-inch) inter-vals, then roast them crisply.

In clear water catfish will be less active, but you have other options: With the small flashlight from your companion bag you search the shal-lows near the shore, which is where the action is late at night. You must move as stealthily as if you were stalking fur-bearing game or birds, and advance your light along smoothly and continuously so as not to spook the fish, alligators, or turtles you may encounter. Save your batteries whenever possible.

When you come upon a fish, you can hit it behind the head with the back of your machete if you've got one, spear it, or shoot it. In the latter case the fish must be in very shallow water and as straight down from your position as possible. You must furthermore aim low: at the bottom line of the fish when aiming from the side, or at the mouth for a frontal shot. No use shooting at a shallow angle out in the middle of the stream. You cannot afford to waste ammunition.

During the time I worked for Fazenda Bodoquena I had several opportunities to shoot fish for lunch in the driest months of August and September, and what fish!

One day I was riding homeward when, on passing a stretch of the Miranda River where there was a rapids, I led the horse in close to the high bank for a look down in the clear water. Behind a trunk of drift-wood I spotted three dorados lying in wait for prey. Since they were rather deep—about 30 centimeters (1 foot)—I aimed my .38 revolver just under the belly of the largest one and fired. The bullet hit the fish right behind the head, and as it turned over on its side I spurred the horse down the bank and into the river before the piranhas caught on to the potential feast. I hoisted the dorado onto the saddle by its gills, amazed at its size: It weighed 11 kilos (24 pounds), and was the largest dorado I ever caught.

Where there are ledges with algae, in falls and rapids, you are like-ly to find cascudos (*Hypostomus* spp.) after midnight, which feed on the algae. This fish looks like something prehistoric, with a very rough skin and large, coarse fins. It has neither teeth nor sharp, cutting barbs on its fins like some of the catfish, its protection consisting solely of its thick skin. You might blind a cascudo with the light and grab it with your hand, for it won't touch any bait. You have to "break" a cascudo to kill it by forcing its head back until it snaps; otherwise it will remain alive throughout the night out of water.

A cascudo has to be cut open vertically along the backbone, from where you extract two very tasty, boneless fillets. These together add up to only about a quarter of the entire fish, but that's all you get out of it, the rest being carapace. For this reason a cascudo smaller than 25 cen-timeters (10 inches) isn't worth taking.

Daytime Fishing

Here you have the option of the line and hook or the gun, if the water is clear. Either way you must always take utmost care not to be seen, for fish like the dorado can spot us from close to 30 meters (nearly 100 feet). Your entire success may depend upon your ability to remain concealed. If there is movement of good-sized fish that don't take a hook, such as plankton-eating curimbatás (*Prochilodus* spp.) which can grow to about 5 kilos (more than 10 pounds) but are usually closer to 1 kilo or (2 pounds), the procedure is to climb a tree that has a thick-enough branch extending out over the fish's playground, from which you can shoot as straight down as possible. Here you wait, without moving, for the fish to resume their movements in the sunlight. Firing at anything deeper than 30 centimeters or (1 foot) is not advisable. After you've shot one, hurry down and scoop it out before it is swallowed by the current, or piranhas come up to dispute it. Should this happen, stay clear of the water, for these fish make no distinction.

My uncle Eric and I were hunting along the upper Estrelinha Creek in south Mato Grosso near Paraguay back in 1960, when we decided to shoot some fish for lunch in the brook, which was about 2 to 3 meters (6 to 10 feet) wide on the average. With my Hi-Standard .22 long rifle pistol—which I still own—it took us less than an hour to collect a large-enough bunch of fish for our meal.

Most fish other than cascudo or corimbatá take the hook, and any worm, larva, meat, or even fruit may do. Fruit are appreciated by fish ranging from common shiners up through medium-sized piraputanga or matrinchã (*Brycon* spp.) to large pacu or caranha.

In case no bigger fish are hitting your bait, you must perform the biblical "multiplication of bread" by tying your smallest "mosquito" hook to a short line and rod and catching tiny shiners near the edge— but always remain hidden behind some bush or trunk. Lambarís are a good universal bait for larger fish, and if nothing else you can always eat them fried, yourself. But keep a supply for the evening fishing, for after dark you will no longer catch shiners, but larger fish.

Evening Fishing
The darkening hours at the end of the day are the best time to begin trying for larger fish, so don't waste time during the day if there is no action. And never leave a baited line in the water on a rod merely leaning against something.

On a trip to explore the upper Cajazeiras River in 1973, I was fishing one evening from the boat tied to a branch, my heavy-duty rod with a large Mitchell spinning reel between my legs. Suddenly the tip of the rod sank into the murky water. The other end flipped up into the air, was dragged underwater, and was gone in an instant, before I could even try to grab it. And thus I had lost my equipment.

Should you be in a group, where larger fish become desirable, you can then once again bait the paternoster as a handline with some of the medium-sized fish and try for the big catfish like pintado (*Pseudoplatystoma* spp.) and others that can weigh right up past the 50-kilo (100-pound) mark.

FINDING THE WAY OUT

In the morning, if you expect to return to this camp, you can place an old stump on your campfire to keep it alive and smoldering while you are away (see chapter 16). Gather firewood first if it looks like rain. Better protect your campsite and wood stockpile with palm leaves, for when you go out into the field you should take your companion bag with you, complete with raincoat: You may find your lost way, or decide to camp the next evening at another site, fail to make your way back to the previous camp, catch rain while out, or what have you. But check the north on your compass in relation to the creek or river by your camp in case you opt to return here, so that you can locate the place again. And clear a good firebreak around your campfire to prevent a possible conflagration while you're out.

If you prepared a spear the previous evening you can now take it along in place of your walking stick, after shortening it somewhat, so that you have it handy and ready if you need it.

The Highest Point

Assuming that you are lost, that the creek by which you camped is too small for boat traffic, and that there is no human vestige around you, such as a trail along the banks, then your first objective this morning should be to find the highest point in the area and climb up to its top, so as to obtain a general view and get your bearings. In this case you will head upstream, in principle, because that is the direction toward higher ground, unless you can actually see a hill.

If on the other hand your objective is to find human habitation and traffic, you head downstream, because your creek will join or receive tributaries and grow into a river. It all depends where you came from and where you were heading in the first place. These are but basic instructions, to be adapted to each particular case.

Should you be the survivor of an airplane accident, the best plan, after water and food have been made available, is to stay withing hearing distance of the wreck if it is visible from the air, for a search will certainly take place. But don't count on it, because distances are sometimes immense.

Of course you may happen to be in the kind of terrain where there is no high point within walking distance. In the lower Amazon or the Swampland, for instance, identical scenery repeats itself time and again; you must stick to the compass to avoid a merry-go-round.

In the Swampland

The Pantanal or Chaco is, but for tourism, exclusively cattle-breeding country, with very large farms and few people. When you leave your camp here, you want to make sure your fire is completely out and there is a safe firebreak all around, for major grassfires are a potential danger as the wind picks up later on in the day—and once they get out of hand, they may burn for weeks.

To find the ranch headquarters you get up at daybreak and head in the direction the cattle are *coming from*. In the late afternoon you *follow* the cattle. Where there are cows, there are trails, which you will use for walking, so you want to pay attention to details: If the trail you are on receives or joins other trails and grows bigger, that means you are approaching something. It may be the farmyard or an outpost, which you can guess from a distance by converging fences. It may, however, be a salt trough, watering hole, or passage in the woods. Whatever the case, go and check where it leads to.

Should you be unlucky with the trail, try the next best thing: a fence. When you detect one, follow it visually until you see a gate—two thick, tall poles with a crossbeam or, on poorer farms, just two sturdy poles and three or four rods. Then head for this gate, because there you will come upon a trail for vehicles.

Signs of Human Presence

In the Swampland it is unlikely that you will find human footprints, because everybody in the region rides. But you should find horse tracks. How do you distinguish the hooves of equines from those of bovines? A hundred years ago any kid knew that, the way they know computers nowadays, but times have changed. The cow's hoof is split in the middle, consisting of two half-moons; the horse's hoof is solid around the front, with only an open triangle in the back.

Follow the direction the last horse took—or car or oxcart—if there are fresh marks. You will know which way the vehicle moved by the direction in which the grass has been bent, or by the tracks of the person who opened and shut the gate: The side of the gate where tracks appear on top of those of the vehicle is the direction taken. Use the opportunity and climb upon the gate for a good look around.

In the Savanna, Cerrado, or Sábana

Although visibility in the cerrado is not as open as in much of the Swampland, the vegetation is generally sparse enough for you to see where you are. This kind of country usually has hills or buttes—testemunhas—that you can climb to obtain a fuller view, or use as points of reference. Water in the central highlands is mostly indicated by the beautiful burití palm (*Mauritia flexuosa*) snaking down the depressions accompanying creeks with large, fan-shaped leaves and long bunches of "leather-woven" fruit. These are edible but require assistance from local people since preparation involves several steps such as precooking and stripping. Veredas, these palm woods are called.

In the cerrado you have more easily identifiable indicators of human habitation than in the Swampland, such as fruit trees and cultivated areas: bananas, papayas, oranges, any rectangle of even-colored green that may turn out to be manioc, sugarcane, or planted grass for forage, or any piece of color that doesn't seem to fit the whole. Also look for the same indicators as for the swamps: cattle, fences, gates, trails, and smoke.

Cuidado!

Straight lines indicate civilization, whereas the absence of geometry suggests Indians. Nothing wrong with that; the days of Indians falling upon lone travelers with stone axes are mostly history now. The modern Brazilian Indian warrior is a man with a degree in law carrying an executive case who knows the way to the forum—the court of law—as his ancestors knew their jungle trails. Still, the taking of hostages to press their claims is not uncommon. These captives are usually prospectors, lumber thieves, squatters, and fishermen invading what the natives consider their territory, often vaguely marked by the government.

The presence of women and children can be seen as a green traffic light—go ahead, it's okay—whereas seeing men only is a kind of yellow light: Better retreat into the shadows and take a good long look, searching for signs of both regular activity, such as work in the field or with animals, and irregular, like the presence of armed, watchful guys, or an airfield. On approaching an isolated human habitation in the depths of this vast South American hinterland you must nowadays always bear in mind the long tentacles of the drug trade. If you happen to come across a clandestine plantation or refinery, you will simply disappear. Period.

In the Forest or Floresta

Down under the double or even triple tree canopy it's hard to see anything beyond 30 meters (100 feet), with luck. The biggest difficulty in the forest is, as a matter of fact, to get a view and an idea of the general layout, as was the case when I got lost off the trans-Amazon highway. I have already mentioned that in order to reach the highest elevation you head upstream. The faster the water runs, the steeper the climb.

But even the top of the highest ridge you are able to reach may be covered in forest. And if there are no boulders to climb onto, you will have to ascend the tallest trees in order to get a more or less unimpeded view . . . which may again show you nothing but endless forest!

What should you look for, then?

The only signs of human presence you might detect under such circumstances are smoke in the air early in the morning and, if you are high enough above the surrounding jungle, perhaps a clearing. Any dent in the canopy should merit your scrutiny, for there is sure to be something interesting there, even if it turns out to be only a rocky outcrop. Mark its direction on your compass and go see. Of course, not all clearings are man-made.

And what to do if there's nothing at all visible? Easy now, for there's always something, once you know what to look for. In case no taller mountain is in sight, you can figure out by the topography and the vegetation where there is likely to be the largest river in the region: Trees are normally taller and greener along its banks because of alluvial buildup through floods, and its natural location will be down in the lowest valley. Shorter, lighter-colored, or even yellowish trees, on the other hand, suggest a swamp.

But while you are on top of a ridge, do not neglect to investigate the other side, too. Although it may be a momentary sacrifice to climb more than one tree in a row, this is the best option you have for the moment and you must explore it to the fullest. Take your time and be thorough. You have a rope in your companion bag to help you.

A River or Rio

Why should you now head for the largest river in the vicinity? Because if there's anyone living in the area, you will sooner or later come upon a fisherman's or hunter's trail along the riverbank or leading to it. Follow the most recent tracks and you are likely to come out on a dwelling or meet someone. The trail will tell you something about what kind of people to expect: Bare feet and no cut vegetation point to Indians, or perhaps caboclos if there are dogs' tracks as well. Shoes and cut branches mean Europeans. The presence of children's tracks is always reassuring.

Should you find no trail, then there is almost definitely nobody in the area. You will have to camp, fish, and collect fruit, then move on downriver until you come upon signs.

18

LOST WITHOUT YOUR COMPANION BAG

In the last chapter you saw how I got lost. It could happen to anyone, doing something as simple as nipping into the forest to go to the toilet and then being lured farther by something interesting. More commonly, it happens through an accident. There have been a number of cases in South America and elsewhere of a commercial flight or a small private plane suffering a failure, resulting in a crash landing in the middle of nowhere. It can also occur with a riverboat or seafaring vessel, delta wing, or paraglider.

Not long ago a small plane was discovered in the Serra do Mar cloud forest east of Curitiba, Paraná state, with the skeletons of its occupants inside, plus a suitcase full of money that, due to years of inflation, had lost all its value.

Somewhere south of Rio de Janeiro a plane is still missing in the same mountain chain with five geographer women aboard, after several years. As is a helicopter with a senior congressman, his wife, and companions.

At the end of winter, in August and early September, before the spring rains put out the last grass fires and clear the skies, there is often so much smoke in Mato Grosso that visibility can fall close to zero and air traffic has to be suspended.

But our wise general manager at Fazenda Bodoquena decided, back in 1967, that there were enough open pockets in the sky to permit us to fly to an outlying section. The pilot did not object. The moment we were airborne a cold front moved in from the south and the sky closed completely, allowing us to see neither land, water, nor the isolated peaks around us as we flew first west toward Corumbá, then northeast in the direction of the Rio Negro, without ever seeing a thing.

Fuel shortage forced the pilot to do the only thing possible: pray—and go down! As luck had it, we did not crash into a tree or hill; we leveled out just above the forest, and after locating the railroad tracks we even succeeded in finding our way home. The pilot hung the keys in the office and marched off to the railroad station, never looking back.

This is why you should always carry your companion bag fully packed and handy by your feet, even if your expected destination isn't the jungle.

FLIGHT TO DEATH

This episode happened many years ago but remains vivid in my memory as a dramatic example of what can happen when people are unprepared and have no idea what to do.

A small private plane with two occupants flew west from the interior of São Paulo and, without checking in at Corumbá and obtaining adequate information, or clearance, crossed the border into Bolivia on a clandestine mission to pick up some contraband at Santa Cruz.

Despite the railroad tracks connecting that city to Corumbá they managed to get lost, and with the approaching dark were forced to perform an emergency landing. The next day the plane could not take off with both men on board, so one stayed behind while the pilot tried to find out where they were. Seeing nothing, he made the incredible decision to turn back and land at the same place!

Why he ever did that, knowing that it was impossible to take off with two people on board, has remained a mystery. Anyway, he damaged the aircraft on landing, so there was no question of taking off anymore. And that was the end, just like that: One drank airplane gasoline, the other died of thirst.

What Should They Have Done?

Since something like this can happen to anyone, here is an excellent opportunity for us to explore the procedures to follow if you have no companion bag, just a pocketknife.

They went down in the semidesert, or caatinga. There are two such regions east of the Andes. One is a very large swath extending throughout the interior of the northeast of the continent from the middle of Bahia across Pernambuco, Paraíba, Rio Grande do Norte, Ceará, and Piauí to the south of Maranhão; the other, somewhat milder region, is found in the ancient limestone mountains west of the Swampland around Corumbá, from where it expands into Bolivia toward Santa Cruz de la Sierra.

Without going into all the preliminary mistakes these young fellows made, let's carry on from the point where they were grounded, the plane spoiled. This is what I would have done: During the hot hours of the day I would have rested in the shade of the aircraft in order to lose as little body moisture as possible, occupying my time preparing a sturdy walking stick with my pocketknife and searching the surrounding landscape with my eyes for woods or thickets or cliffs where lianas might grow. That's because in this part of the world we have a water-containing liana—cipó d'água—that is an important thirst mitigator on high and dry ground.

A Water-Containing Liana

The cipó d'água (*Amphilophium vouthieri*) has no special identification marks that I can think of; it's gray-brown in color with no thorns. You cut it down by your feet with a single blow, and immediately up above your head as well. Hold the severed piece upright, and in a moment it will start to drip clear, tasteless water. Should the sap be either milky or of a dark color and bitter taste, discard it; that's not the one.

The next piece you cut will have to be from another shoot of the plant, not the same one you've already cut, for the sap in this one has seeped up to the tips of its branches.

Another plant to look out for is wild bamboo, which—though its occurrence is unlikely in semi-arid country—also contains water in some of its partitions.

There being no cipó d'água in your vicinity you might, if necessary, chew some cactus for liquid. The mandacaru (*Cereus jamacaru*), which has a number of arms pointing skyward like the western American saguaro, is a common inhabitant of this kind of country.

In the northeastern Brazilian caatinga the lifesaving tree is the imbu—*Spondias tuberosa*. As its name implies, it has tubular roots that store water, while in summer it produces a delicious, sour-sweet fruit.

Sleep

One good thing to do during the hottest hours of the day is lie in the shade and read this manual or get some sleep while there are no mosquitoes, for at night you will need all your alertness to detect and pinpoint the rustling of some animal that you might be able to capture, such as an armadillo, or snooping bats that can sometimes be knocked down by wagging a thin, flexible rod like a fishing rod back and forth (similar to a windshield wiper) when you perceive their presence. These can be skinned and roasted like any other mammal.

You need to adapt yourself to the rhythm of wildlife around you, which in the semidesert becomes active at night.

Near evening, as it got cooler, I would have taken a walk in the immediate vicinity, looking for the mentioned lianas, fruit, and some erosion gully to follow at dawn, or even the same night if there was a moon. On the seat of the plane I would have left a message saying which way I was heading.

After midnight I would have gone outside to check whether any dew was forming on the wings, as it usually does on aluminium when there is a drop in temperature and no wind. If so I would have spent the predawn hours mopping the dew up with my shirt or handkerchief and twisting it into my mouth or some container. An airplane has a large surface, so it should gather enough dew to quelch your thirst and build a modest reserve for the next day.

As soon as there was enough light I'd have set out down that erosion gully—there are always such ravines, and following one downhill long enough is your best chance of coming upon some shaded cove holding water or at least moist sand where you might dig for water. When the rising sun became warm enough for me to start sweating it would have been time again to seek shade and rest for the day, aware that my first priority, until I'd come upon water, must be to preserve body moisture.

During the walk and the following rest period I would have kept my ears pricked for domestic sounds such as the braying of an ass, the bell of a goat, a call or the trepidation of a motor indicative of a human habitation. And I'd have kept my eyes open for trails, tracks, fences, fruit. And animals: lizards (lagartos), snakes (easy to kill and skin, and when roasted they taste similar to eels), and tortoises and armadillos, both of which can be cooked in their shells. And bees, for honey (to be stolen after dark, mind you!). Nothing but succulent fruit must be eaten, however, until water has been assured.

Every track found should be identified, which is easier in the morning, before there is any wind. An increase in tracks and animal trails suggests there's water nearby. Such water may not be in this particular gully, so don't go on without first investigating the surroundings to find out where the trails lead to.

Once water has been found and food becomes the first priority, the best place to ambush game will be right there by the drinking hole. Tracks in the sand will show you where animals drink.

Hunting for Survival

The first thing to remember in preparing to wait for game is not to urinate, spit, smoke, or evacuate anywhere nearby, nor bathe where the animals drink. Nor should you peel or sharpen your freshly cut lance, or leave it on the ground. The second consideration is that you must position yourself at least 2 meters (6 feet) above the approach to the water, either in a tree or upon a tall rock where you don't show an outline against the sky. Third, remain absolutely still—no slapping mosquitoes or ants, changing position, or the like. So you must make yourself as comfortable as possible right at the beginning, perhaps padding your seat with grass, then sit quiet.

Assuming that you don't have a gun, you will have to wait for a species that you are able to outrun and capture. The easiest of these would be a land tortoise, which requires no effort at all, or a snake, which must be approached carefully and hit behind the head with three or four well-aimed blows of the walking stick. Other slow animals are armadillos and the small anteater—tamanduá mirim (*Tamandua tetradactyla*)—though only in extreme desperation would I even consider summoning the courage to sacrifice this meek creature, which is already so persecuted by the big felines and hit by automobiles. Opossums and porcupines are also rather slow.

Wild Animal Tracks and Droppings

Perhaps this is the best moment for us to become familiar with the footprints and feces of the principal animals in the jungle, so as to know what we might encounter. Chapter 7 has more information on many of these beasts.

Tracks of the giant anteater are the most interesting, showing how the animal walks on the back of its hands in order to save its large claws for opening termite hives. Thus superstition has it that the mysterious "bottlefoot" is always accompanied by a child (its hind feet).

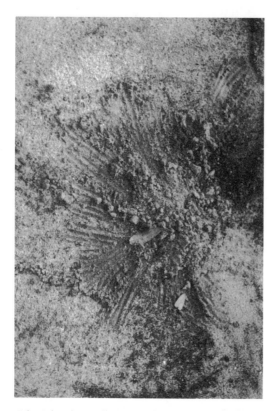

Like a dog, this small anteater (Tamandua tetradactyla) *was deciding where to defecate, but similar to a feline it scratches up dirt to cover its feces.*

One mysterious being that the superstitious are awed by is the bottlefoot—pé-de-garrafa—which leaves either a ball-shaped imprint or something turned backward, and is always accompanied by what look like a child's tracks. These are the marks of the giant anteater, or tamanduá bandeira, which saves its powerful claws for breaking open termite hives by walking with them turned up and inward, stepping on the backs of its hands, while the child's tracks are of its feet.

We have several three-toed animals, the largest of which is the tapir, or anta, whose droppings are like a donkey's or a yearling foal's. Next in size is the rhea—ema (*Rhea americana*)—always out in the open savanna where it outruns any other animal. Then we have the world's largest rodent, the capybara—capivara (*Hydrochoerus hydrochoeris*)—usually associated with water, but sometimes found right up on top of mountain ridges where there isn't even a spring. Its feces look like dates, gradually turning black under the sun. Next comes the paca (*Agouti paca*) and the agouti—cutia (*Dasyprocta* spp.)—whose feces are like a small deer's, in decreasing order of size. The armadillo's, or tatu's, imprints usually show just three of its five toes, bent outward, used mostly for digging.

Another interesting set of tracks are the mane wolf's—lobo guará—which look like those of a large dog, but it is the spacing between the tracks that calls your attention: They're nearly twice as long as a German shepherd's, because of this beautiful animal's extraordinarily long legs. Its droppings contain fruit seeds and residue. Smaller dog's

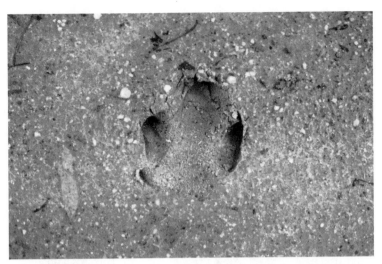

Very similar to this tapir's footprint—which shows the small, fourth (fetlock) toe that doesn't usually appear—are, in descending order of size, the capybara's, paca's, and agouti's. Armadillo's toes, used for digging, are bent inward or outward.

tracks, about the size of a dachshund's, belong to our two foxes, the gray lobinho (Mato Grosso) or cachorro-do-mato (*Cerdocyon thous*) and the vinegar-colored cachorro-vinagre (*Speothos venaticus*). All three are Canidae, whose footprints show the claws.

Felines' tracks, on the other hand, don't show claw marks, as these are retractile. Their hands are somewhat larger and rounder than their feet: An adult jaguar's are about the size of a man's fist, followed by the puma's matching our largest dogs', then the ocelot's—jaguatirica (*Felis pardalis*)—and smaller jaguarundis and

The mane wolf's tracks are distinct from a large dog's because of the distance between footsteps, due to its long legs.

The puma, like all felines, retracts its claws when walking.

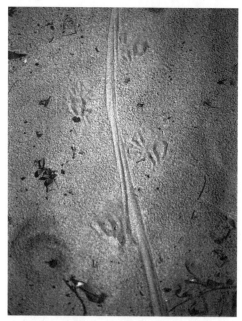

A teju lizard's (Tupinambis nigropunctatus) spoor, like that of its larger cousin, the alligator, is usually straighter than a snake's, and you can see the footprints.

wildcats. Their excrement is rarely seen since felines scratch up dirt to cover it. But a concentrically scratched area emitting a strong, sharp smell is suggestive.

The footprints of saurians—from alligators in decreasing order to camaleão (*Iguana iguana*), víbora (*Dracaena paraguayensis*), teiú (*Tupinambis teguixin*), and other, smaller sand lizards and geckos—are easily recognizable by their long fingers and the furrow made by the tail between their tracks.

Then there are three sets of webbed mammal's tracks, all of them found near water, belonging to the giant otter or ariranha (*Pteronura brasiliensis*), and the common otter or lontra (*Lutra platensis*); the coypu or ratão do banhado (*Myocastor coypus*); and the raccoon or mão pelada (*Procyon cancrivorus*), whose prints are disproportionately large in relation to the animal's size.

Long, narrow tracks without a web belong to the irara (*Tayra barbara*), which looks very much like an otter and loves honey; the coatí; the porcupine—ouriço (*Coendu prehensilis* and C. *villosus*).

That leaves the split-hooved deer and peccaries, beginning with the large Swampland cervo (*Blastocerus dichotomus*)—droppings look like those of elk and the larger deer of temperate zones—followed by the white-tailed veado campeiro (*Ozotocerus bezoarticus*) of the open fields and savannas; the forest deer, or veado mateiro (*Mazama americana*); and the scrub deer or veado catingueiro (*Mazama simplicicornis*). The feces of all are similar to a hare's. The hooves of the peccaries are more rounded than those of deer, and always found in larger numbers, as these pigs live in herds and often follow well-marked trails.

And this ought to suffice to give the layman a foundation concerning animal signs.

Jim Corbett, who shot India's most infamous tigress, noted in his fascinating narrative *Man-Eaters of Kumaon* that as a boy he used to walk a trail across the jungle near evening dragging a branch to erase the day's tracks from the sand, so that next morning he could see which animals had crossed during the night. That is a practice I have also adopted, with commendable results.

Furthermore, Jim said that he was able to tell which way a snake had crossed by the direction in which the sand grains had been tumbled and smoothed, perceptible by their reflection of the sun. This I have not had an opportunity to duplicate, though it makes sense.

Ants, too, make trails that can fool you at first, some nearly the width of a large anaconda's.

Wild Fruit

The treasure in edible fruit that the tropical South American jungle has to offer the attentive walker never ceases to amaze me—an avid consumer since my earliest years.

To get a general idea, I have drawn up a list of no fewer than 130 species of fruiting trees, shrubs, vines, and cacti. The numbers are more or less evenly distributed throughout the various botanical regions—the Swampland and scrub savannas, semi-arid caatinga, coastal cloud forests, and Amazon basin rain forests—so that there are always some forty to sixty species present in each, since many overlap.

That's what I have here before me. There are sure to be a good many more, as I possess only scattered information on native fruit up in the tepuys or cliff mountains of Roraima, the Pakaraima and Tumuc Humac, and the headwaters of the Rio Negro, all north of the equator, where even the rainy season differs somewhat from that in the rest of the basin.

Ninety-three of these fruits ripen in summer (December, January, and February), followed by forty-three in spring (September, October, and November) plus an equal twenty-four for autumn (March, April, and May) and for winter (June, July, and August). In the Tropics we don't have a winter interval, as occurs in temperate zones.

This is no more than an approximation, however, for not only will the same plant bloom and give fruit at slightly different times in different altitudes and climatic conditions, but there are also prone to be yearly seasonal advancements or delays, plus temporões—rare-ripe fruits—more or less out of season.

The Amazon basin is a gigantic region, encompassing close to half of the South American continent and measuring in the vicinity of 3,000 by 2,700 kilometers (1,875 by 1,690 miles) inside Brazil alone. This world contains all kinds of formations, including tidal floodplains and rising through rain forests and savannas right up to 3,000-meter (10,000-foot) altitude cloud vegetation, as well as the savannas, or cerrados, stretching some 2,500 kilometers (more than 1,500 miles) from central Maranhão state to the Swampland . . . How can I generalize?

So no matter where you may find yourself—in rain or cloud forest, savanna, the Swampland, or semi-arid caatinga—native fruit will constitute an important complement to your survival diet.

By paying attention to birds and monkeys and bright colors in trees and shrubs and on the ground underneath, you will never have to walk long before happening upon some edible fruit or other. If the fauna eat them, they're okay. Should there be no visible sign, however, then be careful: Milky, latex-containing fruit and plants are to be avoided, along with very small berries lacking a juicy, sweetish pulp.

Palm nuts give you two edible areas: the outside and the inside of the kernel, which must be broken open, but has the advantage of remaining edible after the season has passed.

But this list of mine will serve you no purpose. If the subject interests you, I recommend Dr. Harry Lorenzi's excellent two-volume work, *Árvores Brasileiras*, wherein you will find each arboreal species fully illustrated—the tree, a branch, the fruit, the seed, the bark, and the wood—with all the desirable information. And on the Swampland in particular—though also valid for the savannas—Drs. Arnildo and Vali Pott's *Plantas do Pantanal* is not as fully illustrated but contains smaller shrubs and vines as well (see appendix).

How to Find and Prepare

I am therefore going to discuss only those fruits that are either difficult to spot or else require some preliminary preparation before eating.

In low-lying, riverside forests you will find a small, thin, but extremely prickly palm, the **tucum** (*Bactris* spp.) which forms extensive and practically impenetrable thickets. The Indians—as well as you, if necessary—extract the fibers for their very resistant bowstrings from the leaves: You fold the tip of the leaf back and pass your fingernail over it (as you'd do on a sheet of paper you wished to detach a piece from), then pull down parallel to the leaf, and you have the fibers, to twist. And from the stem the Indian polishes his bow.

In summer and autumn this palm produces a small bunch of grape-sized coconuts that you can eat directly, since their husks are soft enough to break with your teeth. Like coconuts, they are edible even if unripe.

Another interesting fruit often found along rivers—but it also occurs elsewhere, even in the semi-arid caatinga—is the genipap, or **jenipapo** (*Genipa americana*). This tree has a light trunk and large, lance-shaped leaves, producing a tennis-ball-sized fruit that, when ripe, has a dull yellowish brown color in spring and summer when it becomes soft to the touch, its pulp a light orange with a strong peppery taste when eaten fresh. This can be made milder by quartering the fruit and coating with sugar, then allowing it to "sleep" overnight.

In the sandy areas of the Swampland and savannas you will come upon a tree whose smooth, gently curving branches beginning close to the ground are an invitation to climb it. Its fruits, ripe in summer, are about the size of the genipap (above) and a dirty green on the outside. This is the **pequi** (*Caryocar brasiliense*). By cutting it open, however, you come upon one to four large seeds involved in coral pulp—this is the edible part. You must be careful because it's prickly under the pulp, for which reason it is normally eaten cooked in rice or with chicken or meat, and you will do well to scrape the pulp of the first one with a knife to see at what depth the black thorns are located.

The same area also breeds islands of an aggressive-looking bromelia, **caraguatá** (*Bromelia balansae*), under the protection of whose swordlike, thorny leaves many small animals have their homes. From summer through winter it produces easily visible bunches of bright yellow, peach-sized fruit. You will first have to put on your gloves and carefully cut your way to the fruit with your pruning shears, always looking out for snakes. By quartering the fruit with your knife you can eat a bite or two raw; it tastes like extremely sharp pineapple. You cannot eat much more because it may cause the tongue and gums to bleed, especially if yours are as sensitive as mine. But by cooking it in water with sugar or rapadura it becomes edible, and the resulting syrup you must save in a bottle, because, taken in teaspoonfuls, it is one of the best known medicines for sore throat.

The **mangaba** (*Hancornia speciosa*) is slightly smaller, of a more opaque yellow, and often dotted with brown or russet spots. It can be eaten raw but only when completely ripe—that is, when it drops by itself. Before that it contains some white "milk" that is laxative. The mangaba can also be cooked.

In the Amazon forest there are some fruits that cannot be picked off the tree: You harvest them on the ground. One is the Brazil nut (*Bertholletia excelsa*), for the obvious reason that no one can climb this giant of the forest, which stands among the world's largest. As has been mentioned elsewhere, you don't want to loiter under a **castanheira** in the summer, for the kilo-heavy fruit pods come crashing down like cannonballs. Guided by the impact, you go pick one up and then execute a hasty retreat out from under the tree's wide umbrella. The asbestoslike pod is unbreakable. It must be either hacked open with a machete or heavy knife, as the nut pickers do, or else sawed open with your foldable saw. The fresh nuts are milky, like fresh *Araucaria* pine nuts in the south, though the two trees are completely unrelated. They can be eaten either raw or cooked.

Another fruit native to the Amazon that you don't pick off the tree, though for a different reason, is the **cupuaçu** (*Theobroma grandiflorum*), a large, brown, cylindrical fruit that falls by itself when ripe and emits a strong smell to help you find it. If prematurely harvested from the tree it simply spoils. You hold it upright and cut off the top, like a coconut. Inside, the pulp-lined seeds swim in juice. To this you can add manioc flour, oats, or bread, and eat it with your spoon. One single fruit makes a delicious and satisfying meal.

There is also a fruit in the eastern Amazon called pepino-do-mato (*Ambelania acida*) because it looks like a cucumber with a ridged, dirty yellow skin. This you cut open lengthwise and scrape off the milky latex before eating.

In the southern region we have the Paraná pine—**pinheiro do Paraná** (*Araucaria angustifolia*)—whose pod, likewise impossible to harvest from the tree due to height, looks like a pineapple, which is where *Ananas comosus* probably got its common name from in the first place. This pod does not drop whole, but rather begins to break open in April while remaining in place, helped by wind, gravity, and birds. The shiny, yellowish brown fruits look like little bombs, and can be eaten raw, roasted, or cooked. Pinhão, they are called. Wash both the fruit and your hands before eating, because of hantavirus (see chapter 9).

Annonaceae and Myrtaceae
These are the two largest families of native fruit trees and shrubs in tropical South America, the former with twenty species, including soursop and sweetsop, and the latter with forty species, including guava. Important to know here is that the Annonaceae are laxative and should therefore be consumed with moderation—unless a laxative is desirable—whereas Myrtaceae have the opposite effect, especially when the seeds of guava and jabuticaba (*Myrciaria cauliflora*) are swallowed.

Eating After Starving
Since I'm talking about survival, it is opportune here to alert you to the danger of overeating after being deprived of food for several days: It can kill you more promptly than starvation! If for some reason you've been unable to take in any food at all for several days, once you do come upon edibles—such as fruit—these must be properly ripe, for you cannot risk an intestinal infection in your debilitated state. Also, ingestion must begin with very small amounts—a handful at the most—at hourly intervals, gradually increasing the amount, but without decreasing the interval, as long as you don't feel any adverse effects.

19

DEALING WITH **I**NJURIES

You may be able to foresee ninety-nine contingencies," my boss on the opening trans–Amazon highway used to warn, "but fate keeps a one hundredth up its sleeve that you cannot foresee!"

After a while you may think yourself secure enough to do without some of the recommended equipment. But that is an intermediary illusion, similar to that of the young driver who may become momentarily overconfident before new experiences convince him to settle for a constant, sober routine of permanently alert, defensive driving.

It's also an illusion subject to being shattered in a matter of seconds. One moment everything is okay; the next you're down, stuck in mud, thorns, a hole, driftwood, or boulders and requiring—with luck—some light medication. That was my case when I first wrote this chapter on the banks of the Rio Claro below Chapada dos Guimarães in Mato Grosso.

While climbing down a very steep bank of a creek one morning I lost my foothold as some silt piled up by a past flood gave way. I instinctively stretched out my other leg and sank deep into soft mud across the creek. No problem there. But what had held the silt in place emerged as a sturdy vine with grappling claws at intervals, which closed around my lower leg and with the jerk dug in deep and tore furrows across like eagle's talons.

What should you do in a situation like this?

Preferably nothing at all, if you can afford to stop and rest. Humans have a built-in computer, called the immune system, that is programmed to take care of injuries and ailments, and it generally does so very competently when we allow it to go about its job without our "wiser" interference.

The fact that there are thousands of medicines on the market does not mean that each time our health is somehow affected we've got to rush and gobble down, smear on, or inject some kind of chemical product—just like we are not obliged to take a car or bus each time we go out simply because the streets are full of them.

On the contrary: The more we interfere through medication, the greater the chances that our immune system may just close down shop and go out of business . . . And no longer be there when we need it!

When the wound is in your leg, like mine, the next best thing to do is give it a rest, for it is unlikely to heal under the stress and pull of the trail, with salty sweat running into it.

In the minor accident described above, I washed my leg and shoe—though the one that had sunk into the mud, not the injured one! This clawed leg I examined, and saw that there was no dirt in the wounds that were already covered in blood and serum, thus no need to do any disinfecting; for that was what the blood and serum were already doing.

You should avoid, whenever possible, washing out fresh wounds, be it with water—a contaminant—alcohol, iodine, mercury, or what have you, all of which interfere with the body's own curing job, to which we should give first precedence. When there is dirt in a wound, its removal should always be first attempted dry, with clean tweezers, needle, or cotonets. If that won't do, then try cotton or a clean handkerchief moistened with saliva. When as a last resort water must be used, then—provided it is clean—let it run, without rubbing, as in the rapids of a river or under a tap. On the other hand, no dirt should be left inside a wound or under the skin, such as a thorn or splinter, for it will surely start a local infection.

Neither should a wound be dried by hand or tied up, unless such protection is absolutely indispensable, such as when you must continue your walk across underbrush or tall grass, or there are maggot and other flies present. Whenever possible, leave the wound open to dry by itself. We are here talking of relatively shallow injuries, it must be remembered.

Later in the day, if there are still wet or festering areas in your wound, you can give these a dusting of dry sulfa powder, provided you are not allergic to this product. It is sold in the Amazon in finger-sized cylinders called Anaseptil em pó and constitutes one of my indispensable first-aid ingredients. It dries up the wound and helps form a protective crust.

Only at night, when you are about to retire, should a dry bandage be applied. Wrap it around plenty of times so as to pad the wound well and avoid friction. In the morning you may find, upon unwrapping the bandage, that the last turn or two have become glued to the wound. Do not pull, for you will then tear off part of the protective crust, thus retarding the healing, besides causing yourself unnecessary discomfort. Moisten the bandage with water from the outside on the spot where it sticks until the crust has absorbed enough moisture to release its hold. In case there is still some liquid festering, give it another dusting with sulfa. That's what I did that day of the accident, for in midafternoon I still had two wet spots. If, on the other hand, the area of your injury begins to grow red, remove the sulfa; this may be a sign of allergy.

Then place a pad with white, refreshing hipoglós (vitamins A and D) salve over the wound and attach it with adhesive tape or a flexible bandage. This will keep the wound crust elastic enough not to crack if you must continue walking, besides its healing and insect-repellent qualities.

In order to take a shower it's best to tie a plastic bag above the injury with adhesive tape so as to keep it dry and free of soap.

The most aggressive thorn in the savanna is that of the caraguatá (*Bromelia balansae*), whose fruit—yellow when ripe— is incidentally one of the best medicines for throat ailments (see chapter 18). The claws on its leaves are bent back and forth, so that if they don't get you one way they get you the other—even after the leaf is dead. Kadiweu Indians inhabiting the foothills of Serra da Bodoquena east of the Brazilian Swampland use them to imprint designs on their pottery. They are not poisonous, however, causing no consequences other than drawing blood and spoiling clothes.

The thorns of Bromelia balansae *are the most aggressive, though nonpoisonous; if they don't hook you one way, they hook you the other. But the syrup from its fruit is the best medicine for sore throat.*

Blood Loss or Perda de Sangue

We've become so accustomed to seeing medics begin by attaching a drip to the wounded that a reminder of the real importance of minor blood loss may be in order.

Patients with deep, profusely bleeding wounds such as some victims of car crashes no doubt need drips. But for the comparatively superficial injuries we are discussing in this chapter—cuts, scratches, excoriations, and bites—where blood loss rarely amounts to much, we should not give it a second thought. Bear in mind that the adult woman regularly loses blood every month in her menstrual cycle and still outlives men on the average. As a matter of fact some blood loss—which in the past used to be a medical prescription for a number of ailments—is a stimulation to blood production and renewal.

Why am I saying this? Because the psychological affliction of seeing your blood spilling out may cause much more damage—if you're not accustomed to it—than its minor physical loss. Of course a hemophiliac or diabetic must take his special precautions and specific medicines.

A Broken or Twisted Limb

This kind of injury can easily happen, as the result of a fall or a misstep into a crack or hole, severely jeopardizing your walk. What you have to do is immobilize the limb. For this purpose you need a few sticks—of which there is no shortage in the jungle—plus some rope, which you carry in your companion bag. With the foldable saw you cut the sticks to the size needed. Should round sticks become uncomfortable under the pressure of the rope tied around them, you can trim the inner surface with your machete or hunting knife so as to flatten it. After this it is a matter of rest.

A Cracked Rib or Two

Here is another common sort of injury. It requires exclusively rest. Back in the mid-1960s I was searching for stray cattle in a hilly, densely overgrown kind of savanna called cerradão in the region of the Rio Perdido, near the southern tip of Serra da Bodoquena, Mato Grosso do Sul, when my left stirrup leather snapped. I automatically pressed my leg against the rather skittish mare's flank. She sped forward, jumped over a fallen trunk just under a low branch that swept me off her back, and I fell sideways onto the trunk. Luckily. For if I had fallen on my back I might have injured my spine very seriously.

I got myself up, slow motion, while the sharp needle stabs indicated I had one or two cracked ribs. The mare having disappeared, it took me some four hours' slow and careful walk to get back to the farm. There I let myself down in an easy chair for a nap, and that was a mistake: When I tried to get up—my body having meanwhile cooled—the intense pain forced me to get out of the chair sideways, onto my knees, and then slowly up, holding on to things. During the next week I had to do the indispensable tasks at a sloth's speed, but around the tenth day I was practically all right . . . though I still had to avoid making any effort for the rest of the month.

A Cracked Elbow

I was riding my motorcycle north across mountainous Ecuador when in the vicinity of Cayambe I approached an Indian couple driving two herds of pigs, each on one side of the road. But as I was about to pass, the woman decided on a whim to shift her pigs across to the man's side . . . I braked and crashed onto the little black stones Ecuadorian roads are paved with, the motorcycle on top of me. The pig herders moved on, not looking back. People peered from doorways and stared out of a passing bus, but nobody gave a hand. Then a pickup came to a halt and the gentleman immediately put his peons to work loading my bike onto his vehicle, gathering my things, seating me inside, and in an instant we were off to Cayambe, where I was left in the care of some missionaries. The next morning I was driven in to a hospital in Quito, where the X ray revealed a cracked elbow.

I explained to the friendly doctor that I was traveling with little money and could ill afford to rest at a hotel, while I did not wish to lean on this missionary family any longer than minimally necessary. The doctor thought for a moment, then asked me to hold my arm in the position I would need it on the motorcycle. Thus it was immobilized in a cast. Back in Cayambe I had the bike basically repaired, and since my other injuries did not impede indispensable movements, I was able to proceed with my trip, albeit rather precariously, that same afternoon.

Insects in the Eye, Ear, or Nose

It's easy to deal with insects in the nose: You can simply blow it energetically, closing the other nostril with your finger. But the eye and ear require great care. Captain John Speke, who was the first to correctly identify the source of the Nile River, told of his trip that while camping on the island of Ubwari in Lake Tanganyika, a small, black beetle entered his ear, causing him distress to the point where he attempted to dig it out with his pocketknife. He thereby injured his inner ear, leading to inflammation and suppuration resulting in a most painful tumor that made him nearly deaf and ended up opening a passage between his ear and nose, so that whenever he blew his nose his ear whistled embarrassingly. Six months later there were still bits of beetle coming out in the wax.

An insect in the ear must either be allowed time to come out on its own—turn the ear up, not down—or carefully tweezed out by somebody else. If you are alone, any caboclo woman is your next best bet, since she usually has experience with her children. Do not try this yourself if you cannot see.

With an insect in your eye you must under no circumstances rub, for that would irritate the eye and aggravate the condition. The best procedure is to dip your head in clean water, preferably the running water of a creek, open your eye wide, and with your fingers carefully turn back the eyelids by holding on to the lashes. Shake your head a little if necessary. Beware of small fish and things in the water. That should do the trick. When you are not near water, use your mirror, fold back the lids, and remove the intruder with a saliva-moistened cotonet or a match with a bit of cotton wrapped to the tip; or else wash it out with drops of Lavolho or any clean water, by means of a dropper, if it is in the lower fold. This must be done promptly, before irritation sets in and makes it difficult to see. Then rest the eye by covering with gauze or cotton or sunglasses.

Conclusion: Where and How to Walk in the Jungle

JUNGLE "RULES AND REGULATIONS"

Someone coming for the first time out of roadless jungles to a traffic-oriented metropolis is sure to be absolutely bewildered by what may seem endless confusion and danger from all sides, until he begins to grasp the rules and regulations of city life, the rhythm it moves by.

The same happens to the city dweller upon his first contact with the jungle, until it dawns on him that there must be a system here that needs to be grasped and followed.

And that is your challenge: to understand the jungle, for then it will appear much less agressive to you. Since this guidebook is called *Walking the Jungle*, let's talk about that.

A country driver unaccustomed to a large city's one-way streets is sure to become frustrated by the lengthy roundabout maneuvers he will be obliged to perform, at times, in order to get his car to a place he can see just a few hundred meters (yards) away in a straight line.

In the jungle it's the same: You cannot follow a straight line. Where, then, do you walk in the jungle?

WHERE TO WALK

Riverbanks, Beira-Rio, or Orilla de Rio

Riversides offer a promising place to walk, for if there are any people living in the area, the river will be their main lifeline, along which they fish and hunt; closer to their home, the women wash clothes, collect water, and bathe. And if the river is navigable there is sure to be a canoe you may hire. So you are likely to end up coming upon a more or less well-used and walkable trail along at least one side of the river.

235

Mountain Ridges, Espinhaços, or Cordilleras

These are the next best places to walk, where you may also find hunter's trails. One reason people walk along the crests of elevations is comfort, as any American or Canadian walking the long Appalachian or Rocky Mountain trails will tell you. You are stepping on more or less flat and even ground, as opposed to the slopes where your feet are almost constantly inclined, which—although healthier for the feet than stepping only on flat, paved streets—can become stressful to the ankles after some hours and deform your shoes when wet. Besides, the ridge is better ventilated, drier, and you can see and hear farther to obtain a better idea of your surroundings and whereabouts, the layout of the terrain, the vegetation, and so forth, while also gaining an altogether greater sense of freedom. You are not oppressed under the enclosing forest, if this sort of claustrophobic sensation bothers you. It is also easier to establish a landmark—tree, cliff, rock, or hill—that you either want to reach or guide yourself by. Down under that's impossible; you have only the river.

Mesa Mountains, Testemunhas, Chapadas, or Mesetas

In the case of abrupt terrain such as crags and precipitous formations with high, vertical cliffs rising several hundred meters—including the tepuys along Brazil's border with the Guianas and Venezuela near Angel Falls, and the edges of most plateaus and table mountains like Chapada Diamantina in Bahia and Chapada dos Guimarães in Mato Grosso—it is along the base of the cliff, where the ancient vertical wall joins the slanting talud gradually building up from falling matter, that you are likely to find an easy-to-follow game trail. Most of the animals have their dwellings here and feel less exposed than up on the windy and mostly bare savannas, grasslands, or marshes that usually top these formations.

For the explorer, too, this is an interesting and exciting environment, not only because of the more intense animal and vegetable life, but also in view of the potential for discovering fossils, minerals, and other curiosities in the cozy lap of these lime or sandstone walls, often ancient seafloors.

The Dangers in Cliff Climbing

In such terrain you are likely sooner or later to be faced with the temptation or the need to climb up or down one of these cliff walls.

Here the most important thing to look out for is the kind of rock you are to support yourself on, avoiding all loose rubble, flaked, or layered material coming apart. Such formations are in the process of decomposition and collapse, in which you can easily become an incidental victim.

I was climbing the wall of a cauldron at the foot of Serra da Bodoquena's wild, west-facing cliff inside a natural "chimney" that seemed to facilitate my progress when, some 50 meters (150 feet) up, I felt with a shock that the rock was coming loose under my feet and dropping away into the void. I had inattentively climbed into an outcrop of loose shale . . . even if I survived a fall here, no one would find me.

At such moments we must face the danger as a challenge that we were given a brain to cope with. My first, instinctive reaction was to stem both elbows and knees against the side walls of the chimney in order to take the weight off my feet. Then, craning my neck, I peeped outside the well I was in, searching for something I might hold on to.

There grew a shrub from the rock, just out of reach. Slow as a sloth I worked myself into an oblique position in relation to the funnel, which, by pressing my head against the wall, allowed me to swing one arm out over the edge toward the thumb-thick stem of the bush. This I managed to reach after several minor readjustments in my precarious position. Fortunately it was well enough rooted to support me as I swung, slow motion, out of that death trap.

I had not stopped to think that that chimney, which at first facilitated my climbing, had actually been formed by decomposing rock. When I am physically tired out I tend not to think enough.

Tall Forest Versus Scrub, Capoeira, or Breña

A third guide to walkable ground is the height of the vegetation. Tall forest means the sunlight is disputed high above the ground, so that down on the floor it is fairly dark, with little vegetation, and therefore quite comfortable to walk.

Low growth, on the other hand, such as you find along the fringes of forests, in swamps, and in various scrub formations, means the sun has good penetration and is savagely disputed right from the relatively poor ground up, each plant for itself and bristling its weapons: thorns, poisons, snares. Here you find no trails except for those of short-legged animals beneath the thicket. There will also be many more snakes since they are better protected from aerial predators and such inveterate field roamers as emu, or ema (*Rhea americana*), and seriema (*Cariama cristata*), and there are more mice and frogs to eat. If man is present there will be a well-cleared path.

If not, it's best to give this kind of formation a wide berth since you are neither equipped nor meant to penetrate it. You cannot see what is down near your feet nor up in the shrubbery at elbow level.

Still, you may have to, for some reason. Then it is a must to go about the business with care and patience, raising your feet high and treading down the brush so that you can see where you step, and cutting your way free with your garden shears. Any attempt to hack through with a machete is likely to result in at least an injured wrist from the hundreds of vines crisscrossing your path—many of them thorny—a potential snake or spider attack, a dozen wasp stings, a hundred ant bites, one to two thousand ticks climbing all over you, your exposed skin tattooed, checkered, and cut up by thorns, plus a generalized allergic reaction . . . Boots or leggings are a must here.

An Allergic Reaction

My family and I were camping on the north coast of the state of São Paulo between Caraguatatuba and Ubatuba when, at dusk one evening while walking along a dirt road in shorts, I had to go to the toilet and stepped into the woods. As I crossed a knee-tall kind of grass growing in the shade my legs began to burn intensely, forcing me to beat a hasty retreat out of there. It was only while scrubbing with water and soap later on that the strong reaction began to let up.

At the time it was too dark to see whether that kind of grass was in itself the cause of the allergy, or if there was perhaps some poison ivy or even caterpillars in there that I failed to spot in the penumbra. I never went back to the place, so I was not able to determine the cause. But one thing is certain: To enter the tropical jungle you must always be fully dressed, in long pants, shoes, and long-sleeved shirt.

The Swampland

During the dry months—late July to early October—walking is extremely easy because of myriad cattle trails everywhere. What you have to establish when leaving the ranch or inn where you are staying, by means of your pocket compass or the position of the sun, is which way is back. This is especially important because of the repetitive nature of the landscape.

The water level in the Swampland changes constantly, as well as from one year to the next. I have driven and walked in dust and waded across water in the same place and month. Thus stick to the cattle paths, for if you go dead by the compass you may find your way blocked by water. Often there is so much water everywhere that you have to ride a horse.

HOW TO WALK

I have already discussed the choice of clothes and footwear, and how to keep the latter greased. Let's now look at the act of walking in itself. In my case I walk slowly, choosing the ground with care for every step. As the terrain becomes steeper I automatically shorten my stride, but keep on going all the while as long as nothing of interest appears. That isn't very long at all, though, because the more I study the jungle, the greater the number of things that excite my interest along the trail.

Because of a hearing deficiency I am not fond of large parties. But when I happen to find myself in a group of hikers, my favorite position is bringing up the rear. Here I pick up the stragglers as they fall behind and together we look at things calmly, at our own pace. Those dropping to the rear are pleased to have the attention, and so are the usually younger, more dynamic guides and walkers up ahead who'd rather pay attention to their watches than to nature around. My explanations back there don't interfere with the guide's up front, and he doesn't have to worry about stragglers, so everybody gets something out of it.

Gradually my little community at the tail end grows larger as the hours tick by, especially after lunch break, to the point where sometimes almost everybody ends up joining us, including the guides, when they are humble enough to learn a thing or two.

Our caboclo of the hinterland, on the other hand, throws his upper body with the load on his back forward to the limit of his balance while pushing, so to speak, with short, fast steps, as if running after the trunk about to fall. In this posture he is able to move nonstop for many hours.

This book focuses on the hazards of the jungle, perhaps to the extent that readers may wonder if I am trying to keep them away. Nothing could be farther from the truth. The jungle's beauty—its birds and animals, its plants and its people—are experiences not to be missed. But I believe an enjoyable trip is one well planned, and in planning there is no place for optimism. Rather, one ought always to go more by Murphy's Law: Assume that whatever can happen, will. Save your optimism for the end of a successful trip, as a result of cool forethought and careful preparation.

Thus, while this is a guide to what can go wrong in the jungle, most of the time things go right when you abide by the above paragraphs, so often reiterated and illustrated in firsthand experiences throughout this book. Once you are properly prepared, the appeal of the plants, animals, and people of the jungle make it a place you will want to return to many times. And each time you will feel more at home.

A TRIBUTE TO SILLINESS

In closing, I would like to pay homage to something people normally try to conceal or feel embarassed about. It is thanks much more to silliness (*burrice* or *asneria*) than to any pockets of intelligence in my mind that I owe many of the brief stories of experiences narrated throughout this book. To be quite sincere, I don't remember most of the events that ran smoothly and according to plan. There was no impact to register them. The foolish things I've done, on the other hand, remain vividly imprinted in my memory, because they were followed by a psychological reaction: shame, regret, self-recrimination. And so here they are, fresh and clear as if they'd just happened.

So when walking in the jungle, don't be too hard on people's silliness, especially your own. It will pay dividends later.

Appendix: Books of Interest to the Jungle Walker

FAUNA
Birds

• *Aves Brasileiras* by Johan Dalgas Frisch, 353 pages, field-guide sized, names in Latin, Portuguese, Tupi-Guarani, English, and Spanish, text in Portuguese. No hummingbirds, seriema, or rhea. All others are illustrated, though Johan's father, Svend, copied many of the birds from museums, and that's what they look like. This hardly diminishes the value of the book as a field guide; I've been consulting it for twenty years.

Though personally a bit swaggering, Dalgas Frisch pioneered the recording of bird calls and songs in Brazil. Incidentally, while at Fazenda Bodoquena in the Swampland he recorded a background sound that has since become extinct in the region: the whistle of a Noroeste railroad steam locomotive.

• *Aves No Campus* by Elizabeth Höfling and Helio de A. Camargo, 160 pages, a field guide limited to the birds found on the University of São Paulo campus adjacent to the Butantã Institute. Names are in Latin, Portuguese, Tupi-Guarani, and English; text is in Portuguese. No tinamids. Well illustrated.

• *A Guide to the Birds of Venezuela* by Rodolphe Meyer de Schauensee and William H. Phelps Jr., 425 pages, field-guide sized, text in English, names in English, Latin, and Spanish, well illustrated and described. Princeton University Press, New Jersey. Contains most of the Brazilian birds, too.

A curator in the Ornithology Department of the Academy of Natural Science, Dr. Schauensee has written a number of books on South American birds. Dr. Phelps spent close to thirty-five years in the Venezuelan jungles and conducted twenty major ornithological expeditions to unexplored regions of that country.

- *Ornitologia Brasilerira* by Helmut Sick, 828 pages, large sized, names in Latin, Portuguese, and Tupi-Guarani, text in Portuguese. Describes all species with meticulous care; illustrations are excellent but do not show all the species. Expensive.

A graduate from the University of Berlin, Dr. Sick was the curator of the National Museum in Rio de Janeiro and a tireless field explorer until his death.

FISH

- *Dicionario dos Peixes do Brasil* by Hitoshi Nomura, 482 pages, medium sized, names in Latin, Portuguese, and Tupi-Guarani, text in Portuguese. Illustrations are generally clear but black and white, and some photographs taken of dead fish are rather poor.

Hitoshi Nomura is a professor of pisciculture at the Department of Zootechny, University of São Paulo at Piracicaba.

- *Peixes do Pantanal*, 184 pages, describes 263 species, names in Latin, Portuguese, and Tupi-Guarani, good illustrations. Published by Embrapa—Pantanal in Corumbá, a government institution devoted to agricultural research.

GENERAL

- *Atlas da Fauna Brasileira*, compiled by Melhoramentos editors, São Paulo, various authors, 140 pages, large format but lightweight, names in Latin, Portuguese, and Tupi-Guarani, text in Portuguese. The illustrations range from good for insects, birds, and mammals to mediocre for reptiles and definitely poor for fish.

INSECTS

- *Os Insetos* by Eurico Santos, two volumes totalling 446 pages, field-guide sized, names in Latin, Portuguese, and Tupi-Guarani, text in Portuguese, amply illustrated though mostly in black and white.

Eurico Santos wrote widely on fauna, flora, veterinary practice, and agriculture. I grew up reading his interesting books, which are periodically reprinted.

POISONOUS ANIMALS

• *Aculeos Que Matam* by Wolfgang Bücherl, 153 pages, field-guide sized, good and clear illustrations. Names in Latin, Portuguese, and Tupi-Guarani, text in Portuguese. African bees, centipedes, scorpions, snakes, and spiders.

Dr. Bücherl was chief of the venomous arthropod section at the Butantã Institute museum, involved in the extraction of poisons, and tells of his interesting experiments and experiences.

• *Serpentes do Brasil* by Afrânio do Amaral, 247 pages, names in Latin, Portuguese, Tupi-Guarani, and English, text bilingual, Portuguese and English. Illustrates and describes all tropical South American snakes. Medium sized.

Dr. Afrânio do Amaral was head of Butantã Institute's Department of Ophiology and Medical Zoology, later called to help organize the Antivenin Institute of America under the auspices of Harvard University and the London-based International Commission on Zoological Nomenclature.

• *Serpentes, Escorpioes e Aranhas* by Dr. Benemar Guimarães, a practical, sixty-four-page field guide, well illustrated and described by this medical writer, names in Latin, Portuguese, and Tupi-Guarani, text in Portuguese. Despite its modest size, this manual covers all the main points you need to know.

FLORA
Aquatic Plants

• *Nos Jardins Submersos da Bodoquena* by Vali Joana Pott and others, 160 pages, a beautiful field guide to the vegetation of those enchanting, crystal-clear waters of Bonito in the Serra da Bodoquena next door to the Swampland. Names in Latin and Portuguese, text in Portuguese. Excellent pictures, helped by Bonito's natural beauty.

Dr. Vali Pott is a researcher at Embrapa—Pantanal in Corumbá and curator of the herbarium, ideally stationed for her specialty—aquatic plants.

- *Plantas Aquaticas do Pantanal* by Vali Joana and Arnildo Pott, 404 pages, photos of 246 species. Names in Latin, text in Portuguese. Science and art combined in beauty.

Bromelia

- *Bromelias na Natureza* by Elton M. C. Leme and Luiz Claudio Marigo, 184 pages, large sized, names in Latin and Portuguese, text in Portuguese. Beautiful photography, the specialty of Luiz Marigo, whose pictures illustrate a number of publications all over the world.

   Elton Leme has revised several genera of *Bromelioideae*, worked with the German specialist Wilhelm Weber, and had close to a hundred works published.

Palms

- *Palmeiras no Brasil* by Harri Lorenzi, Hermes Moreira de Souza, and others, 320 pages, field-guide sized. This book is divided into two parts: native Brazilian and exotic palms. Names are in Latin, Portuguese, Tupi-Guarani, and, in the case of imported species, English and foreign names. Text is in Portuguese, giving characteristics, occurrence, habitat, utility, and production of seedlings. Clear photographs showing the whole tree, crown, and fruit.

   I have had the privilege of accompanying Dr. Lorenzi—a very hardworking specialist who is the director of the Nova Odessa Plantarum Institute of Flora Studies—and Dr. Hermes, who was chief of the Campinas Agronomic Institute's Botanical Section until an accident forced him to retire, across the Swampland.

Plants of the Swampland

- *Plantas do Pantanal* by Arnildo and Vali Pott, 320 pages, large sized, a product of Embrapa—Pantanal at Corumbá. Names in Latin, Portuguese, and Tupi-Guarani, text in Portuguese, giving etymology, type of plant, utilization, occurrence, and distribution. Mostly just one photograph per plant.

   I have already mentioned Dr. Vali under Aquatic Plants. Dr. Arnildo is an agronomist with a doctorate in pastures from the University of Queensland, Australia. His area at Embrapa is native pastures and flora.

Trees

• *Árvores Brasileiras* by Harri Lorenzi, two volumes, 370 pages each, large sized, names in Latin, Portuguese, and Tupi-Guarani, text in Portuguese giving morphological characteristics, occurrence, wood, utility, ecological information, phenology, seeds, and production of seedlings. Extremely well illustrated, showing the whole tree, leaves, flowers, fruit, seeds, bark, and wood.

I have already spoken of Dr. Lorenzi under Palms, above.

Weeds

• *Plantas Daninhas do Brasil* by Harri Lorenzi, 425 pages, medium sized, names in Latin, Portuguese, and Tupi-Guarani, text in Portuguese, giving general characteristics, leaves, inflorescences, origin, occurrence, and importance (such as medicinal properties); a single photo per plant, mostly in bloom. As precise as Dr. Lorenzi's other works (see Palms and Trees, above).

WHERE TO WALK

Beaches

• *Guia de Praias* by Quatro Rodas, 210 pages, field-guide sized, satellite photographs of the whole 8,000-kilometer (5,000-mile) length of the Brazilian coast from Chuí on the border with Uruguay to Cape Orange across the bay from French Guiana, plus the islands. Shows the entire topography, with roads specially marked and beaches numbered and described in detail, quality, location, facilities such as camping grounds and trails, plus additional data on the coast, weather, marine parks, fish, turtles, and marine birds besides accommodations, foods, and sports. Portuguese.

• Quatro Rodas—Four Wheels—specializes in road maps and guides.

National Parks

• *Parques Nacionais—Brasil* by Guias Philips, 384 pages plus map, field-guide sized, amply illustrated with beautiful photographs and regional maps, text in Portuguese giving brief history, landscape, fauna and flora (very superficially), general regional information, how to get there, nearest city, infrastructure if any, whether open to visitors, what to see, and addresses for contacts.

Swampland

- *Bodoquena* by John Coningham–Netto, 575 pages, standard sized, a
  novel of the Pantanal the tourist does not see: life and death among the
  yearly cycles of floods and drought, huge cattle ranches, territorial dis-
  putes, jaguars, and women ranchers. Text in Portuguese, index of fauna,
  flora, and regional expressions in Latin, Portuguese, and Tupi-Guarani.
  Background events and characters are all from the author's own experiences, many of which are mentioned throughout this guide.

- *Pantanal e Bonito* by Guias Philips, 310 pages, organization similar to
  Parques Nacionais above, includes the cities adjacent to the Swampland
  and Chapada dos Guimarães National Park. Also available in English.

Amazon Basin

- *A Ponte Sobre o Tuere* by John Coningham–Netto, 231 pages, standard
  sized, Portuguese. A novel that takes place during the opening of the
  trans–Amazon highway, telling of the natural and human problems
  faced as well as the individuals who flocked to the region, among them
  religious, ideological, and social misfits. As in *Bodoquena*, above, the
  background characters and events are all from the author's bag of personal experiences, many of them recounted in this guide.

- *One River* by Wade Davis, Simon & Schuster, New York. Medium
  sized, in English. A most interesting and well-researched history of the
  Amazon basin's peoples, their medicine men, curare poison, missionaries, and the work and suffering of the American botanist Dr. Richard
  Schultes during his basinwide search for disease-resistant rubber trees.

GENERAL TOURIST GUIDES

- There is Fodor's and Lonely Planet series, both in English, plus *Guia
  Brasil*, Quatro Rodas, in Portuguese.

INDEX